THE WORLD WITHIN THE GROUP

NEW INTERNATIONAL LIBRARY OF GROUP ANALYSIS

Series Editor: Earl Hopper

THE WORLD WITHIN THE GROUP
Developing Theory for Group Analysis

Martin Weegmann

Routledge
Taylor & Francis Group

LONDON AND NEW YORK

First published 2014 by
Karnac Books Ltd.

Published 2018 by Routledge
2 Park Square, Milton Park, Abingdon, Oxon OX14 4RN
711 Third Avenue, New York, NY 10017, USA

Routledge is an imprint of the Taylor & Francis Group, an informa business

British Library Cataloguing in Publication Data

A C.I.P. for this book is available from the British Library

ISBN-13: 9781780491981 (pbk)

Typeset by V Publishing Solutions Pvt Ltd., Chennai, India

CONTENTS

ACKNOWLEDGEMENTS

Martin Bharruth, Erica Burman, Guy Davidson, Monica Doran, Arnold Goldberg, Earl Hopper, Leisal Hearst, Ryan Kemp, Edward Khantzian, Dieter Nitzgen, Malcolm Pines, Alistair Sweet, Maggie Turp, Gary Winship, Martin Wrench, Suzanne Zieger.

ABOUT THE AUTHOR

Martin Weegmann is a consultant clinical psychologist and group analyst, with thirty years' NHS experience. He is a well known trainer, delivering workshops and lectures throughout the UK to a variety of psychology and psychotherapy organisations. Martin has co-edited two books, *Psychodynamics of Addiction* (2002, Wiley) and *Group Psychotherapy and Addiction* (2004, Wiley), and published many book chapters and papers in a range of journals.

NEW INTERNATIONAL LIBRARY OF GROUP ANALYSIS FOREWORD

Earl Hopper

The study of the social unconscious and the applications of our understanding of it, especially in clinical work, is one of the characteristics of Group Analysis, which distinguishes it from other schools of psychoanalytical or psychodynamic group psychotherapy (Hopper & Weinberg, 2011). The concept of the social unconscious is embedded in a field theory of considerable scope. However, the utility of this theory depends on an observer's use of binocular vision, the gestalt of his perceptions, and/or the specification of his particular frame of reference, which leads to the focused selection of particular facts from the totality of the magna, the oneness of the universe. The main elements of the social unconscious are the sociality, relationality, and collectivity of human nature, as well as their manifestations in the transgenerational foundational matrices of their socio-cultural groupings. Of course, the restraints and constraints of the human body on the personalities of human beings, and of the human species on society and culture and their component institutions, are also of vital importance. Power structures and power differentials are central in the socialisation processes of all matrices, including those that develop in clinical work. It is, therefore, inevitable that, to a degree, psychotherapeutic work will be political work and perhaps vice versa. The individual person is indeed social through and through: persons engage in interpersonal relations but such relations are in essence transpersonal.

By now, it has become axiomatic that the one and the many are completely intertwined (Tubert-Oklander, 2014). Nonetheless, very few of us seem to appreciate the complexity of the issues involved and the depth of the problems and insights that have been brought to bear in our attempts to solve them. Martin Weegmann is not a member of the cult of group analysts who espouse theories of the social unconscious as a *cri de coeur* of his professional identity. He is entirely committed to the struggle of engaging with his clients and patients in an attempt to understand how their lives and relationships have been co-constructed by social facts, and, in turn, how they have co-constructed their more intimate environment. Weegmann is especially concerned with explaining how these processes become crystallised in more immediate situations, and, thus, how they are available for repetition in clinical work. Although he is prepared to go where it is hottest, he also understands how equivalence is the product not only of projective and introjective identification, but also of unconscious narratives of helplessness and powerlessness, as well as of the search for a clinical guide, who is prepared to listen and to hear, to look and to see, and perhaps empathically to share.

Martin Weegmann has acquired an unusual set of professional qualifications and skills. A sociologist and social theorist, a philosopher, a psychodynamic psychotherapist and group analyst, he clearly prefers Foucault to Freud, Lacan to Klein, Kohut to Kernberg, and Foulkes to Bion. He was introduced to Group Analysis by Stephen Coghill and Harold Behr through a block training in Manchester under the auspices of the Institute of Group Analysis in London. Martin is indebted to Malcolm Pines for intellectual stimulations in their active exchange of ideas. His clinical experience is deeply coloured by his work with substance misusers and those with personality disorders in a range of NHS settings, including the Henderson Therapeutic Community.

To me, it is important to recognise that Martin is an artist, photographer, and musician, with an interest in gardens and the natural world. He understands that, like a garden, a group requires the exercise of benign authority. I suspect that he understands that whilst a garden is structured out of nature, it also remains a part of it. In fact, he appreciates that the person and his groupings are transitional figurations who live between the dominion of the dead (Harrison, 2003) and a world that can be defined in terms of the ability and willingness to exercise the transcendent imagination (Hopper, 2003). Weegmann is alert to the dilemma and paradox that characterise the appreciation of the power of socio-genesis and the possibilities for creativity. However, when I learned of his title for this book, *The World within the Group: Essays on Group Analysis*, I also heard the echoes of a few lines from "Auguries of Innocence" by William Blake (1757–1827):

> To see a World in a grain of sand,
> And a Heaven in a wild flower,
> Hold Infinity in the palm of your hand,
> And Eternity in an hour.

which I (Hopper, 2003) used as an epigram for my own book of papers in the study of the social unconscious.

Martin Weegmann's book deserves to be read, and read slowly, tracing its ideas from one discipline to another and from one intellectual culture to another. The reader will not be able to avoid having to think and re-think his basic group analytical perspectives and ethical values, and to consider and reconsider the location of his clinical orientation within his general world view. I am not surprised that Edward Said is one of his intellectual mentors—if not heroes.

This carefully integrated set of papers is eclectic in the best sense of the term. The glossary is very interesting; as is the range of theorists whose work informs this illumination of society and culture in clinical work.

Earl Hopper, Ph.D.
Series Editor

PREFACE

Reading Martin Weegmann's book has been a pleasure. His assured writing style flows, opening vistas and horizons for group analysis by moving elegantly from philosophy to history to cultural studies. He has an inquiring mind, not hemmed in by established "givens".

My own journey through psychoanalysis and group analysis began some sixty years ago. As an ardent student of psychoanalysis, I found the theory of the time restricting but enjoyed exploring the historical context out of which psychoanalysis had evolved. I discovered group analysis, established by S. H. Foulkes, who was my training analyst. The "givens" of group analysis were bringing together the "vertical" psychoanalytic exploration of personal depths with the "horizontal" dimension of persons as social agents; foregrounds and backgrounds, figures/grounds, our existence as social entities. Group analytic theory licences freedom to search the disciplines of social theory, historical psychology, economics, and neuroscience, the latter as developed by Kurt Goldstein. Foulkes was assistant to Goldstein's network theory of brain physiology which laid the ground for Foulkes' proposal that humans are intrinsically interconnected as nodes, "synapses", in social networks, later described by his collaborator, Norbert Elias, as "figurations". Martin Weegmann draws from philosophers Nietzsche,

Gadamer, and Dewey to illuminate the depths and widths of our subjectivity in ever-moving contexts. I used to wonder at his interest in medieval and reformation history, witchcraft, and the history of addiction, and now I see how they help us recognise shifting social fields of inclusion and exclusiveness.

My own professional journey has led me to explore and appreciate self psychology, as established by Heinz Kohut and his collaborators in the 1970's, finding a "good fit" with our group analytic theory and clinical practices as applied to small groups, and later with median and large groups and therapeutic community practices. Martin Weegmann acknowledges other group analysts who have widened our horizons.

At the same time as reading this deep and sensitive text, I am reading Skidelski and Skidelski's (2012) "How Much is Enough?", a superbly crafted exploration of humans as subjects to economic theory and practices. It is indeed refreshing to follow good, clear expositions of how we are always enmeshed in societies which practice differing economic approaches.

Another book, by Kuriloff (2013), is an important study of how psychoanalysis and psychoanalytic societies have dealt or not dealt with the aftermath of Nazi domination and its atrocities. She has studied the impact on psychoanalytic societies in a range of countries and, to my mind, has shown us how much they differ in their immersion in their cultural histories.

I bring these works in, as they illuminate our recent history, as does Martin Weegmann with his knowledge of early-modern and reformation history. We are always repeating former histories, as Santayana wrote, if we fail to see our historical origins. And the history of group analysis is being written as we better understand our origins.

My own exploration of the place of group analysis in contemporary society has led me to both overlapping and separate narratives. I have gained so much pleasure and knowledge from this book, which merits wide readership and discussion. I deeply appreciate Martin Weegmann's invitation to introduce his essays, explorers saluting each other as our journeys cross and pass.

Malcolm Pines
London

INTRODUCTION

This book is the outcome of a long journey to discover my own thoughts about group analysis—ideas about its claims, how it works and how it relates, beyond the circle of therapy, to the world in which we live. It also reflects dissatisfaction with the relative slowness of theoretical developments within the discipline of group analysis, as I see it.

Writing is an astonishing practice in which, somewhat like the unpredictable generativity of the therapy group, we happen upon unexpected, unbidden associations, the "more than" what we set out with. As I laboured, I found myself drawn by a swirl of connections between group analysis and three loves of old—philosophy, history, and social theory. The result is an interdisciplinary, integrative book that moves between different domains of inquiry, convinced that it is in the borders and interplay of perspectives—clinical, philosophic, historical—that the discipline of group analysis can be strengthened in theory. Of course, Foulkes adapted the models and movements that had made him—psychoanalysis, neurology, gestalt theory, war-time psychiatry, and so on—creating the synthesis which was group analysis. But I am not alone in thinking that we have exhausted the original, founding paradigm of group analysis and that our discipline badly requires paradigm shifts in order to remain relevant in today's world.

The first three chapters explore relationships between group analysis and philosophy, using philosophy as a resource for thinking. The metaphor of philosophy as "therapy" is not new and it is interesting to regard each of us as philosopher in our own right, immersed in a perspective on life, tackling problems of existence, guided by moral themes and seeking solutions to the situations we find ourselves in. Whilst human kinds are seldom philosophers in the grand sense of the word, tackling big questions of Life and Truth, we are nevertheless deeply influenced by implicit "theories" about who we are, models of the world, and stories that help us make sense of living; if we sustain an inquiring, examining attitude, we can revise those models, overhauling received versions of ourselves. Three philosophers—Nietzsche, Gadamer, and Dewey, together with the tradition of intersubjective psychoanalysis— figure large in the first three chapters.

A common component of psychotherapy is to locate a client within the hi(story) that carries them. The past is not inert, but is subject to reinscription, whilst the future is under construction—we are always *en route*, as Gadamer said. None of us is complete, and narrative lies open, with plenty of commas, but no full stops. The same is true of our psychological theories and therapies, which can be seen as models, both explanatory and ameliorative; importantly, they are historical products, relative to context, time, and place. Contesting any strict separation between theory and practice, I will argue that they grow together, in codependence, and this is particularly so in disciplines which are concerned broadly with the "care of the soul".

Group analysis needs to be placed within a matrix of borrowings, metaphors, dependencies, and breaks, within a field of the "psy disciplines". My interest in such contexts was stimulated through many conversations with that eminently history-wise group analyst, Dr Malcolm Pines. The question explored is, that if group analysis and relational psychoanalysis regard human beings as inescapably social, interconnected creatures, what are the implications of Nietzsche's insistence on seeing human kinds as *historical* beings, through and through?

Questions of historicity are addressed in Chapters Four to Seven, offering a new formulation of social unconsciousness as discursive, historical production. Numerous historical case examples are used, ranging from shifts in personal and group subjectivity as a result of the Reformation, in Chapters Four to Five, through to nineteenth-century concerns with degeneracy and abject groups, in Chapters Six and Seven. If I take history seriously, this is not for remote, academic reasons: history does not stop, as a process confined to what is "past"; we are carried along by being part of it. We are always *in* history.

However historical and social we are, there is no avoiding the reality of agency and fact of singularity (what Heidegger called the "ontic" dimension), although these occur within circumstances not of our own making; we are, as Charles Taylor puts it, "self-interpreting animals". Self-interpretation is reflected in our ability to construct and vary narrative accounts of our lives: "We are story-telling animals", says Alistair MacIntyre. This emphasis on story and narrative identity is developed in Chapters Eight and Nine. Our unavoidable immersion in a world of discursively produced stories and values is examined, showing how group analysis dovetails with the highly diversified and plural societies in which we live. However, there is a critical issue in as much as group analysis, like any therapy, is a carrier of ethico-cultural assumptions and regulative ideals. A critical perspective on our own practice is essential; we cannot pretend not to be part of those wider disciplines and practices of self in our modern, therapeutic culture.

Many people have helped my labours, through their interest and encouragement. Some helped without knowing it, through inspiration, as heroes. Paul Hirst, formerly Professor of Social Theory at Birkbeck College, died in 2003, having made a vast contribution to social and political theory. I never formally studied with him, but eagerly consumed his talks and books. He was a friendly and generous acquaintance. A true polymath, I admired Hirst's openness, his rigorous, sceptical pragmatism, and respect for the value of theory, not as an end in itself, but as a mobile vehicle for the development of evermore useful analysis and critique. Amongst other things, it was he who aroused my interest in the Reformation and early modern witchcraft. An interesting aside is that Paul Hirst studied sociology at the University of Leicester, where he was much impressed by the scholarship of that early friend of group analysis and of Foulkes, Norbert Elias. Group analysts have rarely pursued historical inquiry, content perhaps to cite Elias as luminary precedent and co-travellor of the discipline.

Also in 2003, I learned of the death of Edward Said. I had not realised how much this man, whom I never met, meant to me. It was as if he had "been with" me for years, a figure of continuity. In response to grief, I organised a conference, "The West and the Rest—Exploring the Contribution of Edward Said", at the Institute of Group Analysis, London

(Weegmann, 2005a). Said's phrase, "permission to narrate", so apt of his efforts to tell the story of broken Palestinian reality, is equally fitting as subtitle for group analysis, as people talk, listen, exchange, and develop new narratives.

Hirst and Said excelled at traversing disciplinary boundaries, practicing the art of, to use another of Said's expressions, "travelling theory". Both wrote from humanist, worldly convictions, with an eye on the future, as to what might be improved.

It is within such a spirit that I aspire to write …

To Henry Christian Weegmann, who,
in his quiet way,
helped me to notice the world about me,
to look in order to see,
and to listen in order to hear ...

CHAPTER ONE

Working intersubjectively: theory and therapy*

I do not think we should always try to understand … In this connection I tend to leave things unresolved, in mid-air, incomplete ("no closure").

—Foulkes, 1964, p. 287

With his nightcaps and the tatters of his dressing-gown,
he patches up the gaps in the structure of the universe.

—Heine, quoted in Freud, 1933, p. 161

"With his nightcaps and the tatters …" is how the poet Heinrick Heine playfully derided the philosopher. It was one of Freud's favourite quotations. Classical philosophers were prone to the belief that they could arrive at a state of certain knowledge and/or uncover an irreducible principle; some examples are Plato's theory of Forms, Descartes' notion of *cogito*, or Locke's *tabula rasa* self. One can see in such ideas a manifestation of omnipotent thinking and

---

*This chapter is a modified version of Working intersubjectively: what does it mean for theory and therapy? In: E. Hopper & H. Weinberg (Eds.) (2011), *The Social Unconscious in Persons, Groups and Societies: Volume 1* (Chapter Six). London: Karnac.

the search for absolutes: in modern philosophy, such thinking might be dubbed "foundationalism", the notion that what one needs above all else is a secure and knowable foundation, and that once achieved, then all things are fall into place (Rorty, 1980, 1982). At one level, Freud knew such ideas to be pretensions; this is why he resisted trying to convert his psychoanalysis, which he saw as a science, into a new fabricated "view of the universe" or "*Weltanschauung*". In fact, Freud believed that psychoanalysis could find its place within the more modest scientific worldview which already existed. It could be argued, however, that Freud fell into a different, but related trap: he thought he had discovered the irreducible principles of mental life, its ultimate structuring principles (of the unconscious, repression, infantile sexuality) or blueprint of the mind (Spence, 1987). The analyst, by virtue of his training, was seen to be in a privileged position and with his interpretations could patch up, so to speak, the gaps in the structure of the patient's mind. At a theoretical level, Freud conceptualised an isolated mind, a "one-body psychology", and a knowing analyst guided by this new branch of medical science. Of course, this is not to suggest that Freud's thought is consistent or entirely under his sovereign control; clearly, Freud's ideas were constantly worked, re-worked, and amended. In fact, Freud knew something of the irony which links writing and discovering, having remarked, "I invented psychoanalysis because it had no literature" (cited by Roazen, 1971).

At times Freud played at being Plato, or at the very least a searching Sherlock Holmes figure, since the analyst, like the philosopher-king or detective acquired a "special knowledge", the patient by contrast being trapped within the snares of the unconscious cave. There has always been a large tension at the heart of psychoanalysis between (a) an image of itself as privileged view and master therapy, and (b) an unceasing spirit of inquiry and free-floating interest that animates its rationale; a contrast, perhaps, between a rationalist, objectivist version of psychoanalysis versus those that emphasise the infinity of meaning and hermeneutic openness.

This chapter uses ideas from Robert Stolorow's intersubjectivity theory and group analysis to convey an impression of what it might mean to move decisively away from the "myth of the isolated mind" and "one-body" psychology. A significant tilt towards the "relational" is apparent in several areas of modern psychoanalysis: self psychology, attachment theory, empirical psychoanalysis (Stern, 1985, and other infant research), relational-perspectivism (Aron, 1996; Mitchell, 1988;

Orange, 1995), to name a few that are, arguably, compatible with many of the ideas of Foulkes; and contextualism, the figure/ground dynamic, the "meeting of minds" in groups and a dynamic concept of location (Behr & Hearst, 2005). Foulkes (2003), also exposed the myth of "mind" or self as self-enclosed entity, and looked forward to a time when thinking could "get beyond the metaphysics of psychoanalysis" (p. 316). In this reading, Foulksean group analysis is one version of a more communicative, relationally bound unconscious, notwithstanding inconsistencies in theorisation (Stacey, 2001).

"Intersubjectivity" is therefore a concept within an emerging paradigm in psychoanalysis and group analysis. A common emphasis within this paradigm is that of conceiving complex relational fields and organising principles, within which psychological processes come together and through which experience is continually shaped and reshaped. There is a move away from postulating a dynamic unconscious, storehouse of mental conflict, as the only form of unconscious mental life (Spence, 1987). Stolorow and his colleagues (Stolorow & Atwood, 1992) add two more types of unconscious life. First, there is the "pre-reflective unconscious", constituting the building blocks of psychic life, organising principles that, whilst not directly reflected upon, govern how we see ourselves and our expectancies of being with others, and that are not primarily the product of defensive activity. An example of this is early communication between caregiver and infant, conveying ways of being together, responding to distress, playing and enjoyment, and boundaries; symbols, or symbolic thinking, from the middle of year two, make possible "a sharing of mutually related meaning about personal experience" (Stern, 1985, p. 172). Organising principles are implicit, inferable, and operate throughout life. Second, there is the "unvalidated unconscious", representing a landscape of possibility. This concerns unused elements of psychic life, not so much "repressed" as unarticulated, unnoticed, and thereby by-passed. Although Stolorow and Atwood (1992) suggest that this realm is particularly important to bear in mind with those who have suffered developmental disadvantage, it is surely of universal relevance, since none of us is completed and there is always unused potential. Importantly, in these formulations of unconscious mental life—and this is also true of the group analytic view of the social unconscious—matters are not seen as exclusively derived from the infantile experience, as they were for Freud.

Human development and pathology are seen as irreducibly relational, embedded in varying intersubjective contexts. Stolorow and

Atwood (1979) argue that as psychoanalytic ideas are too profoundly influenced by the personal and training worlds of their creators, they cannot be entirely objective and that treatment can only be conceived as an "intersubjective field", involving reciprocal principles and influence, an intersection of two differently organised subjectivities—that of the analyst and that of the patient. As just one instance of this, they claim that, "Not only does the patient turn to the analyst for selfobject experiences, but the analyst also turns to the patient for such experiences ..." (Stolorow & Atwood, 1992, p. 396).

This broad approach not only helps reconceptualise psychoanalysis anew, but also sheds light on the historical context within which Freud's "discoveries" were made. Something of Freud's attitude or relationship to his ideas was mirrored, for example, in his stance towards the fledgling movement he created, to the early circle of analysts and the organisational structures that functioned to contain the new doctrine. Partly this was protective, even necessary, but had long-term negative effects for psychoanalysis of creating relative isolation, insulation, and an attitude of immunity. A norm-creating culture of thinking was established in the early analytic world, held together by the sheer moral and symbolic function of Freud, the man and his ideas (Frosch, 1997). The early analysts were a community of inquirers, held together by a highly distinctive discourse of description and explanation. This included the use of the privileged wisdom of clinical cases, Freud's case studies, and similar rhetorical conventions that analysts deployed when practicing and discussing their work. Thus, intersubjectivity theory can illuminate group as well as individual processes, whether those of historical groups, such as Freud's circle or the International Psychoanalytic Association, or of groups of individuals who come together with the aim of seeking therapy and personal change.

What follows is an inevitably schematic description of some key features of the classical psychoanalytic orientation. It is acknowledged that one of the risks of presenting it in this way is that it could be accused of creating a convenient stereotype.

Classical theory

During the 1890s, the cornerstones of Freud's "discovery" were set in place. Freud moved away from his interest in hypnosis and cathartic techniques to encouraging "free association" and listening. Through his researches in treating hysterics (all the early patients of "psychoanalysis" were female hysterics), a new method emerged, with a new significance attached to "phantasy", often seen as coterminous with Freud's abandonment of the "seduction hypothesis" around 1897. With these changes we see the formation of the new domain of psychoanalysis, christened "the talking cure" by Anna O., the first patient, as it were, of the new approach. For our purposes, in this brief excavation of psychoanalysis, we shall refer to Freud's topographical understanding of the mind and his leading metaphor of archaeology, his notion of resistance and the transference, and, by extension, the special, surgical-like stance of the analyst.

The archaeology metaphor

An archaeological metaphor is used frequently by Freud to describe mental life—a psychology of "depth", whereby later stages of development are overlain on earlier ones, just as the archaeologist unearths traces of earlier civilisations. History, in Freudian theory, is governed by endogenous drives, with treatment aiming to resolve the deeper "infantile neurosis", thus restoring the patient, and to "fill the gaps in memory". The reality produced by psychoanalysis is "discovered" or "recovered" in the archaeological metaphor; Wolberg (1976) likens the classical view of treatment to that of a mining operation, aimed at reaching the psychic core and latent content. The Freudian "self" was based on the idea of a self-enclosed subject, organised predominantly around sequential intrapsychic structures and driven by instincts. Second, the perspective is a vertical one, from top to bottom, with the analyst, as psychic archaeologist, presiding over the treatment, over the patient, as it were; "... this aligned the patient closer to the primitive and overemphasised the neutrality and imperturbability of the analyst" (McLaughlin, 1981). Stolorow (Stolorow, Branschaft & Atwood, 1987) indicates that the intersubjectivity concept is in part a response to the tendency within classical analysis to view pathology "in terms of processes and mechanisms located solely within the patient" (p. 3).

The resisting patient

> I had explained the idea of "resistance" to him at the beginning of the hour ... (Freud, 1909, p. 166)

The concept of resistance was there from the beginning and was integral to understanding psychoanalytic treatment and obstacles to it;

overcoming resistance is a "law of treatment" (ibid.) and failure to do so is the factor which "finally brings treatment to a halt" (Freud, 1905, p. 71). Importantly, and this fact may help throw light on Freud's own subjectivity, not only did he use the term to refer to obstacles in gaining access to the unconscious, but he used it also to refer to resistance to psychoanalysis by its critics, those who had encircled his "embattled science". It linked into Freud's own myth of the isolated hero.

The concept of transference is tied to the concept of resistance. Freud writes: "This transference alike in its positive and negative form is used as a weapon by the resistance; but in the hands of the physician it becomes the most powerful therapeutic instrument ..." (1923a, p. 247).

Consider briefly Freuds (1905) case of Dora. Freud makes several references to the "incompleteness" of that case, to what was left unanalysed, its omissions. In his postscript to the case, we are told of the one central omission to explain this incompleteness, this being the concept of transference. In a phrase which might reveal a lot about Freud's own position and desire, he writes that in the case of Dora "I did not succeed in *mastering* the transference in good time" (1905, p. 118, my emphasis). In psychoanalysis, from this time on, what was previously regarded as the biggest obstacle to treatment (the "un-welcome" factor which Joseph Breuer alluded to; Breuer & Freud, 1895), became "its most powerful ally", if sufficiently mastered. Transference is the "carrying over" of the past, stimulated, but not invented, by the treatment. Linked to libido theory, it is understood within conflictual terms, with the analyst representing the figure on to whom libidinal wishes are transferred, the focus of a transferred, inner "battleground".

In 1919, Freud distinguished "the pure gold of analysis" from the "copper of direct suggestion"; what distinguishes psychoanalysis from other psychotherapies, is the role of interpretation and, increasingly central, interpretation of resistance and the transference. The vertical perspective is clear, with the analyst making the interpretations (because he is in charge) *to* the patient (who resists). In Strachey's (1934) famous contribution, he argues that only transference interpretations have mutative power. Hearst (2000) comments on Strachey's language of trench warfare and summarises the outlook then as one where "it is the task of the analyst to penetrate step by step through the minefield of the analysand's resistance to the source of the neurosis. The analyst's weapon in the correct, and correctly timed, transference interpretation" (p. 2). Foulkes (1975a), in his writings, never agreed with "the monopoly conceded in certain techniques to the transference and its interpretation" (p. 116).

Intersubjectivity theory, by contrast, views the analytic situation with greater mutuality, but not naive equality, where the patient is seen as co-constructing his treatment and who "interprets" the analyst's behaviour as much as the analyst interprets him. "The concept of transference as displacement (or regression or projection) has perpetuated the view that the patient's experience of the analytic relationship is solely a product of the patient's past and psychopathology and has not been determined by the activity (or non-activity) of the analyst" (Stolorow, Branschaft & Atwood, 1987, p. 33). It now becomes possible to think that some of the very concepts used by the early analysts, and the treatment ambiance they fostered, helped to create some of the resistance they claimed to have discovered. And, far from being neutral, the stance of the analyst entailed an assumption of a superior point of view or epistemology. There was then, a silent metanarrative of truth and power, operating at the heart of psychoanalysis (Foucault, 1978b).

The surgical metaphor

> I cannot advise my colleagues too urgently to model themselves during psychoanalytic treatment on the surgeon, who puts aside all feelings ... (Freud, 1912, p. 115)

Consistent with his topographical model and archaeological stance, Freud believed in the essential exteriority of the analyst (of which, sitting behind the couch might be seen as an expression), who carries out treatment "in abstinence" (this idea being based on the instinct model). His recommendation in 1912 was that the analyst "Should be opaque to his patients and, like a mirror, show them nothing but what is shown to them" (1912, p. 118). The classical theme of surgical detachment was consistent with Freud's identification with the scientist who bases his approach on objective treatment.

In this model, with its vertical perspective, the authority of the analyst is enshrined. Although we have little direct sense of how Freud worked in practice (and he certainly did not advocate coldness), the tone of writing and interpreting in his case studies often appears as one of "explanation", "pointing out", "demonstrating to". Foulkes (1975a) comments on the term *Deutung* and suggests that the interpreter in the

Freudian conception has "a specific knowledge ... by no means open to everyone, but only to the select few who have been initiated on the strength of a quite peculiar ability" (p. 114). Foulkes' (1964) reference (see quotation at start of chapter) to the importance of incompletion and values of non-closure, typifies a stance (in theory) of hermeneutic openness. The contrast to this is characterised by Arlow (1995) as the tradition of "stilted listening" in psychoanalysis, with implications of infallibility, or at least of an incremental notion of the truth, with the good analyst in an increasing relationship of truth to his patient. From the early phase onwards, dissenters begged to differ, and analysts, such as Ferenczi, found themselves in increasing trouble with "loyal" analysts.

The surgical metaphor, then, is tied up with the power of the physician (the early generation of analysts were all physicians, and Freud uses the terms interchangeably). The historical context in which this occurs is important, a culture which enshrined a strict hierarchy and elevated the authority of the physician over the patient. In the early phase of psychoanalysis, and often since, there was simply no acknowledgement of the socially constituted nature and location of analytic authority and the analytic dyad.

On history and the psychoanalytic movement

This is not psychoanalysis ... (Freud, quoted in Eisold, 1997, p. 97)

The history of the psychoanalytic movement is of considerable interest to the student of intersubjectivity and group analysis. I have suggested some parallel between some of the theoretical concepts and metaphors of psychoanalysis, such as archaeology and surgery, and Freud's stance as the leader of the movement he founded. As with all movements, we see the creation of "foundation" myths, legendary aspects through which the ideas and individuals involved are seen. Perhaps in Freud's own preferred myth of isolation and resistance around his discoveries, he comes close to identifying with his boyhood idol, Hannibal, who challenged an empire and conquered Rome. Sterba (1982), in his fascinating recollections of the early Viennese days, talks about the analysts, like himself, as a group of exceptional, "*gebildete*" people, individuals who are well-educated, able to speak languages, and are familiar with high culture, literature, and art—and, of course, in this regard, "Sigmund Freud was above us all" (p. 87).

In the early years, with the creation in Freud's flat of the "Wednesday Evening Society", the early psychoanalytic ethos was reflected in some aspects of the proceedings. Kanzer (1983) observes, for example, that, "Freud always presided, so that a distance was established between himself and his followers" and that following presentations he "alone had the privilege of intervening at will" (p. 8).

The relationship of Freud to the psychoanalytic movement that unfolded, and to the organisational structures devised, is a complicated one and we know that in many ways Freud was a reluctant leader. With the creation, in 1910, of the International Psychoanalytic Association, a complex co-relationship existed between Freud and those to whom he turned to safeguard and to continue the enterprise of psychoanalysis. Eisold's (1997) fascinating research suggests that Freud gravitated towards becoming, in Bions terms, a "fight leader", with himself and his Viennese followers needing a culture of allegiance (the members being still dependent on Freud) as well as needing to promote the professional aspirations of the membership. An "unconscious pact" resulted, argues Eisold, "in which they sought and rooted out "enemies" within the movement ... who questioned his basic concept of childhood sexuality and would lend support to the external enemies of psychoanalysis" (p. 87). This can be linked to the notion of resistance to psychoanalysis from outside and from within.

The notion of "orthodoxy" is an important one in understanding the behaviour of groups. Who has the power to sanction orthodoxy, and what is the shibboleth distinguishing the adherents of a movement from its opponents? (Roustang, 1980). Using an intersubjectivist viewpoint, how might we understand the selfobject needs of the members of a movement or emergent orthodoxy? In many ways, the fledgling or fragile movement reflects the fragile self; for example, Freud's own anxieties about what he had discovered, the dependence of his colleagues on his support, his dependence on friendly allies, and a host of other narcissistic needs: for recognition and admiration and for the consolidation in this first generation of analysts of a new "analytic identity" (Bergmann, 1997).

Summary

There were many problematic consequences to the early analytic framework and institutional stance, even though it was born accompanied by an understandable "euphoria of discovery" (Greenberg,

1999a) Amongst these were/are: the privileging of intrapsychic and archaeological materials; the implied hierarchical relationship between the uncovering analyst and patient; the implied epistemological objectivism of the analytic stance, both with respect to the patient's experience and in relation to other therapies; the creation of prototypical case-histories as instruments of dissemination, knowledge, or insight (perhaps seen in male mode as a stance of "mastery"); images of bold analyst as heroic outsider; and foundational myths about the nature of psychoanalytic knowledge. All have contributed to a significant degree of intolerance and isolating within psychoanalytic groups. The idea of the behind-the-couch, out-of-sight analyst in psychoanalysis had metaphorical dimensions, linked to the idea of the uncontaminated analyst, always, ultimately, one step ahead paradoxically by virtue of having a view from behind; the idea of the "behind" also fits in with the early psychoanalytic preoccupation of "latent" and "manifest" and the analyst as occupying a superior perspectival position.

In an interesting comparison to medieval morality plays, Greenberg (1999b) touches upon the inescapable moral dimension of the analytic situation, and whilst the patient is telling her story, the analyst is also telling his own, using his own narrative conventions and figures of discourse. Greenberg rightly notes that "relational psychoanalysis" likewise carries a different set of moral values. And yet, the "writing analyst" is always different from the practicing analyst. The risk is that different psychoanalytic models will structure the patient's "free associations" differently, with all schools tending to create prototypical case histories. Wittgenstein (in McGuiness, 1982) suggested that there were both helpful and harmful aspects to Freud's mythology and claims, that something is gained, but also lost, in any act of interpretation, according to the classical regime.

Therapy implications

The philosophical and theoretical influences upon, and implications of, intersubjectivity theory are manifold and can be linked to many developments in late nineteenth and twentieth-century philosophy: the ideas of Nietzsche, Husserl, Heidegger (*Group Analysis*, 1998; Orange, Atwood & Stolorow, 1997) to name a few. Some of these links are explored in this book. The following discussion, relevant to group analysis as much as to individual psychotherapy (Nitsun, 1989; Stacey,

2001), describes how intersubjectivity theory contrasts with the classical paradigm. Rather than being a new "technique", the intersubjective—contextual paradigm cultivates a particular *sensitivity* to the work of therapy and understanding and is one that is more diverse and pragmatic in aim.

A changing view of interpretation

Foulkes' (1975a) encouragement of psychotherapy "by the group, for the group, including the conductor" (p. 3), rather than merely between analyst and group, was an important divergence from the classical psychoanalytic stance. Foulkes' "conductor" had many capacities besides making interpretations, such as confrontations, clarifications, acknowledging and receiving contributions, and so on. Furthermore, by getting away from the idea that group analysis was more than "a hunt for unconscious meaning" (1971), he opened up the transforming power of communication, theorised as the opening up, the ever-widening and deepening of a group "matrix", a horizontal perspective conjoined with the more traditional vertical perspective of individual psychoanalysis.

In spite of these advances, when it came to an understanding of the patient's *individual* pathology, Foulkes was a committed Freudian, retaining a rather insular view of human development and accepting the pre-eminence of the psychosexual stages as universal psychic contents. Dalal (1998) refers to this as the "orthodox Foulkes", contrasted with the "radical Foulkes". It is curious, perhaps, that Foulkes the analyst (he was a training analyst within Anna Freud's "B" school in Britain) was not more explicitly influenced by the emergent Independent School of psychoanalysis, which, amongst many things, theorised the role of other agents of psychic change, besides interpretation (Stewart, 1990).

Stern (Stern et al., 1998), working from a contemporary interpersonal and intersubjective perspective, has researched "non-interpretive mechanisms" in therapy. He talks about the notion of a "something more" than interpretation, noting that patients frequently recall, after treatment, not only "key interpretations" that might have affected psychic change, but also special "moments" of "authentic person-to-person connection". Hence, he suggests two mutative phenomena, interpretation and "moments of meeting", the latter involving what his research group term "implicit relational knowing" and complex "affect attunement", ideas based upon investigations of infants. Yet, even interpretations, good or bad, are a relational process and not disembodied observations *about* the patient, as in a vertical perspective. In the traditional episte-mology of psychoanalysis, the "word" (the voice, the interpretation) was seen as different from the "act" and was conceived as informative rather than performative (Aron, 1996). Pines (1996a) offers a Bahktian view of interpretation as an act of revelation, of the therapist *and* patient, the momentary instance of an unfolding dialogue.

From analyst to conductor

Consider the possible impact, on a group, of adopting a classical stance, taking as example the work of some clinicians working at the Tavistock Clinic, during the 1950s. Clinicians such as Ezriel and Sutherland took inspiration from Bion's ideas, which had been developed with training groups, and applied these to therapy groups.

Ezriel (1950) described efforts to apply a "strictly psychoanalytic technique" to group therapy, with, amongst other things, a "rigorous technique of transference interpretation". Building on the tradition of Strachey and Rickman before him, Ezriel assigned overriding impor-tance to transference interpretations in the "here and now" of the group session. The task of therapy is universalised by Ezriel, as to do with the resolution of infantile, oedipal conflicts, and so the material is always viewed in this light; to quote Ezriel (1952), all the material "is consid-ered as the idiom used by the patient to give expression to his need in that session for a specific relationship with the therapist" (p. 120).

Isolating some key aspects of Ezriel's approach with respect to the role of the analyst, ultimately centres the communications of the group on the analyst himself and, by extension, on the analyst's overarch-ing framework. Ezriel goes as far as contending that the other mem-bers of the group are reducible to co-present "stimuli", there to attract the projection of internal defences. Brown (1979) argues that this type of analyst-centred mode fosters another kind of "basic assumption dependence" and thereby infantalises the patient. It radically reduces the importance of understanding and engagement from and by other members, as an end in itself.

As with Freud's idea of abstinence and neutrality, the analyst's own organising principles (including theory and training) are bracketed out of the equation, with the therapist viewed as being external to the setting. The framing of all material in terms, for example, of unresolved infantile conflicts is, from an intersubjective viewpoint, already a structuring and organising (and, thereby, constraining) viewpoint contributed by the analyst, and is, because of that, far from being "neutral". In Malan's (1976) empirical evaluation of the Tavistock groups, he points to the resentments often encountered by patients to an unduly impersonal psychoanalytic approach and to the emphasis on conflictual object relations alone. In a (mild) recommendation, he says, "… it does seem possible that therapists ought to feel less constrained by what they have learned from their classical psychoanalytic training …" (p. 1315). Using an understanding of groups afforded by self psychology, we could see such resentments as expressions of protest at the imposition of a "technique" and as a reaction, in some cases, to a felt undermining of the total self and the group's efficacy as a whole.

It needs to be noted, however, that although Foulkes had a lot to say about the "dynamic administration" of groups, he did not specify the actual qualities required by the conductor. In this regard, there is a similarity with the neglect, in classical psychoanalysis, of the real or desirable qualities of the analyst (Kantrowitz, 1986).

The transference: an intersubjectivist view

There are several drawbacks to the classical view of transference and its role in treatment. The early generation of analysts (and many who came later) tended to see themselves as representing a position (*in potentia*) of objective truth, vis-à-vis the patient, taking their own conceptions of the main contents and structurations of mental life as already established and valid. This resulted in many extremes, and Ferenczi, as one example, challenged this prevailing epistemology by disagreeing with the implied infallibility of the analyst and in taking the patient's criticisms as valid. This led him into severe difficulties with his peers and with Freud himself (Eisold, 1997). Another problem was the failure to recognise how dependent patients could be on the acceptance of the analyst and, through this, the patient's dependence on seeing "reality" through the basic concepts that organised the *analyst's* observations and interpretations. Ferenczi's pupil, Balint (1968), took up this theme in his warnings against the dangers of "over-insistent interpreting" and the "obtrusive analyst", and Stolorow (Stolorow & Atwood, 1992) expresses the dilemma in the following way: "This is the requirement with which patients often felt compelled to comply as the price of maintaining the vitally needed tie to the analyst" (p. 91).

If we take "field complexity" and the "uncertainty principle" of science seriously, then modern analysis, be it in groups or with individuals, has to fully incorporate the idea of the analyst as being a subjectivity in his own right and to acknowledge the essential indivisibility of observer and observed (Stacey, 2003; Stolorow, 1997). Interestingly, the word "understanding" has different connotations to the term "interpretation" and may convey this indivisibility more clearly: as Orange (1995) describes it, "The term 'understanding' thus refers to both person and process, to both self and relation" (p. 5).

We are indebted to Kohut (1977) for a systematic attempt to clarify different kinds of transference and for broadening the concept away from an exclusive emphasis, as with Freud or Klein, on intrapsychic conflict (and this narrowly conceived in feeding, sexual, and aggressive terms). Through his work with narcissistic patients, he discovered so-called "selfobject" transferences, where the individual attempts to find experiences which will help him have, or maintain, a basic sense of cohesion and well-being. These transferences stem from areas of unmet need, particularly around the formation and cohesion of the self. So, in addition to what the person might *wish* for, the area of repressed desire, there is also the question of what the patient *needs*, the area of developmental deficit; as Stolorow and Lachmann (1981) put it, "experiences that the patient legitimately needed but missed or prematurely lost are understood in the transference in order to assist the patient in his belated psychological development" (p. 309). Kohut (1977) postulated a variety of basic, narcissistic needs and a relationship to the analyst as a "selfobject", which is distinct from the analyst as an object of instinctual conflicts. Symptoms and fears can be understood more widely and affirmatively, as "developmental and restorative necessities" and not merely as "compromise formations" based on psychic conflict, as Freud believed (Lachmann, 1986). Within a group, other members also continually evoke and respond to these selfobject needs, creating a new matrix from which new development might proceed, if all goes well. The group is a complex spatial and temporal reality within which recurring, restorative, and emergent experiences unfold.

The relationship of selfobject to other dimensions of the transference can usefully be framed in terms of a continually shifting figure-ground relationship, with different constellations at different periods.

It could be argued, for example, that until a person is assured through a selfobject experience that her self is supported or cohesive enough, the less likely she will be in being able to tackle psychic conflict in a safe manner. Furthermore, selfobject needs are not confined to the overtly "narcissistic" patient, but apply to areas of narcissistic need in *all* individuals.

There are rich implications for the understanding of groups, although the literature in this area is still relatively new (Harwood & Pines, 1998). The group conductor is faced with the complex task of responding empathically at different levels, both between different members of the group and within the same individual at different times (often within the same session). Howard Bacal (1998) has suggested the term "optimal responsiveness" to describe this flexible capacity in the therapist, replacing the traditional notion of neutrality. The group therapist helps foster spontaneous reactiveness and responsiveness taking place unconsciously, and preconsciously, at all times, between the members.

The irreducible subjectivity of the therapist

Freud (1919a) distinguished the "pure gold of analysis" from the "copper of direct suggestion", to differentiate psychoanalysis from other forms of psychotherapy and suggestion. This was linked to the concept of the "neutral analyst" and the idea of fostering the "transference neurosis" of the patient. However, as Gill (1982) contends, when the analyst does intervene, and even when not doing so, "he may be experienced as suggesting a direction for the patient to pursue" (p. 171).

Orange, Atwood, and Stolorow (1997) questioned what they term the "myth of neutrality" in psychoanalysis. They argue that "each time the analyst offers an interpretation that goes beyond what the patient is consciously aware of, he or she invites the patient to see things, if ever so slightly, from the analyst's own theory-rooted perspective" (p. 39). In the intersubjectivity model, by contrast, the analyst has no "objective position" from which she approaches the patient, and what is crucial is the ability of the analyst to be reflective in such a way that includes an awareness of the values and theoretical frameworks which guide him. Theory, or "internalised theory", more precisely, is not only a model for thinking, but has an important psychological presence, contributing, as Almond (2003) has argued, regardless of particular orientation, to "a sense of conviction, affective stability, reassurance and self-esteem" (p. 130). Criticising both the notion of neutrality and that of the "uncontaminated transference", intersubjectivists draw attention to the unavoidable organising principles of the therapist, including the proposal that transference can be understood as an "organisation", to which analyst and patient both contribute (Fosshage, 1994), a notion similar to Aron's (1996) insistence that the treatment is mutually constituted, but asymmetrical.

What then of the conductor's or analyst's contribution? Orange (1995) argues that the term "countertransference" needs to be replaced by "cotransference". In this view, the cotransference is defined as the analyst's perspective, with the argument being that it is often impossible to quite know what is "counter" to the patient's material, as if each party were independent of the interaction (McLaughlin, 1981). An apt question raised by Goldberg (2007), relevant to such arguments, is that of "who owns the countertransference"? Although Goldberg is specifically addressing publishing, and dilemmas surrounding the writing up of case experience, it can be seen as representing a wider philosophical question, once "mind" is no longer seen as independent substance, encased within someone's skin.

Not only this, but the analytic dyad, and the therapy group, do not exist in isolation from a wider organisational and social context that also nourishes and influences the relationship (Zeddies & Richardson, 1999).[1] Orange (1995) thus declines the temptation to ground some ultimate objectivity in the lone authority of the analyst. A group analytic, and certainly sociological, view might be that the authority of analysts (individual or group) is simply a product of specific historical networks of relations.

Beyond the particular theory the analyst or conductor may hold—and it is interesting to speculate why different therapists gravitate towards a preferred model—there are wider (or deeper) values which influence conduct and thinking. All clinical exchanges involve some communication of values between the patient and therapist, expressed by verbal and non-verbal means. Lichtenberg (1983) argues that the point is not that the analyst can ever become *value-free* (or theory-free), but that he can become more *value sensitive*. This is where the concept of the "social unconscious" has an important clarifying role, helping us to better locate our patients and ourselves within a cultural matrix and attendant world of values that help produce us.

Metaphors for unconscious life: house, home, traffic

In their seminal contribution to relational psychoanalysis, Stolorow and Atwood (1992) offer a building metaphor with which to encapsulate their proposed "three realms of the unconscious" (dynamic unconscious, pre-reflective unconscious, and the unvalidated unconscious). They incorporate the Freudian, dynamic unconscious (associated with repressed, intolerable impulses, etc.) below ground within the dwelling, consistent with an original psychoanalytic image of mind as rooms within a house, locating the unconscious, as one might expect, in the basement. The pre-reflective unconscious, by contrast, has no physical place in Stolorow and Atwood's metaphor, but corresponds to something like the "architect's plan" from which the building has been erected. As organising principles, they inform the construction of the building and the relationship between the various parts of the building, so whilst not "seen", their manifestations are all around. In this regard, the Stolorow metaphor is already an improvement on Freud's, in so far as the house is not a once and for all structure, but involves an ongoing process (design, building, improvement, etc.). The unvalidated unconscious is represented by the "bricks, lumber, and other unused materials" left lying around, "materials which were never made part of the construction but that could have been" (Stolorow & Atwood, 1992, p. 35). In psychological terms, the latter are not (to date) articulated or integrated into mainstream psychic life, but might be so at some future stage; they represent potential, possibility, future horizons.

Does the building or house metaphor need further modification to incorporate subsequent insights of relational psychoanalysis and group-analysis? Perhaps we can no longer see the house, representing mind, as a detached dwelling, separate from its neighbourhood (or, indeed, as inspired by a lone architect). In philosophical terms, to displace the detached house image corresponds to displacing the detached Cartesian subject, the independent, "punctual" self (Taylor, 1989). In similar vein, Foulkes (1974) argued that mind is not simply a quality "inside the person as an individual" (p. 277). Theorising a "multipersonal" dimension, Foulkes (1974) said that there cannot be a "conventional, sharp differentiation between inside and outside … What is inside is always also outside, and what is outside is inside as well" (p. 280). One solution therefore, is to see the dwelling as terrace house within a street, within a neighbourhood, and so on.[2]

Foulkes (1975b) proposed a traffic analogy of psychic and social life, consistent perhaps with the analogy of terrace house within a street, within a town, with a region, within a country, and so on. Emphasising notions of interconnection, network, and transpersonal process, Foulkes pointed out the "The traffic (i.e., 'transpersonal processes') is not an isolated fact and closed system"; there are other towns, many road users, and routes in and out.

Retaining, but expanding upon Stolorow's notion of the "architect's plan" (pre-reflective unconscious), we can posit an architectural team whose influence is exerted at different stages of construction; it takes a village (or neighbourhood) to raise a child. Development is crucial. So too, a house begins with one idea, until it is modified by one builder, downsized by another, extended after five years, and so on; behind every person is a group; human development is a continuing affair. This sense of movement and potential, Stolorow's unvalidated unconscious, is imaginatively analogised by his image of the unused materials lying around the site.

The group analytic concept of "social unconscious" traverses the repressed unconscious, the pre-reflective unconscious, and the invalidated unconscious, in so far as these can be separated at all; it constitutes the kind of transpersonal "traffic" through which individuality is formed, maintained, and transformed. At the same time, it does not deny the importance of singularity or creative reinterpretation of one's conditions of existence.

Conclusion

This chapter describes the emergent paradigm of "relational" thinking as it occurs within psychoanalysis and group analysis. This is contrasted with the classical framework of psychoanalysis, which exercised considerable influence on the formation of Freudian and post-Freudian orthodoxies, including much of early group analysis. Intersubjective perspectives offer exciting possibilities for reconceptualising our practice, as does the group analytic insistence on the spirit of "no-closure" (see Foulkes quotation at start of chapter) and the value of evaluated, reciprocal dialogue.

It is to related concepts of dialogue, historicity, and the role of personal/cultural horizons that we now turn.

CHAPTER TWO

Personal horizons, unformulated experience, and group analysis*

Hans-Georg Gadamer (1900–2002) is one of Heidegger's most famous students (Gadamer, 1985; see introductions by Johnson, 2000, and Lawn, 2006), whose work is situated within Germanic traditions of existentialism and hermeneutics. Gadamer lived through four regimes—Weimar, Third Reich (briefly), Communism, and the Federal Republic—which make his writings all the more interesting, even though social reality was not his object of inquiry. An influential figure, with pan-disciplinary appeal, he has been criticised for, on the one hand, conservatism, with his emphasis on tradition and authority, whilst praised for the precise opposite, his valuation of freedom, trust in dialogue, and rejection of closure (Gadamer, 2006, in conversation, explores such controversies).

As we saw in the preceding chapter, there is considerable interest in applying hermeneutic (and narrative) ideas to the psychoanalytic project (Spence, 1982, 1987; Steele, 1979), which in part is a reaction against Freud's ideal of the analyst as detached observer and of

---

*This chapter is a substantial reworking of ideas originally published in 2004 in "You're not finished yet": personal horizons and unformulated experience. *Psychodynamic Practice,* 10: 5–26.

psychoanalysis modeled on the image of the conquering scientist. This chapter shows how Gadamer's hermeneutics has an equal and compelling relevance to group analysis.

The concept of horizon

The concept of "horizon" is used by several twentieth-century phenomenological philosophers, but it is to Gadamer that we can turn for a more systematic definition. Gadamer situates the concept squarely in the domain of philosophical hermeneutics, which is concerned with issues of how we come to an understanding of historical texts, cultures, and people. The stance of Gadamer radically departs from Cartesian and rationalist philosophy, with its idealisations of "Reason" and denial of the historicity of being. For him, horizon is like a non-fixed vision, with Gadamer defining the quality of "truth" as openness to experience and a willingness to modify one's horizons.

One can link the idea of horizon with Stolorow's "organisation of experience", discussed in the previous chapter, or to Nietzsche's "perspectivism", discussed in the next. Horizon concerns our inevitable historical situatedness, indicating the ground on which we stand and our embeddedness in what we inherit; context is everywhere, forever behind one's back, as it were. Understanding and interpretation always stems from a particular perspective and tradition within this historical matrix, upon a background of pre-understandings. Gadamer used the term "tradition" to express this dimension of legacy, as the something we always stand within: "it is always part of us, a model or exemplar, a recognition of ourselves ..." (Gadamer, 1975, p. 282); we are always situated somewhere in relation to what we seek to understand or to know. Weinsheimer (1985) writes: "Horizon is another way of describing context. It includes everything of which one is not immediately aware and of which one must in fact remain unaware if there is to be a focus of attention; but one's horizon is also the context in terms of which the object of attention is understood" (p. 157).

Attempting to free the word "prejudice" from its negative, Enlightenment associations, Gadamer argues that prejudices are an inevitable part of the fabric of involvement and interaction with the world, and influence our presuppositions. He argues: "Prejudices are biases to our openness to the world. They are simply conditions whereby we experience something—whereby what we encounter says something to us" (Gadamer, 1966, p. 8). When we are better aware of the historicity of our background beliefs or prejudices, alternative organisations of meaning become possible and with this can arise a greater understanding of the context within which the other's meaning exists. Gadamer calls this shift "fusion of horizons", which is not an end point but is part of many further, incomplete acts of understanding.[1] Understanding, at bottom, involves a relation between horizons that is continually subject to revision.

Understanding (*verstehen*) in Gadamer's work is premised on involvement, in which we "reach" and "develop" contact, a term which refers both to person—as in a "person with understanding"—and process—as in "we reach an understanding" (Orange, 1995). Arguing against objectivist versions of science, Gadamer was interested in the process of understanding and not its static and precise product. Understanding emerges in the play of dialogue, in conversations which are neither predictable nor possessed by either party. We need, he argues, to retain a constant openness to the other, to the text or other culture, to what is being said, in order that the contours of our own prejudice (background beliefs) can appear. Simply put, one opens oneself up to other possibilities, including new prejudices, productive or otherwise.

Clinicians can surely relate to a notion of horizon. Therapeutic conversation or dialogue promotes fusion of horizons in a lively back and forth process in which it is trusted that something new can emerge (for each party). We know that patients can only see as far as they can look and we hope that, through therapy, any given individual will emerge with broader horizons and a greater flexibility of perspective. Patients (indeed, humans) are metaphorical "world-makers", beings busy at toil within their own epistemological circles, hampered and hexed by the repeating problems to which they seek solutions. Horizons of a particular present are like defences, in that we need them but are constrained by them, they both reveal and conceal aspects of reality. Speaking as a philosopher, not as a therapist, Gadamer (1975) recognised that, "we are always affected, in hope and fear, by what is nearest to us" (p. 305). A narrow field of vision can help in some circumstances (e.g., fight-flight acts of survival) but, in others, is non-adaptive: where no "fusion of horizons" is attempted, critical understanding and the possibility of alternatives cannot emerge. True understanding and change necessitates some awareness of our own horizons and a capacity to decentre from them in order to be influenced by the horizons of the other. This decentring is relative, since we cannot but remain ourselves when we encounter someone else or another culture. Yet that encounter can help, one hopes, to modify our stance, even our identity, depending on what is at stake in that encounter.

It is useful, therefore, to compare the work of the psychotherapist with, say, that of the historian. Crucially, the psychotherapist reaches for successive understandings of the patient's inner culture just as the historian recreates and researches a culture of the past. Of course, all patients carry complex cultures within them, as do their therapists. Therapists enter any clinical situation informed by their traditions, prejudices, and horizons, and so one challenge is: how do we begin to understand the reality of another person's subjective world and horizon? How do we relate to the stranger, the other, and how do we develop an understanding in which dimensions of familiarity and unfamiliarity are inescapably present? Such issues are an intimate part of the challenge of empathy. Derived from the German, *Einfuehlung*—"to feel into"—empathy involves elements of understanding what it might be like to be in someone else's place or shoes and of "becoming aware of someone strange or different" (*Fremdwarhrnehmung*) (Basch, 1983). Yet, as Orange, Atwood, and Stolorow (1997) suggest, in the clinical situation the challenge involves developing "an attitude of continuing sensitivity to the inescapable interplay of observer and observed. It assumes that instead of entering and immersing ourselves in the experience of another, we join the other in the intersubjective space" (p. 74), or in the case of group, the intersubejective spaces of a multi-person situation.

The horizontal in group analysis

> The psychoanalytic process might be called a *vertical* analysis. It goes from surface to depth, from present to past, thinking in terms of hierarchical layers and levels inside the patient's mind. By contrast, group-analysis might be termed a *horizontal* analysis …
> (Foulkes & Anthony, 1957, p. 42)

Foulkes used the notion of horizontal perspective to characterise group analysis, involving analysis of individuals as constituted by the matrix, that is, within a network of relations and cultural inheritance, contrasted with the psychoanalytic perspective, which operated on an archaeological or vertical plane (see Chapter One). Foulkes sought to bring the planes together—the horizontal and vertical—and in so doing displaced any absolute division between the interpersonal and the intrapsychic. He believed that it is through progressive expansion of communication that the different experiential worlds of patients within a group are clarified. If horizon is landscape, then horizontal understanding involves a kind of survey; we might call this a wide, "horizontal seeing", to adopt Barthold's (2010) suggestive phrase. True to Foulkes' therapeutic pragmatism, horizontal seeing is not a God's eye view or a commanding viewpoint, but is forever located within particular moments of seeing, acts of intervention, located within the context of ongoing clinical dialogue. Hence, whilst *theoria* allows a necessary degree of separation and distance, our acts and expressions of understanding do not arise *sui generis*, because we operate within the context of pre-involvements and the horizons of specific traditions of training, convention, and so on; "The conductor, like the author, does not occupy an Archimedean point outside of the group from which to make pronouncements" (Zinkin, 1996, p. 351).

Several group analytic concepts seem compatible with the idea of horizon. Foulkes (1975a) deployed the image of the "figure and ground" relationship from Gestalt psychology. This visual, spatial metaphor illustrates how a certain position or practice acts as "ground"—a silent, background horizon—within which particular objects are experienced, but that if the former comes into direct awareness, then this becomes "figure". Group analysis, with its emphasis on a plurality of perspectives, can be conceptualised in terms of an ever-changing figure-ground constellation; Foulkes referred to "configurational analysis". The idea of horizon both describes the kind of enclosure that each group member brings with him into the group, but, as group, it also describes the resultant totality of enclosures, though these are not necessarily homogenous. Groups might start with narrow, fearful horizons; groups with "no horizon", in colloquial terms, do not see far enough and cannot accommodate change. Thus, we justly worry when the horizons in any given group are narrow, repetitious, and when there is a lack of fluidity between figure and ground. On the other hand, "to have a horizon" means, in Gadamer's (1995) words: "... not being limited to what is nearby but being able to see beyond it" (p. 302). To continue Gadamer's point, ideally, then, "A horizon is not a rigid boundary but something that moves with one and invites one to advance further" (1995, p. 245) and in this respect groups are a rich presence of contrasting and competing perspectives, perspectives which broaden through successive communicative activity, layer upon layer.

We can, I suggest, align Foulkes' emphasis on group powers of communication, free exchange, and resonance with Gadamer's concepts of conversation, dialogue, and dialectic.[2] Gadamer's vision of conversation, influenced as it is by Socratean/Platonic values, holds that understanding between people is dependent on a dialectics of dialogue and the fusion of horizons; each of these steps is unpredictable, given that we "fall" into conversations that lead us to new places, and given the relatively "I-less" quality of language. Gadamer observes, "something comes into being that had not existed before and that exists from now on ... Something emerges that is contained in neither of the partners alone" (Gadamer, 1991, p. 462). In other words, we need others to see what we cannot see, as the possibility of new horizons emerges through dialogue, in a dialectic accompanied by inherent separations, mis- and non-understandings. A fusion of horizons is not a superficial agreement.

A related feature of Gadamer's model is the importance of the engaged trust and play (*Spiel*, play, originally meant dance in German) which carry participants along. Unfortunately, although Foulkes used rich metaphors, such as resonance, he did not clearly emphasise the type of serious play which occurs in analytic groups, which may account for the descriptive flatness in the clinical material which he cites; on the other hand, how therapists write and how they conduct groups are different matters. The play which Gadamer tried to capture, is the sheer buoyancy of dialogue, both patterned and unpredictable, the infinite play of background and foreground, one horizon and another and another, and the interplay of the strange and the familiar; in his words, the "true locus of hermeneutics is this in-between" (1995, p. 295).

Vignette one

Sheila (early thirties), who had missed her group the week previously, sat quietly attending to others. Meanwhile, Andrea (late thirties) abruptly stopped talking, announcing that she had said too much and was afraid the group was fed up with her. Sheila retorted that she felt a similar fear and that for her it was important not to take up group time. As others commented on Sheila's previous absence she looked surprised. She could not see that she was missed, believing that others would have been relieved by her absence because they would have had a respite from her. Discussion ensued, focusing on the difficulty of bringing needs to the group and how to deal with the fear that these might overwhelm others or be met with a non-receptive or hostile response.

I said to Sheila that the idea that she was noticed, let alone valued by the group, seemed unacceptable and that she could not allow herself to think it. She looked dumbfounded and restated her belief that, "I don't think that people would ever miss me—I've always expected other people not to like me."

Later in the same group session, resonating to similar themes of non-acceptance, Andrea said she felt like an uncomfortable child and that often, on first waking, she had a strange, twilight dream from which she needed time to "come around". In the twilight she felt like an awkward schoolgirl and had to consciously remind herself she was a grown woman, as well as parent, in order to face the day.

Sheila and Andrea: organising world views?

Sheila and Andrea lived within narrow horizons; there was something frozen about their respective developments. I had seen Sheila and Andrea in extended consultations before recommending group analysis, that recommendation being based on a conviction that they needed considerable time and experience with others if new development were to take place. Sheila lacked a sense of temporality, as if she had "just arrived", disconnected from her history. Andrea, on the other hand, had a conscious terror of being unable to develop, of being permanently "stuck"; these are, of course, my metaphors to translate troubled mental states. Sheila and Andrea were struggling, I would suggest, with the consequences of limiting internal horizons, unknown yet organising principles of psychic organisation. One of the consequences of living within narrow, over-near horizons, is that people cannot see where they are and populateit with more diverse experiences. Neither of these two women could envisage herself as being significant (e.g., being missed by the group) or as capable of being enjoyed by others. Each had a poor sense of personal agency. The group responded to these psychic constellations as they became familiar with them; as a whole, the group was only able to know and challenge its membership through the acquired confidence of progressive communication. In this way, the expanding horizon of the group is a precondition for the expanding horizon of individual members, and by the same token the work of individual members changes the scope of the group, in a rich contest of figure-ground relations. Individuals shape group dialogue and are themselves shaped by it.

Theoretical reflections

As we saw in Chapter One, intersubjective theory uses the notion of non-conscious organising principles which, in the examples of Sheila and Andrea, governed and limited their view of themselves, their capabilities, expectations, or horizons. Organising principles are pre-reflective and can be thought about as akin to "emotional conclusions" which have consolidated in response to earlier, intersubjective contexts of being (Stolorow & Atwood, 1992). Such principles come to thematise a person's existence, giving us an immediate experiential sense of "how a person is".

I propose the term "population" as a useful way of describing the infinite, intimate ways in which inner horizons are filled. In the faculty psychology of the eighteenth century, minds were seen as "busy places", with individuals "crowded by thoughts", ideas could "throng", and so on (Pasanek, personal communication). We saw in Chapter One how Foulkes used the metaphor of "traffic" to characterise group life, and "population" seems equally apt to depict the way in which horizons encompass specific contents—be they emotional expectations, habitual reactions, evaluations, narratives, and so one. Narrow horizons are equivalent to a thin, underpopulated group matrix, where there is little room to move, whilst broad, flexible horizons are equivalent to a richly populated group matrix in all its diversity.

While it was not entirely clear at the time of the individual consultations—like all understanding, analytic understanding is a constant dialectic of before-and-after, part-and-whole—Sheila evoked a subtle, nonverbal sense of unimportance and invisibility (a self-effacing manner, an unemotional exterior). Andrea seemed anxiously suspended in time, looking as if she did not feel substantial (a frightened face, a discourse of grave hesitancy, graphically illustrated by the twilight state upon waking).

Let us further elaborate on their respective ways of organising experience and selfhood.

Andrea: not enough light

Plants with insufficient light may survive, but will not flourish; deprived of what they need, the active synthesis required for good growth does not take place. Adaptation to poor light carries a cost.

The reference to light is not incidental, in that one of the themes and metaphors that emerged in Andrea's therapy was that of "living under mother's shadow". It was likely that at some nonverbal level, Andrea had accommodated a depressed and depleted mother who had not, herself, grown. This impression was captured in many evocative, "small" memories of interaction and recollections of family life—the "unthought known" (Bollas, 1987). There was something telling about Andrea's face and eyes, her tendency to look down, and an attitude suggestive of in-built fatalism. Perhaps she had adapted to her mother's state of mind and learned not to ask for much, all of which contributed to Andrea's stunted growth. What you do not see and what is not seen by the other, you cannot take in and use and, indeed, it took Andrea a long time before she could visually connect to (directly face) the others in the group. In that way she remained in the shadow of the group; not being able to look directly or to make a claim on group time was linked unconsciously to a fear of being overwhelmed by pressing needs.

In the transference, as I understood it, Andrea tried to reactivate a more responsive mother. Interestingly, she complained that in dealing with "large bodies", such as the schools, public organisations, etc. (and of course symbolised by the group), she felt acutely small and vulnerable, perhaps expressing the kind of relationship to the mother inside her. At some level she experienced herself as an awkward child, on the brink of teen age, unable to progress. There were important cultural contributors to this, associated with a particular concept of being female and an educational horizon which limited her view of what might be possible with her life. Although she did not expect others would listen to her, as in the group vignette, Andrea was nevertheless responsive to others articulating her fear about being in touch with her relational needs. Picking up, for example, on her implied expectation at the end of the individual consultations that I would not plan to see her again, I commented, "I think you find these sessions and my interest in your life novel and look eagerly, hoping that I'll be like an interested mum, devoted to what you need, looking forward to what you bring each time. But I suspect you're fearful that this won't happen and that you'll become a burden on me ... like I've noticed how you seem to think that every appointment here is going to be our last."

Also of note was her anxiety about the institution within which the psychotherapy occurred, her view being that the NHS would not regard her needs as deserving provision, let alone priority. This could reflect a number of concerns, not to mention realities, and perhaps I represented both a parent and this larger institution within which she felt lost. I explored her feelings towards other institutions in the past and in doing so, a memory emerged: of how, as a girl, she had not felt helped by home in dealing with "big school" and how depressed her mother could be on her return from school. There seemed to be a chronic lack of mirroring as she grew into an older child, and little help adjusting to the new school and peers. But there was also the influence of an older-style, working class, deferential stance towards authority that was expressed at home. Such social horizons are a critical dimension of that which (in-) forms the patient's world.

Andrea seemed influenced by a variety of pre-reflective principles, the dominant ones being: she was a dull person; she was small and the world was large; you get on as best you can and serve others. When Andrea entered the group (another "larger body"), feelings of small-ness and anxiety about having to claim time were once again reacti-vated, this time with siblings and companions to contend with. Whole areas of her life were ill-defined and, consequently, she doubted her judgment. "Frozen self-states" (Bollas, 1993) drastically constrained her assumptive world, her very horizons of being. Reactivated in the transference, she was not sure that either I or the group would have sufficient interest to sustain a relationship with her but equally seemed not to have given up hope that someone could finally attend to her needs and not close the door on her development, as it were. She was able to respond to Sheila, and vice versa, because of a clear crossover in these pre-reflective principles, for example, their common expectations of not being noticed and adaptation of being very careful about the time they could claim. Having said this, they were equally able to note, if not challenge, the assumptions that each other was making, which was the beginning of therapeutic mirroring: "This seems to be how you see yourself"; "Interesting you made *that* assumption"; "You're like me, I'm always doing that"; and so on. In fact, they became good therapists to each other, a sub-pair within the group, able to sense and increasingly identify each other's personal horizons. With this, figure and ground, problem and presentation could begin to shift, with silently organised states of mind slowly symbolised.

Sheila: being a nonentity in a world of people

When Sheila was dumbfounded and convinced that group members would neither notice nor miss her, I knew I needed to take this at face value. Rather than "denying" her significance or "defensively" holding back from the group, I think she was communicating experiential limits of her world, her horizon. However, with others saying that they *did* notice and did have feelings towards her, Sheila was challenged by counter-expectational responses.

As for her background, Sheila had grown up in a household dominated by drink problems, with parents whom she described as "functioning alcoholics". It is interesting to speculate on how family systems adapt to, and accommodate, alcoholism as an organising and hegemonic principle of family life; what becomes central or normative, like the presence of the bottle and drinking behaviour at the heart of family life in Eugene O'Neill's (1959) masterpiece on addiction, loses visibility because it is part of the natural ground (Weegmann, 2005a). I had no doubt, from my knowledge of Sheila, that whilst her material needs had on the whole been attended to, many of her other needs had been neglected and curtailed, particularly those which might have come between her parents and their drinking. On holidays, for example, she had to entertain herself for days on end whilst her parents visited pubs. Being ill during school term might be met with annoyance because, in Sheila's experience, her mother would have then to be available to look after her and mornings were difficult because of hangovers. Sheila had lived with, but did not reflectively know how to think about, the centrality of drinking in home life and only recognised her parents as having such problems years later, after recovering from her own subsequent drink problems (Sheila was now abstinent). Much drama passed unnoticed because of its very familiarity. Her recovery brought clarity, as the clouded reality of family life started to settle, but this was only partial. In fact, the metaphor of "clouded" experience was a productive one for the group as a whole, not only Sheila.

My understanding of Sheila's developmental self, was that she had found ways of not being noticed at certain times, such as during intoxication or illness following intoxication and had acquired some self-esteem and efficacy through cleaning up mess around the house. She described "dry periods" where she sensed her parents were ashamed and her "good behaviour" was rewarded; mother would say, "You're a good one, we don't have to worry about you", and from father, "Anything you want, just say the word." A sensori-motor adaptation to life resulted, which, if verbalised, might translate as something like: "If you make yourself a nonentity in various situations, then you minimise the chances of being injured. Play it safe, don't be noticed." The timeless quality to her initial presentation made sense to me in terms of a process of dissociation and mindless accommodation to experience; protectively, it meant that there was no future to disappoint.

In spite of the presence of drinking during upbringing, she nevertheless had a wider variety of developmental experiences, positive and negative, inside and outside the family, but certainly within a context of a significant degree of deprivation. The notion of being missed, let alone positively valued by the group, was an alien notion. However, once this was exposed and explored, it became part of a process, a referent or a potential theme within the life of the group. What had been ground, a wordless aspect of Sheila's inner horizons, could become figure, populated or filled by new meaning.

The therapist's horizons

Therapists work and interpret within a variety of horizons—personal, professional, and cultural. Such horizons are necessarily perspectival and, of course, therapists are profoundly affected by the "pre-understandings" of their trainings. The latter contain not only formative experiences and cultivated capacities, but also values, allegiances, modes of comportment (e.g., the use of couches, circles of chairs, nods, notes, expressive/receptive orientations, active/passive approaches, etc.), and so on. Clearly, psychoanalytic enterprises, such as group analysis, need to be placed in the socio-discursive contexts in which they originated. We always think within some tradition or other, which limit our horizons and "determine our history from a position within it" (Warnke, 1987, p. 29). The therapeutic authority with which we are endowed is similarity located within pre-existing practices, traditions, and precedents which help govern the very modes by which we live and see ourselves, for example, as autonomous, freely choosing, psychological beings. In other words there is an ethical dimension, a sense of working towards a desired horizon, an area explored in the final chapter.

Take the example of the therapist's theory, which can be understood as a horizon within which we gain distance and formulate understanding. Theory is often a preferred viewpoint—"In this sense, 'theory' can be understood not only as a model of thinking, but also as an internal selfobject, so to speak, helping the analyst to feel secure and coherent in his/her functioning" (Weegmann, 2001, p. 527). But there is always limitation with theory, which can also create a loss of sight or become encrusted. Gadamer (1991) was well aware of this paradox and of how both an opening and a concealing of horizons occurs "in all our experiences of interpretation".

We are all capable of retreating into the comforts and consolations of own world horizon, and much of the historical intolerance amongst different psychoanalytic groups or schools could be conceptualised in these terms (Eaton, 1998).[3] Spurling (1993) calls attention to the role of tradition within psychotherapy and the inherent ambivalences within the term, which connotes a "handing over", or delivery and continuity, but also risk, *tradere*, to betray. Relationships between different schools or individuals can, in these circumstances, become characterised by non-conversation (no fusion of horizons), since no one is willing to risk their horizon being challenged. Therapeutic authority can be used and misused, and in its worse light, such traditions simply shore up fragile, defensive solidarities between members.

In the cases described, the use of self psychology and intersubjecvity theory is apparent, influencing my approach to the transference and relational needs. The questions I ventured reflect this, such as: What had been the quality of some of Sheila's and Andrea's formative selfobject experiences? What had been the developmental costs of these? Was there still a sense of hope in finding, through therapy, an appropriately responsive human milieu? Attending to relational needs involves understanding a wider picture, influenced by cultural construction, that people have about themselves; for example, expectations of femininity and what can be conceived educationally (Andrea), or playing a serving role in life (both Sheila and Andrea). Such needs are not fixed once and for all, but can evolve within complex, shifting relational contexts, of which the group is a new, hopefully transformative, one.

The question remains: what are the limitations of my theory and traditions and what might have been better opened up through the influence of another perspective?

"You're not finished yet": the role of unformulated experience

On joining the group, Andrea was demoralised for long periods, and declared, following a humiliating set back, "I guess that's me, how I am, all I can expect", to which a fellow group member, Peter, retorted, "Yes, but you're not finished yet … none of us are." It took me some time to register Peter's response to Andrea, but once I had, it underlined the fact that his simple words were a fine description of psychotherapy, which, after all, concerns psychological development and the prospect of what might "come next". None of our stories are complete. One patient's horizons, of which he or she is unaware, are more clearly evident to another patient, or patients, and vice versa, who can, with horizontal seeing and unfolding dialogue, help give it form.

Stern's (1997) concept of "unformulated experience" is comparable to the pre-reflective unconscious, concerning as it does those raw materials or building blocks of subjective life that lack clarity or articulation. Andrea's pessimism, for example, reflected fatalism and a crushing sense of being an undeserving person, undeserving of attention and improvement. Stern explains the concept as "the label I have chosen to refer to mentation characterised by lack of clarity or articulation" and goes on to contend, "unformulated experience is the uninterpreted form of those raw materials ... that may eventually be assigned verbal interpretation and thereby brought into articulate form" (p. 37). Bringing into articulate form is seldom instantaneous, akin to the flick of a light switch. In this regard, it is interesting to note that Foulkes valued the non-explicit, the inconspicuous, the unfinished moment, as well as the reciprocity of "the need to understand and be understood" (Foulkes & Anthony, 1957).[4] In Gadamer's language, we would talk in terms of the value of non-completeness and an open dialectic.

The analyst, likewise, trades upon his own unformulated experience of the patient, trying, through sensing, clarification, and interpretation, to articulate what is important in the group at any given point; this is accomplished, partially and provisionally, through the endless creation of reflective spaces, promoting a "meeting of minds" (Behr & Hearst, 2005).

Moving horizons: therapeutic change

Central assumptions governing Sheila's and Andrea's respective psychic lives, constituting horizons of experience, were modified as a result of three years of group analysis. Both were better able to initiate, and inhabit, less rigid worldviews; with the broadening of horizons, people acquire a new perspective on their former problems and encounter the world differently. Horizons travel, once they are freed up from fixed viewpoints, once the work and play of the group enables wider, newer contexts of meaning.

Vignette two

On one occasion, the entrance to the clinic was changed due to building work, and Andrea asked an official the directions to the psychotherapy department, knowing, as he spoke, that she was forgetting what he was telling her. Andrea was thrown by this exchange and arrived at the group acutely embarrassed, complaining, "I felt stupid not knowing the way, so very stupid."

It seemed as if the experience had precipitated a momentary crisis in her sense of self, enfeebling confidence. With discussion, there was some partial realignment, especially when others expressed their parallel difficulties following the route. There were many conversations about this representation of herself, in this and other groups, but eventually she was able to question the immediacy of her views: "I always think first, 'It's me. I'm the thick one. Other people know how to do things and know how to deal with officials'."

I would suggest that, in this example, we see a reactivation, under a condition of stress, of a particular way that Andrea organised her experience, albeit it a self-defeating one. The incident brought a characteristic reaction to the fore so that others were able to see how this operated in Andrea's mind. There was a transference aspect: her experience of me as an important official who might easily overlook or fail to see her importance; consistent with this, she saw me as "clever", in complete contrast to herself.

Psychic patterns, by definition, are enduring and "people repeat because they organise their experience according to the principles available, until other alternative principles are established" (Stolorow, 1997, p. 429). After much work in, by, and through the group, Andrea was better able to value her views and mind, enjoying a previously unfamiliar sense of effectiveness. She moved beyond a view of herself as a dull, crushed individual and her self-esteem was less dependent upon a role of serving others.

Vignette three

There was a heated discussion between two group members, with Sheila sitting anxiously between them. In a familiar pattern, Sheila often held herself responsible for such "rows" breaking out, related historically to a fear of rowing parents and the wish to hold the peace. On this occasion, however, she said nothing until much later in the same group: "I've been sitting thinking about the anger earlier and for the first time I didn't feel as worried about it ... my heartbeat went up and then I thought ... 'Hold on, this is just two people expressing their views. I don't have to be threatened'." She smiled, adding, "I enjoy this group. We can all have our say and we come back each week with new things to deal with. I think I'm changing because people take me seriously, which never happened at home. Something artificial, booze, always got in the way of my parents and me."

This example illustrates considerable change from the extremes of dissociation which had characterised Sheila's dealings with the world, suggesting an increased ability to embrace more complex segments of experience. Dominant, hegemonic principles influencing her internal horizons could be rearticulated and life populated by richer experiences. Sheila made impressive strides in locating her history, her effective history—traditions, prejudices, if one wills—and thus seeing her past in a different way; past and emergent horizons merged through dialogue, so that the old and the new were seen differently, certainly in less violent or exclusive terms. Her confidence and assertion grew and she was far less afraid to have an impact on others.

Circles of the unsaid

It is probably impossible to capture complex qualities of group life in writing, and, clearly, to isolate particular individuals for purposes of clinical illustration is problematic. It is artificial in that, even though it is individuals who seek group treatment, "individual processes" cannot be conceptualised independently of the group matrix in which they occur. That matrix shifts continually, and effective therapy groups are always on the move, occupied not only by present content, but by that which is not-yet said, continually pushing and bumping the edges of the "circle of the unexpressed" (Linge, 1966, p. xxxii); each group calls forth another occasion, a further conversation, a next time. As a consequence, group horizons expand and allow "corrective developmental dialogues" to occur (Tolpin, 1971). Developmental dialogue "gives us the opportunity to look forward and not exclusively backwards and to bring movement rather than petrification to the patient's experience in therapy" (Pines, unpublished, 1996b, p. 11).

Although movement is integral to any process of change, there is the important question of what gets in its way, of hope versus stagnation. Just as group analysis has been open to the criticism that it is based on a communicative optimism, Gadamer's approach has been criticised for its benevolence, his being a hermeneutics of trust rather than one of suspicion. There are, when all is said and done, many conversations which seem to land nowhere, with no one being the wiser; in the realm of human transaction, con-fusions of horizons are as likely to arise as fusions of understanding. And just as group analysis has to grapple with developmental refusals and powerful retreats, "anti-group process", if one wills (Nitsun, 1996), so too Gadamer's ideal has to deal with "anti-dialogue", consisting of a refusal to learn and a ruthless non-openness to experience which simply reinforces (unthought) known prejudices. Both approaches have to be acknowledged, including negative dimensions and distortions of power/domination.

In defence of a Gadamerian version of how group analysis proceeds, it would be simplistic to imply that developmental dialogues simply unfold, evenly and progressively. Misunderstanding is constant companion to understanding, with psychotherapy having its productive origins and very effectiveness "in *breaches* in intersubjectivity" (Linge, 1966, p. xii, my emphasis). Efforts to repair such breaches are central to an analytic process in groups, with its unending cycles of dialogue and exchange premised upon "the continual iterative process of taking in different 'explanations', with its implications" (Thornton, 2004, p. 311).

Conclusion

Peter's simple observation, "You're not finished yet …", was a challenge to finitude or closure, to how as people we can be stuck around the limited horizon of a particular present. The quiet dominance of any person's organising principles often makes particular life experiences seem inevitable, just as in societal terms, a particular world-view can seem part of the natural order. Sheila and Andrea were suffering because their internal world-views were crippling, but were assisted through their immersion in the unfolding articulations of group dialogue and shared understanding. Although writing as psychoanalyst rather than group analyst, Stolorow (Stolorow, Atwood & Orange, 2001) makes the valuable point that all being involves a "multiply contextualised experiential world … Horizons continually form, modify and transform within a 'nexus of living systems'. Groups represent live contexts within which old problems are re-contextualised and new trajectories consolidated" (p. 47). Gadamer taught us well, when he insisted on the continual buoyancy and interplay between spaces of experience and horizons of expectation.

A Gadamerian view of group analysis emphasises the playful and serious intimacy of dialogue and of dialectic as the condition for the expansion of horizons. Dialectic in this view is not premised on any simple schema of overcoming, but on the acknowledgment of the inevitable, mixed up nature of human "throwness" and exchange. Retranslating back to Foulkes words, (Foulkes & Anthony, 1957, pp. 149–150), "Therapy lies at both ends of the communication process … communication becomes plastic, relative and modifiable by group experience, not rigid, absolute and repetitive". Further, I would argue, this time against a Foulksean ideal, that group analysis is seldom characterised by the equivalent of psychoanalytic "free associations" (i.e., "free group associations"); there has never been a "blank group" in the way in which there have been "blank screen" analysts. Rather, group analysis is characterised by the serious work and play of articulation, of group dialogue in which all participants are inevitably affected (constrained and enabled) by the realities of addressing and answering.

Group health is characterised by ever more richly populated horizons, which contain an expanding field of possible experience, moving patients beyond what is present and familiar. In the evocative words of one commentator, "Gadamer's hermeneutics preserves the tension between our finite, practical existence and our desire to transcend it causes us to see Hermes anew. He is no longer just an unknown messenger sent from on high, but our own kin: as understanding beings caught 'in-between' we are the offspring of Hermes" (Barthold, 2010, p. xxii).

CHAPTER THREE

Perspectivism, pragmatism, group analysis

Foulkes wrote little on his philosophy, and what there is dispersed and suggestive rather than systematic (Cohn, 1996). This is consistent with a man who travelled light regarding theory and whose pragmatic approach resulted in his keeping a distance from any overarching viewpoint. Dahlin (1991) contends that, "Foulkes might have not felt the need for a covering metatheory. Consequently, he never composed one and left the problem to his followers" (p. 28). Is this a weakness, the consequence of an absence of theory, or a strength, a refusal to be bound by the omnipotence of "one" theory? This chapter favours the latter view, seeing it as advantageous that Foulkes did not anchor group analysis to a master perspective or any single foundation, but by the same token, group analysis cannot be a theoretical and nor can it afford complacency about its existence and need for development (Weegmann, 2004b). Unfortunately, perhaps, group analysis moved rather slowly away from its parent discipline, psychoanalysis, in its quest to develop new models of understanding and languages with which to characterise group life. Foulkes' loyalty to psychoanalysis, even "loss of nerve", may have inhibited attempts to draw upon other potential models or to exploit them more fully (Dalal, 1998; Stacey, 2003). If group analysis stands in need of new developments and ways of conceptualising and researching its practice, then philosophical perspectives are one way of prompting this.

Several commentators have explored links between group analysis and philosophy, the first major attempt being that of de Maré (1972). Since then, other connections have been examined, such as the compatibility between Foulkes' ideas and those of the existential-phenomenological tradition (e.g., Cohn, 1996; Cohn, 1997; Diamond, 1996; Gordon, 1991; Maglo, 2002), links to Bakhtin's philosophy of dialogue (Pines, 1996a; Zinkin, 1996), and to Wittgenstein's philosophy of language (Cooper, 1996; Wyse, 1996). So far, however, no one has addressed what group analysis could learn from the philosophies of Nietzsche and Dewey, a surprising fact in the light of the interest that has been shown in the links between such thinkers and individual psychoanalysis (e.g., Goldberg, 2000, 2002 & 2007; Mace, 1999; Orange, 1995; Rorty, 2000).

As one of the nineteenth-century "masters of suspicion", Nietzsche came to see the whole enterprise of philosophy as interpretation (*Deutung*) and moving picture, rather than a special view or privileged vantage point (Ricoeur, 1970). In this sense, Nietzsche was a profound radical and sceptic, his image of philosophy different to the classical romance of philosophy as "mirror of nature" and its quest for "true representation" (Rorty, 1980). Dewey's pragmatism is equally far-reaching. Although "pragmatism" has acquired connotations of expediency and mere practicality, Dewey rejected divides between theory and practice and did not think that by rejecting supposed "ultimate foundations", philosophy would usher in a mirror opposite of "anything goes"; we still need, in his view, rigour and the demands of what he called "warranted assertability". Here, I characterise Dewey's approach as one of "principled, reflective inquiry", which, like Nietzsche's perspectivism, has a rich import for understanding the psychic life of therapeutic groups.

Nietzsche's perspectivism

> The human intellect cannot avoid seeing itself in its own perspective forms and *only* in these. We cannot look around our own corner. (Nietzsche, 1882, p. 239)

Nietzsche's output is extensive, as are the many traditions that have engaged with this work (see Sedgwick's 1995 overview, and

Stern's 1978 introduction). We shall confine ourselves to Nietzsche's perspectival view of knowing and being, a fraction of his output, even though it can be argued that the perspectival spirit pervades his work as a whole, however inconsistent in his use of it he might have been. In biographical terms, Nietzsche dramatically displaced the perspective of his family and social heritage—the Christian religion, the world view of his zealous Protestant pastor father, and the expectation that he, too, would follow in the paths of the several clergymen in his family ancestry. In this regard, his famed ability to deconstruct the dominant rationalist and theistic paradigms of his time could, in part, be viewed as a personal struggle for self-invention/repair, a will-to-be-different (Arnold & Atwood, 2000; Hollinsdale, 1996; Hoover, 1994). Nietzsche (1882) was acutely aware, however, that as human beings move away from the familiar, structuring horizons of life (e.g., a religious outlook), anxiety follows, expressed exquisitely in relation to his own anti-Christian project: "Who gave us the sponge to wipe away the entire horizon? What were we doing when we unchained the earth from its sun? Are we not plunging continually? Backward, sideward, forward, in all direction? Are we not straying as though through an infinite nothing? Do we not feel the breath of an empty space? Has it not become colder?" (p. 119).

Nietzsche had no patience with classical metaphysical doctrines, including the distinction between a "phenomenal reality" (mere appearance) and a supposedly "transcendental reality" (essential order) which lies behind it. He believed that philosophers had set themselves apart, stationed themselves in contemplative isolation, "before life and experience ... as though before a painting which is once and for all time unrolled" (1881, p. 19). There can be, he argued, no abstract "problem of knowledge", but only the production of knowledges in the plural, which are bound up with use and the wish to master some domain of reality. Coplestone (1965) clarifies Nietzsche's notion about human desires to impose order on chaos, ordering the world: "reality is Becoming: it is we who turn it into Being, imposing stable patterns on the flux of Becoming. And this activity is an expression of the Will to Power" (p. 183). In this sense Nietzsche privileged transience, contingency, multiplicity, and flow, above the fixed and categorical; in his view, it is only through human, linguistic activities and forms that we are lured into thinking *this* is the one picture, the true word, the real world. Perspectivism refuses such stopping points and conclusions, no "world left over once you have taken away the perspective" (Nietzche, 1967a, p. 567). Hoover (1994) advances the interesting idea that Nietzsche reverses Locke's famous thesis, in so far as it is not the mind but the world that is *tabula rasa*, awaiting our constructions, our "scrawl". In this view, every thought is part of a living perspective on the world, an exegesis, and each word is dependent on another, a further view, a "prejudice", if one will, which we cannot get out of in order to find the one "true" perspective. Thus, for Nietzsche, "There is only seeing from a perspective, only a 'knowing' from a perspective ..." (1887, p. 107).[1] Hence, convinced about processes of "becoming" and the role of "will" in shaping the world, Nietzsche radically displaced the classical philosophical, static notion of "reality".

Axiomatic to Nietzsche's approach is the idea that experience *of* is an experience *from* and that this *from*, this "somewhere", is inscribed in perspective. As all interpretation issues within perspective, he saw no possibility of an external viewpoint or of a correspondence with ultimate reality. To say this, however, does not mean that all perspectives are equal; a pragmatist before pragmatism, as it were, Nietzsche maintained that some perspectives are better, simply more useful, than others. Context and aim ("will") are paramount, so that whereas poetry is of no value to the building of a bridge compared to engineering, engineering offers no praise in its final, aesthetic form, unlike poetry (Hatab, 1999). Perspectives are more than mere cognitive frames, as existence and the passions of daily living are intimately bound to them. Humans are constructed within perspectives, multiple meanings, which are continually shifting, overlapping, and transferring around us (Granier, 1985a). All human activities and distinctions have an interpretive character, so it is not merely a question of different ways of seeing, but also of different ways of being, the "perspectival character of existence" (Nietzsche, 1882, p. 239). We construe with passion, we hold on to myths, and we fight within perspectives, holding possessively to our version of "truth". Further, we do not hold to perspective in isolation, but in opposition and contrast to perspectives held by others; Nietzsche's enigmatic, often reductive "Will to Power" concept is still a relational term, signaling obstacles, fields of force, and overcoming.

Nietzsche was deeply drawn to the role of models, metaphors, and the inherently "concealing" effects of language, linking this to how human practice constructs life, the matters that we live by (Nehamas, 1985). Philosophy had, he argued, always used, but denied, its basis in metaphor and figural representations. Nietzsche rejected simple oppositions of concealed/revealed, literal/literary, which, in his view, stemmed from a nostalgic desire ("will") for the "true word" and "thing-in-itself" (Derrida, 1976; Kofman, 1993; Nietzsche, 1886). Language is integral perspectival equipment, cementing human self-images and fictions: "In all our language we give expression to our *relative* view of things and project that view onto life" (Houlgate, 1986, p. 47; emphasis in the original). Metaphor is constitutive, not secondary, and so language infinitely thickens perspective to the point at which perspective appears inevitable and eternal. The metaphorical is seen and experienced as literal, whilst the "forgetting" or dying of old metaphors is regarded as the result of perspectival shifts which renders a previous view obsolete (Kofman, 1993; Rorty, 1989). It is through such processes that dominant meanings come to reign, the power of the actual. As Nietzsche (1967b) poetically asserted, "What then is truth? A movable host of metaphors, metonymies and anthropomorphisms: in short, a sum of human relations that have been poetically and rhetorically intensified, transferred, embellished, and which, after long usage, seem to a people to be fixed, canonical, and binding. Truths are illusions which we have forgotten they are illusions; they are metaphors that have become worn out and have been drained of sensuous force, coins which have lost their embossing and are now considered as metals and no longer coins" (p. 467).

The marketplace of meaning

Perspectives are not merely "windows" or "viewpoints" through which the individual peers and moves on. Perspectives are lived, concerning things that matter, but whose net result is often to simplify the world and thereby create a sense of comfort within it (Granier, 1985b). Consolation is the name of the game, even when it takes a negative form, such as always seeing one's enemy in the same light. If perspectives are "occupied" there can be no meaningful separation between the observer and the observed; we all commit, in some way or another, and in so doing we are mostly committed or attached to our perspective, because it *is* ours.[2]

Nietzsche's (1881) parable of laughter in the market place vividly illustrates the perspectival nature of experience and the complex influence of shifting relations of desire and drive—we are animated, energised by perspective. As the parable goes, a passerby hears the sound of laughter in a crowded market place. Nietzsche contends that depending on which drive is "at its height" at the time, the significance of the sourceless laughter to the traveler will vary; there is only perspectival seeing (or in this case, hearing!). Using the graphic term *inpsychation*, he describes an active process by which human beings digest their experiences. Thus, one passser by would barely notice the laughter, shrugging it off as if it were a "drop of rain"; another hears it injuriously, "as he would an insult"; another is goaded and is ready to "pick a fight"; a fourth checks to see if his clothes are properly arranged, whilst another reacts benevolently, hearing the laughter as a sign that all is good in the world. In each case, the drive is "on the lookout", as it were, and so there is no simple access to "what really happened"; "the drive seized the occurrence as its prey ... because it was thirsty and hungry" (p. 119). Whilst a perception is descriptively what we "see" (hear, etc.), a perspective is the hypothetical position behind the eye (ear, etc.).

Although seeing things in a particular way often occurs because it has "worked" before (e.g., the conviction that "people are always putting me down" may become automatic), the world (the world of others) is resilient and answers back (Parkes, 1994). Thus, our perspective is open to challenge, contest, and disabuse. We get things wrong, and right, all the time.

Life as literature: human beings as creative

Nietzsche rejected the view of self as an eternal soul, constant substance, or substantial identity, instead regarding self as something one becomes, a project, an invention of kinds. Perhaps his is a "bundle" theory of the self, the person conceived, using a political metaphor, as loose confederation of drives, purposes, and fluctuating forces (Hales & Welshon, 2000). Rather than supposing an objective, continuing identity of a person over time, for Nietzsche there is a multiplicity of selves. Consistent with this, he sees man as ultimate metaphorical animal, able in his labyrinthine existence to "compose" the worlds in which he lives (Parkes, 1994). There is an important double meaning in this notion of artistry and invention, in so far as "man is the clever animal" amongst species; on the one hand, cleverness refers to creativity and the inventive, and on the other, it signals potential for self-deception. Referring to the tension at the heart of self-representation, Holingdale

(1995), reading Nietzsche, suggests: "We can 'know' only the simulacra of being which we ourselves have constructed" (p. 115). We are always stationed, always in position(s). So, it is suggested, the perspectivism of Nietzsche dovetails with his contingent, history-bound view of human kinds. The positive message is that, given sufficient freedom and courage, we can remake ourselves in helpful acts of self-overcoming. This can be liberating: "Nietzsche's perspectivism is, amongst other things, a technique for revealing the possibilities open to all of us" (Hales & Welshon, 2000, p. 202). The negative import, by contrast, is that we are easily ensnared and prone to repeat the conclusions that we are used to drawing, ever convinced of our own myths.

Dewey's pragmatism

The historical context of American pragmatism is a fascinating subject, involving, as examples, the influence of secularisation, the movement away from singular world-views, and (in theory) from *a priori* notions of belief and a search for national identity, all of which helped forge what William James called a change in the "temperament of philosophy" (Rosenthal, Husman & Anderson, 1999). John Dewey ran full force with the pragmatist baton that had been held aloft by his eminent predecessors, Charles Pierce and William James.

There is interesting, if largely unexplored, common ground between Nietzsche and Dewey. They write very differently; Dewey's prose is stolid, even turgid, and Nietzsche violates all norms of philosophical writing, with his poetic approach, aphorisms, and refusal to be bound by the conventions of orderly discourse. Dewey reads optimistically, to the point of innocence, while Nietzsche's dramatic style revels in the pessimistic and irrational. As for content, however, the "German pragmatism" of Nietzsche and the seemingly Nietzschean elements of the pragmatist tradition have been noted (Rorty, 1999).[3] To spell out some possible commonalities: similarities between Nietzsche's perspectivism and Dewey's instrumental notion of truth; Nietzsche's view of metaphor and Dewey's notion of language; the critique of classical philosophical dualisms; the rejection of the notion that humans share an ahistorical nature; and an insistence on the inescapably situated, "interested" nature of human inquiry. Rorty (2006) suggests that, "Dewey and Nietzsche wanted to see the quest for knowledge as an attempt to satisfy human needs, not to find the true nature of reality" (p. 93). Both narrowed the forced gap that philosophers had created between utility and truth.

Dewey was a prolific philosopher as well as a theorist of democracy and education (see Hilderbrand, 2008 for an introduction to his ideas). A great deal of his early and middle writing takes the form of a critique of classical philosophy, which he believed resembled repetitive and barren "family quarrels" (e.g., Dewey, 1958, p. 47). Dewey argued that the "general problems" posed by philosophers amounted to abstract, non-problems, confining the philosopher to contemplative isolation (he mocked what he called the "spectator theory of knowledge") (ibid.), and consigning thinking to a series of unhelpful polarities, such as: subject and object, thought and action, pure and applied, reason and experience, individual and society. Abstract philosophical approaches hurry away from that which is in effect irreducibly "tangled and complex" (Dewey, 1958, p. 26). In displacing such dualisms, Dewey fashioned a local, piecemeal approach to the tackling of problems and domains of inquiry, emphasising the thinker's continual involvement and connection with what they seek to understand. One of the names he gave to this version of philosophy was "empirical naturalism".

Experience and Nature (Dewey, 1958) aims to reinsert the ordinary and the contextual back into philosophy. True to pragmatist credentials, only a philosophy that asks useful questions is worthy of its name; "… a first rate test of the value of any philosophy which is offered: does it end in conclusions which, when they are referred back to ordinary life-experience and their predicaments, render them more significant, more luminous to us, and make our dealing with them more fruitful?" (p. 7). The word "experience" is no simple passive imprint or a process hived off from "reason", but refers to man's being within the world, with what he strives for and suffers, his needs, loves, actions, and imaginings; it is a veritable "planted field". The language we use brings order, through categorisation, distinction-making, predicating, and so on. All this changes with time, with context, and so Dewey rejects the eternal or essentialist assumptions of other philosophers; not for him, the quest for certainty or any vision of a final resting place of knowledge. Impressed by the work of Darwin, Dewey came to see knowledge as an adaptive human response, linked to use or instrumentality. Inquirers define and explore particular subject areas and view these in the light of specific objectives, and man, as organism, is both changed by and changes his environment. "The influence of Darwinism on philosophy"

(Dewey, 1977a) is a fine paper, deriding as it does the "sacred ark" of permanency, which in philosophy takes the form of privileging the fixed and the final, all species and categories in place and immune to change. Darwin's work not only scandalised theology, but had implications for how philosophers thought about the world; if there were no fixed species, eternally present or ordained, then our categories of thinking might also be subject to evolutionary change. Species adapt and adjust to their environments. Minds intervene in the world because they are part of the world and thinking is itself a procedure, an instrument, which works with material that is both relevant and at hand and local. Stressing this malleable, adaptive dimension, Rorty (2000) observes that, in the Deweyan scheme, "we should think of moral and intellectual progress not as getting closer to a pre-existent goal, but as a process of self-creation ... dialectical synthesis, incorporating these into our self-images and thereby enlarging ourselves" (p. 280). In other words, man as animal creates, to some extent, new environments, rather than being merely subject to them.

Principled, reflective inquiry

Considerations of lived experience and real-life problems, and problem-solving, are what matters to Dewey, rather than "big style" epistemology. Human experience is an active and constantly organising affair, with pragmatist expressions such as "field", "stream", or "circuit", pointing to that experience as ongoing and relational, not to be falsely abstracted into discrete units (Pettegrew, 2000). Experience, whether implicitly or explicitly, is tied to a spirit of experimentation. Experimentation concerns a capacity to question, to refuse final answers; in his words, "experience in its vital form is experimental, an effort to change the given; it is characterized by projection, by reaching forward into the unknown" (Dewey, 1977b, p. 4). The sequence of "reflective thinking" as a method of inquiry involves the following steps, even if these are not necessarily neat or consecutive in practice: to start with, there is a sense of doubt or query, an inkling that "something is wrong". Doubts arise concretely when our habitual ways of dealing with the world fail us, prompting one to define this sense of "not working" more clearly; indeed its problematic status is progressively articulated as it is subject to inquiry. Through reflection, a hypthothesis emerges, an imaginative leap, involving ideas, theories, and models—"Could it be this?", "Is x causing y?", and so on. These notions are subject to further analysis, to controls of some sort, so that the emergent hypothesis needs to be plausible rather than fanciful; "A problem well put is a problem half-solved", as the saying goes. Judgments about plausibility are not universal, but situated in acts of specific inquiry. To Dewey, it is the *process* of inquiry that really counts. Things do not stop, even if they rest temporarily: "A new order of facts, suggests a modified idea (or hypothesis) which occasions new observations whose result will determine a new order of facts, and so on ..." (Dewey, 1977c, p. 37). There can be no disinterested inquiry and, far from being merely cognitive or intellectual, the process is seen as a response to pressing practical and existential issues. Moreover, acts of inquiry are seldom lone ventures, but involve a community of inquirers, a shared paradigm of questions that emerge at a particular historical juncture.

Philosophy as equipment for living

Dewey's model of interested and engaged human inquiry brought into purview a range of interconnected themes in his writings: the notion of inquiry as embedded (communal), fallible (Pierce, the father of pragmatism, had proposed "fallibilism" as crucial to philosophy) (Hausman, 1999; Orange, 1995), subject to revision (what Dewey called "warranted assertability"), and the importance of learning over knowing and the human being as socially constituted ("transactive"), located within continual fields of communication. Rather like Foulkes in a therapy context, Dewey offers an ecological perspective, in which "mind" is no long privately owned and separable from "surrounding" dynamic processes; for him, language was crucial to the emergence of mind. Dewey asks questions as to how we improve ourselves, even though his moral theory claims to reject general answers to this. In a valuable reading, Fishman (2007), argues that Dewey's emphasis on "living in hope" (realistic, rather than "pie in the sky" hope) qualifies him as a kind of ameliorist, concerned with how we evaluate our current actions and take the next step. In this regard, neo-pragmatist Rorty (e.g., 1980, 1982), who counts Dewey as his foremost hero, sees him as "revolutionary philosopher", who, like Nietzsche, changed the way we think about human issues of inquiry and living; more later, in the final chapter, on Dewey's ethics and democratic selfhood.

Perpsectivism and pragmatism

This summary integrates some central elements of perspectivism and pragmatism:

- The "world" is seen in terms of an indefinite, inventive process of "world-making" and, correspondingly,
- The "world" is not seen as given.
- These traditions have a historicist emphasis, in that both question that entity known as a "knowing subject", posited as free from the constraints of time, space, and chance.
- Rather than dealing with "universal problems", these traditions concentrate on the elucidation of particular problems and objectives. Hence, there are no final descriptions or meta-vocabularies, only what is fashioned relative to a changing domain of inquiry and language; no "one way" the world is or "one way" that human beings are. Similarly, there is no "end point" or general evolutionary direction, whether one of guaranteed improvement or of increasing rationality.
- There is a rejection of classical dualisms and the appearance-reality distinction, replaced by an emphasis on useful (or less useful) descriptions of the world and ourselves.
- With an unrelenting relational view of human beings and "entities" in the world, there can be no simple criteria of objectivity or uncovering "how things are".
- Alongside this is a key emphasis on the flexibility or plasticity of human selfhood. We are complex bundles or assemblages, immersed in a "community of partaking" (Dewey, 1958, p. 185).
- In this reading, perspectivism[4] and pragmatism are consonant with pluralism and diversity.

Perspectivism and pragmatism in therapeutic work

Vignette: a team in trouble?

A mental health team asked for help, "to look at how we work and to take stock", the manager adding, "There's a lot of hurt in the team". The consultation took the form of (a) a whole team meeting to formulate an agenda and (b) a day of exploration to look at problems and solutions.

I isolate two dominant views, expressed, with considerable passion, by the team.

One part of the team, mostly senior, emphasised a historical transition, from a time when the team was well supported, held in high-esteem and innovative, to a present in which they felt demoted, reduced in scope and caught in a "straight-jacket" of external requirements. One person put it thus:

> We have been put in our place by people and policies that are short-sighted … I've suffered a lot as a result, in fact quite a number of us have, but it's the service to the clients that's more important, and what they've lost in terms of resources and our expertise.

His colleague, adding to this theme of history and decline, added:

> One of my old clients the other day said, "They wouldn't have stood for this ten year ago, when they had that other [such and such] service. I recon they have you by the balls. They don't want to you to help us now, only control us. It's all about shoveling the mess out of the way."

I describe these views as "dominant" because the theme of a previous era, dressed in glory and followed by decline, was reiterated and underlined several times. It raised obvious emotion and reminders of injury ("I've suffered a lot as a result …"). In spite of this, another part of the team, predominantly junior, and reticent at first, expressed pride in current innovation and achievements. Ray said:

> It's really good—we've not done it before. I feel good about it and the feedback from the users is positive. It's not the only thing—our new policy on [such and such] has made a whole lot of things more accessible. Let's hear a bit more about that for a change.

In the "middle", other workers felt that, complaints aside, they were doing "reasonably well" and were keen to "get down to our core business … to deliver [such and such]". Their language was one of "realism".

As the day grew to a close, two set of views emerged regarding a way forward. One worker said:

We have a lot to look at—there's a lot of baggage in this team. Unless we start doing it, we won't move on. It's like we need to grieve so that we can move on.

Others felt that the day had already been beneficial and that, to quote again, "Dwelling on things will not help". Their viewpoint was that the team had the talent and resources to continue with its task and that the team should therefore, "look forwards".

Discussion

I adopted a group-analytically informed approach, aided by a mixture of discussion exercises, creative enactments, and free, unstructured dialogue. I listened out for resonant and dissonant themes, noted patterns of group exchange (including tone, sub-groups, power-relations, etc.), noting key metaphors and storylines, seeking a "locational" view of disturbance, that is, understanding given problems and their proffered solutions within the context of definitions, history, service networks, and demands. A pre-eminently pragmatic and contextual notion, Foulkes' (1968) notion of "location of the disturbance" invites participants into each other's shoes and positions, inviting joint effort to figure out that which hinders and that which helps practice. Location is not thought of so much as like a place on a map, a fixed point, but as part of a configuration that can change and can be seen from different angles. This approach to consultation has pragmatic, therapeutic value in itself, in so far as "defining a problem" already begins to change how those things are seen and appraised. "A problem well put, is a ..."

Using perspectival understanding, it seemed that the team was torn between warring definitions of its core troubles. Each version of the "rights and wrongs" had a life of its own, associated with passionate attachments, suffering and striving (e.g., "I've suffered a lot as a result ...", "Let's hear a bit more about *that* for a change", etc.). Some members emphasised a historical journey (designated as "baggage" by others), populated by themes of injury and loss, with stark contrasts between a "then" and a "now" and images of an appreciative versus a hostile world; the subjectivities, if one puts it this way, associated with this were of an angry, injured, and mournful nature and the moral themes were of "good past" and "honourable leaders" versus "bad present", and so on. One could hear this in terms of storylines (e.g., "grandeur and decline") with particular definitions of the world and the agents in it. This view was well asserted, but to others it represented a lost cause and constraint. The reference to grief in the discussion was doubled-edged: grief respects memory, reopens past pain, whilst at the same time anticipates a "letting go". Pain is a powerful constituent of memory and can become a focus of identity, constituting a wound or a "grand cause". Hardly surprisingly, an observation I ventured about a risk of being "stuck in nostalgia" must have felt like a criticism to some.

If the "loss and decline" perspective was clearly expressed, the perspective that emphasised current talent and achievement was voiced tentatively, partly explained by a senior/junior distinction in the team. In not wanting to be "held back" by past struggles, theirs was a perspective driven by the wish to "get on" and put enthusiasm to work. The subjectivities associated with this were eagerness and optimism, but also frustration when thwarted, the moral themes being ones of "lost world", "old cause", or "old guard" versus "new world/dynamic staff", and so on. The storyline suggested "world as opportunity and adventure", and was certainly forward-looking.

The scenario may point to nothing more than a polarity of perspectives, in which the dominant perspective carried a surplus of pain, too much history, as it were. And did the contrasting perspective carry too little history, even "forgetfulness" about the historical context, but also require recognition? There seemed to be a struggle of perspectival projections, the wish to hold the world to one's will: for example, one group might see the others as an old guard, clinging to the past, whilst they might in turn be seen as naive, inexperienced workers not wanting to know about the losses. Those who simply wished to "get on" represented a third, mixed perspective, presumably containing some reactive frustrations to the other two. They represented themselves as the "realists" and "level-headed", operating in a world of "opportunities and challenges".

My objective was to model and foster a spirit of inquiry and, within the constraints of one day, to respond to their requests, knowing that requests are always already refracted by struggles for definitions and power-relations (e.g., the manager has the right to authorise a consultation, and to give the "first view"). I aimed to foster different kinds of conversational and conceptual space, the objective being to help the team to identify those constraints, losses, and repetitive processes that caused suffering and were standing in the way of progress. I had no privileged viewpoint or meta-position, but tried to gather the implications and possibilities of each perspective, hopefully a more integrated view. A situation constituted by chronic conflict calls for more varied perspectives and unblocking; if group life is seen as a field of becoming, then, in a case such as this, the consultant has to keep note of which perspectives assert themselves, those that do not, and at what value and cost to all. When conflicts are articulated and valued, they may in time lose some of their potency to dominate a field of relations. At the end of the day there is seldom "one problem" to be identified, but perhaps there can be a more workable and newer nexus of relations and definitions.

Vignette: a therapy group

The group in question was a slow-open, group-analytically informed group for people with substance misuse. Its members were people abstinent of drugs and alcohol (the background to the group is discussed in further detail in Weegmann, 2006b). The following occurred some years into the life of the group.

Jeremy was anxious and began the group by reporting, "I have something to say, I think it's best to be honest and not do what I used to, which is to tell everyone after the event when things only get a whole lot worse." He continued, "I've had some difficulties since I stopped medication [Jeremy was drug free for three months] and find it hard to deal with the stress I am under. I used twice last week, but not since".

Elliot inquired, "What did you use, the usual …?." Jeremy replied, "Yes, the usual [an "over the counter" drug] … I got it from a different chemist, but felt guilty when I went in twice during the same week … it was like, they can see through me, what I'm up to'". He described recent decisions in his life and an uncanny feeling of being on the brink of either a success or disappointment—things could go either way. Elliot was keen to hear how much he consumed and what it felt like going into the chemist shop, adding, "Do you feel we can see through you as well?" Jeremy said that people in the group don't see through him, because, as they actually know him, he does not need to pretend. Jeremy was "hyper", suggestive of an excitement mixed with fearfulness.

Robert said, "It is no use lecturing you, as you are aware of what you are doing and your patterns ... I'm glad you told us at the start." Robert talked about his own sense of foreboding: "I can't put my finger on it, but something you said, Jeremy, about being on a kind of brink ... with me I get high if I think I've had a success and that's dangerous if it gets a hold ..." Robert told the group more about "unstable feelings" and how difficult it is for him to judge his actions realistically: "It's like I'm so unsure, I get discouraged when things are not going well and artificially lifted when they are—then I start to dream of all kinds of things, that I've really made it—like the world's best teacher—on a different plane of reality and all that nonsense." Others nodded in seeming identification. Meanwhile, Sarah spoke of her previous "experiments" with alcohol, thinking each time that she could get away with using it without adverse consequences. She illustrated what she meant with amusing tales of old, bringing a few smiles.

Inwardly, I felt concerned about Robert—was he on the brink of a relapse and trying to communicate the danger he was in? I was struck by the shared mood of uncertainly and semi-excitement, as though it was hard for group members to trust their feelings. I addressed Robert, saying, "Robert, your situation reminds me of the words of the poet, who says 'He who would ride a tiger must make sure he can first dismount'" and followed this up by wondering aloud whether his was a stage of psychological readiness to relapse that, unless checked, might lead into actual, full-blown relapse.

Group members knew the meaning of the tiger metaphor. Robert agreed he was "riding on something", and wanted to pull back. Elliot introduced another story, emblematic he said of the addict, in which a frog turns to a scorpion for a ride across a swollen river. The scorpion assures the frog that he won't sting, but then he does: "Why did you do that?" asks the frog, to which the scorpion retorts, "Sorry, but it's in my nature."

At this point others came in and spoke about ongoing difficulties in life and whether they could be faced. Short cuts and avoidance was tempting. "We are all addicts at the end of the day," said one, echoing the theme, "it's in our nature". At this point, I said, "Today, I sense that Robert's situation has made people feel excited—like Robert himself—and the group was kind of high just talking about slips and using. Maybe there is a temptation in times of stress to join the opposition and find short cuts? But I think Robert is also trying to help us to think through the sober side, the real worry that you can get side-tracked into thinking that using drugs again is the best way out. So there may be a lot of uncertainty for people here—how do I keep my feet on the ground? How can I encourage myself, without going overboard? What is manageable for me?"

> The group moved on into other areas, with one member talking about an impending holiday. There was discussion about the idea of "taking the group with me" and what this might mean. One person spoke about how they try to "conjure the group" in some situations, in order to remain "clear and clean".

Discussion

Thiele (1990) contends that for Nietzsche, "the multiple soul with its endless internal strive is the defining characteristic of man" (p. 58). Substance misusers, in recovery or otherwise, vividly demonstrate internal strife, a "two-ness" in which a "sober" or "straight" person wrestles with another, an "addict" who wishes to use drugs. Arguably, this theme of duality, of contradictory aims and selves, is at the heart of addictive suffering (Weegmann, 2005b). In the vignette, Jeremy is in turmoil, having re-tasted his drug of choice. The group responds to his struggle around "giving in", resonating to themes of temptation and fear of relapse, and to just how insidiously it happens. I was mindful of the lapse processes and how "psychological relapse" precedes actual use, even if the sequence between the two is not inevitable. Jeremy could pull back. The tiger metaphor is an attempt to encapsulate the struggle about using or not using, with its seductive beliefs about control ("I can handle this ..."). Metaphor can constitute a transpersonal aphorism, positing important general questions about human desire and limitation; it can promote understanding and soften self-blame. Elliot's reference to the "scorpion" tale added further wisdom, illustrating the power of self-seduction and forgetting ("denial").

I suggest that the group, in all its medley of communication, can be thought of in terms of shifting intensities of affect, and "the struggle of competing perspectives and their coalitions" (Thiele, 1990, p. 53). The intensities include temptation and indulgence, danger and excitement (e.g., Jeremy at the start), fear and arousal, (Jeremy, Elliot, Sarah), grandiosity (Robert), nostalgia, and "getting high without the drug" (Sarah and the group as a whole). There is a struggle for supremacy between an internal "drug user" and a person seeking to be abstinent; this occurs within given individuals, such as Jeremy or Sarah, and at the level of the group, as when the group orchestrates a nostalgic "high". In another instance, a usually level-headed and cautious person (Robert) is unsettled by feelings that might eventuate in grandiose fantasy or acting out, with or without picking up drugs. Finally, is there a turning to the group as object of assistance and inner resource?

The battlefield and coalition analogy is apposite, as the members bring to the group those very aspects that might threaten its safety and containing role. There is a bidding for the ruling passion, for example, between the excitement and relief of using drugs to the enjoyment and achievements of ordinary, sober living. Will "drug talk" and fantasy dominate the group or be corrected by "sober dialogue" (Weegmann, 2006b)? The memory (e.g., "It wasn't *that* bad ...") and desire (e.g., to give in to drugs, or to consolidate recovery) of people in recovery can change dramatically, depending, to use Nietzsche's (1967a) market-place analogy, on which "drive" is uppermost: "Every drive is a kind of lust to rule; each one has its perspective that it would like to compel all the other drives to accept as norm" (p. 481). Continuing the political analogy, one could talk in terms of "regime changes" (Thiele, 1990, p. 63), such as from "I'm going to use and stuff your group" to "I'm here and determined to stay clean". Does the group and the therapist represent a position to be opposed, or is the group and therapist seen as a vital ally? Indeed, sometimes the group and therapist represents a helpful adversary. In dealing with fast moving shifts and transitions, the therapist's role could be likened to that of a diplomat, "attempting to acknowledge different parties within the personality and offering dialogue with both sides" (Weegmann, 2005b, p. 289). Partly this relates to "stages" of recovery: "Whilst in the earliest stage of recovery, there is usually an immediate struggle with addiction (rawness, cravings, conflicts about still wanting to use), this may give way in time to more of a struggle *away* from addiction (more confidence, rebuilding, a better sense of not *having* to use)" (Weegmann, 2006b, p. 62). Hatab (1999) uses the Nietzschean image of an "agonistic force field", underlining, rather than seeking to eliminate, the importance of opponents and the play of opposing forces. Indeed, it could be said that it is only out of the mix of such struggle, that a person, hopefully, constructs a viable trajectory of recovery.

The therapist is occupied (rather than, hopefully, preoccupied) by a perspective. In this case, I am hardly neutral but represent a position which was/is sought by the membership as part of their joining, a position broadly of "living life without drugs or alcohol". How this position is "carried" can be very varied indeed, but in this case, as an abstinence-based psychotherapy group, my approach operated within clear boundaries and careful administration (time, expectations, rules around non-using, sharing information about lapses promptly, and honestly, etc.), encouraging active reflection and due permissiveness with respect to possibilities of dialogue. In the scenario, furthermore, perhaps there was a kind of "safe using", but one bordering on actual use, at least for one group member. At the end, we glimpse a perspectival shift, from one of dangerous or complacent excitement over drug use, past and present, to reflection upon anticipated absences. A new feeling sweeps the group, of how to cope and contain needs when the group is not physically available?

Group analysis: a multi-lateral reality

Group analysis typifies an unremitting relational stance, continually moving in and out of the perspectival worlds, those variously organised subjectivities, of the participants. The skilled conductor, as due contextualist, holds lightly not only theory, but any particular view of meaning in the patient's experience. Foulkes' notion of the horizontal viewpoint encourages historicist, locational understanding, dispensing with any final, absolute view which could charactersie the group once and for all. This involves pragmatic inquiry and constant openness, and a willingness to develop warranted, imaginative formulations. The heat of exchange and perspectival shifts are all too apparent in groups, where, to adapt an idea from Nietzsche (1882), we stumble into a "world of evaluations, colours, accents, perspectives, affirmations, negations not found in nature, but based on the values that humans bestow" (p. 241). Foulkes did not cite Nietzsche (although, according to Elizabeth Foulkes, he had read him; personal communication), but I like to think that the following (Foulkes, 1975a, p. 131) is a vague nod in his direction: "Different interpretations are not contradictory but correspond to particular perspectives ... the language of interactions is not confined to words, but extends to inflexions of voice; manner of speaking, looking, expressions, gestures; actions ... emotional reactions of all sorts—sympathy, condemnation or contempt, attraction or disgust, love, hatred and indifference".

CHAPTER FOUR

The articulated space of social unconsciousness

A lthough Foulkes (e.g., 1973–1974) proposed a concept of the social unconscious, traversing an individual, "dynamic unconscious", it was not developed in theory. Exploring textual tensions within the corpus of Foulkes' work, Dalal (1998) argues that Foulkes ultimately collapses a potentially radical concept of the social unconscious into a more biologically derived, relatively static, "foundation matrix"; a foundation matrix where, in the minimal description of Foulkes (1971), group members, "have the same qualities as a species, the same anatomy and physiology, and also perhaps archaic traces of ancient experiences" (p. 212). As all theories are developed in response to that which is missing, Dalal (2001) reminds us that "the notion of the social unconscious seeks to compensate for ... the absence of the social in much psychoanalytic discourse. Thus at the very least, the phrase brings some notion of the social into the discursive frame" (p. 539). However, in Dalal's judgment, Foulkes' concept of the social unconscious remained "weak".

Dalal (1998, 2001–2002) joins a host of other group analysts (e.g., Brown, 2001; Hopper 2003; Hopper & Weinberg, 2011) who have developed the theory of the social unconscious. This chapter will not review these approaches, but, given the premise of intertextuality, my ideas are enriched and made possible by them; however, the focus and most of my terms are different. I draw upon sources of philosophy and social theory rarely used in the group-analytic literature; the question as to whether the ideas presented here are different in kind or emphasis to that of other group analysts is one I leave to readers to judge.

It is suggested that social unconsciousness is an inherently elusive, "empty signifier", to use a term of Laclau's (Laclau & Mouffe, 1985). With this fluidity in mind, I use the verb form, social unconsciou*sness*, rather than the noun form (Weegmann, forthcoming).[1] Social unconsciousness is always already "there", all around and yet nowhere in particular; it is not an indicative phenomenon that one can simply "point to", capture in "an" influence or regard, as Foulkes implied, as a discrete "level" of explanation to be added to other levels.[2] We can never "know" it as evident, transparent object simply because we are part of it and, whenever we try to speak of it, we are in positions, involvements, and a language provided by it. As Heidegger's (1962) work makes abundantly clear, humans have a primordial involvement, a *readiness-to-hand*, whereby we live in a world already drenched in meaning. His term to capture human existence as being-in-the world was *Dasein*.

Consider an analogy: How does one describe a landscape, without already being part of it? The position one occupies—for example, farmer, prospecting geophysicist, painter, or subsistence nomad—influences what one sees, its meaning, as we look at things in different ways. The landscape is perceived relative to particular projects and activities, what Heidegger calls *equipment*, such as survival, potential for exploitation, passing on to the next generation, poetic inspiration, and so on, and as the observer stands on the earth described, indeed is part of it, it is impossible to adopt a non-perspectival view; Orange (1995) makes the Gadamer-inspired point that "our present understanding of anything or anyone is only a perspective within a horizon inevitably limited by the historicity of our own organised and organising experience" (p. 89). At the same time no one can dispute that rocks, fields, trees, distant hills, etc. exist, except that even here some, if not all, of these features are already the product of human cultivation and construct (e.g., Turner and other Romantic painters "opened up" mountains to vision in a way that had not been "seen" before and which reflected changes in human activity, e.g., changed leisure time, physical and engineering conquest, etc.). We cannot avoid our particular "background", since it is the background that conditions our (under-) standing and influences our ways of noticing. *Dasein* and world are not separate entities, but are coexistents and complementary.

Hence then, we are all products of social unconsciousness, and can never "get back" far enough, so to speak, to apprehend its full range or fully know its constituent makeup. As discursive, meaningful beings, we are "pre-constructed" (Pecheux, 1982), "thrown" into a world already made.

Helping us conceptualise this realm of the discursive is Derrida's work (1976, 1981) and what he has to say on the concept of identity. As is well known, Derrida problematises any idea of identity as presence or self-sufficient meaning, on the grounds that any identity involves terms *other* than itself, yet this very "outside" or "elsewhere" is part of what it means to assert or to be someone. Centres of civilisation, such as the city state, or "Christian lands", presuppose other regions, such as "wilderness" or "Barbarous lands"; but each signifier is overdetermined, so that, for example, the American Puritan settlements connoted civilisation, redemption, and light (as in Wintrop's "city on a hill"), the outside of which was not only wilderness, but spiritual darkness and nakedness and hardships of survival, refracted with Biblical images, such as Cannan (Bercovitch, 1975). A complex and elusive concept, Derrida refers to "differance" spelled with an "a". This notion is an emblem, containing three other moments which "differance" suggests: "differing", "deferring", and "detour". The other is always different, nonidentical by virtue of identity-in-difference, so identity does not have the character of a substance. One result is that identities are never complete or final, but surface as contingent products in continual evolution and struggle. There is no agent able to gather up meaning as if it were independent of it; "There is no subject who is agent, author and master of *differance* ..." (Derrida, 1981, p. 28).

Derrida shows how the constitution of an identity entails an exclusion of something else. Traditional polarities, philosophic and otherwise, do not meet each other on neutral ground, but are set up in terms of what Derrida calls a "violent hierarchy" (Cousins, 1978; Derrida, 1976), terms such as: matter/form, essence/accident, reality/image, philosopher/ordinary citizen, or, of particular interest to Derrida, speech/writing. One of these terms is privileged in a particular way. Outside the dualisms of philosophy, we could include oppositions such as white/black or man/woman (Dalal, 2002; Hall, 1996). In any violent hierarchy, one term is superior, while the "other" term is subsumed in some way, although in historical struggle a great deal of change can occur, including a sudden attempt to invert the hierarchy, as in the idea of revolutionary mutation or overthrow. The "world" can be turned upside down, along with its defining words and metaphors; revolutions deploy meanings as much as weapons. Hegemonic meanings are dominant versions of "standard lives", versions that repress and occlude alternatives, with social unconsciousness similar to "a discourse that hierarchically orders other discourses" (Dalal, 1998, p. 212). The "outside", or "other", of meaning is thus an integral part of this continual process of definition, a "constitutive outside", naturalised by the dominant vision.

Consider the signifier "East". Said (1978) offers a detailed analysis of how a particular politico-cultural horizon came about: how western powers, artists, and writers constructed a vision of the "East" or Orient, acting as its adjacent other. Orientalism, that study of the East, denoted not only a geographical region but also supposed moral, cultural, and intellectual attributes, such as "benighted", "primitive", "threatening", "exotic"; to be oriental was to be "overcome by intellectual or moral darkness", a view informed by the dominant discourses, such as, but not exclusively, western Christianity. The project of orientalism was part of a discourse and operation of power and domination, and so, in this way, a certain category of familiarity, or of strangeness within familiarity, the "essence of the orient", was constructed. The "East" was represented and regulated—administratively, militarily, textually, and visually. Drawing on Gramsci (1985), Said uses the notion of "hegemony" to describe the process by which particular views become dominant, articulating organising principles based upon an ensemble of social relations and practices. The silent relational power expressed within this particular cultural and political horizon was formidable; as Terdiman (1984, p. 29) expresses it, "Some see, some are seen". Significantly, the European countries that ran empires were called "the Powers", acutely protective of their interests in the Middle and Far East, and elsewhere.

In other words, West is the master, unmarked term, with East as its marked, constitutive outside; Laclau (Laclau & Mouffe, 1985) argues, "Deconstructing an identity means showing that the 'constitutive outside' that inhabits it—that is, an 'outside' that constitutes that identity, and, at the same time, questions it. But this is nothing other than asserting its contingency—that is its radical historicity" (p. 189). Hegemony and violent hierarchy are only one way in which meanings are constructed; more basic still is the notion of "articulations".

Articulation can be thought of as like a "hinge", in which different elements of meaning are brought together, meaningfully connected. Elements do not pre-exist the relational matrix, but are constituted by it. So, rather than consisting of positive terms, self-present or atom-like, meaning is relational and undecidable, being both relatively fixed, but also the product of, and itself productive of, dislocation. Articulations occur all the time, but do not necessarily take on hegemonic, hierarchical form; neither are they necessarily the product of violent dislocations or traumatic disruption.[3] Individuals, groups, and other agents are continually defining the world and making sense of their situations. Importantly, whilst the relationship of signifier and signified might logically be "arbitrary", in social terms it is not, otherwise it would be impossible to see life as organised or meaningful at all. This does not mean that given articulations are *necessary*, as this would be the mirror reverse of arbitrary; "world-making" cannot be an indifferent assignment of symbols or elements, any more than a carpenter could throw random pieces of wood together and call it "furniture" (Goodman, 1978). Meanings, then, are neither simply chance designations (*nomina*), nor natural footprints, with all given societies acquiring a recognisable shape and self-image.

The concept of the discursive, or the meaningful, exceeds the linguistic, in other words, is not confined to speech or writing. There are important qualifications here; the first is that language itself does not exist independently of its realms of use and action; as Heidegger puts it, "words and language are not wrappings in which things are packed for the commerce of those who write and speak. It is in words and language that things first come into being and are" (Heidegger, 1961, p. 11). Second, discourses or discursive formations do not hover, as pale reflections or mere rationalisations of another, more solid reality somewhere else. Discursive products do not have a second-rate existence, suspended as if mere commentaries "about" human practices, because they are part of those very practices (Cousins & Hussein, 1984). Albeit a rarefied word, "discourses" are part of wider beliefs, conventions, roles, and institutions. For example, a generalised expression such as "medieval monastic discourse", is inscribed in a whole materiality of sermons, devotional guides, the ethos of different monastic orders, everyday codes and rules of devotional living, images in books, walls, and windows, and in all the designs of architectural space (Gilchirst, 2000). From walls to veils, books to behaviour, discourse forms and informs the fibres of life, as much as, and even more than, any grand visions of theology (Salih, 2001). At the same time, it would be foolish to deny facts of singularity and the scope of individual or group "self-fashioning", reducing a given nun or monk, in this example, to mere "container" of discourse (Roper, 1994).

Laclau's (Laclau & Mouffe, 1985; Laclau, 2005) concept of contingency attempts to transcend the polarities arbitrary/natural, accidental/integral, nominal/essential. This is because contingency is the expression of an outcome that involves competing and surrounding discourses, resulting in a relative stabilisation of meaning. History is up for grabs; in the words of Gramsci (1985, p. 31), "In history, in social life, nothing is fixed, rigid or definitive". When agents resist established meanings, by overturning previous interpretations and practices, inventing new names, fighting for different causes, and so on, they do so (partially) within terms already established by the former, whose shadow remains.

The idea of an empty signifier points to a social unconsciousness "filled" or fleshed out by, but impossible to complete and exhaust, different "contents" that are the result of struggle, succession, and mutation. In this conception, there is no plentitude of meaning and there are always dominant/subjugated elements, as well as coexisting elements. If meaning is predicated on difference, rather than substance, then that which is signified is a question of articulation, rearticulation, and contingency. Incompletion and failure to articulate full, "once-and-for-all" meaning characterises social unconsciousness, and it follows that "identification" cannot amount to a final or definite "identity". Although writing as philosopher not social theorist, what William James (1909) says, with great flourish, could apply: "Things are 'with' one another in many ways, but nothing includes everything, or dominates over everything. The word 'and' trails along after every sentence. Something always escapes" (p. 321).

Social unconscious as imaginary

Taylor (2004) offers an interesting view of social imaginaries, defining it as "ways people imagine their social existence, how they fit together with others, how things go on between them and their fellows, the expectations that are normally met and the deeper normative notions and images that underlie these expectations" (p. 23). Not so much an abstract idea, "rather it is what enables, through making sense of, the practices of a society" (p. 2). In different words, practices "carry" an understanding, (in) forming contexts of action and reflection; human beings and groups, "trade on familiarity with a background" (Taylor, 1993, p. 326). The social imaginary can be likened to an enterprise of "world-building", the creation of meaningful orders (*nomos*) within which individuals and groups live out their lives. Berger (1969) uses the evocative expression "sacred canopy", to characterise this process, although secular societies are no less "world-built" than religious ones. The key phrase in Taylor's definition is *imagine their existence*, referring to those metaphors, images, and stories whose occurrence nothing could predetermine or predict. In this way, the social imaginary is not simply a "cover" or "reflection", which like a *camera obscura*, misrepresents reality or legitimates "something else", considered more important and determining (e.g., class interests, the economy, repressed wishes, etc.).

Like Taylor, Ricoeur (1984a) regards social imaginaries as involving active myths, ideals, collective stories, and symbolising identities. An example is the category "nation", imagined, "because the members of even the smallest nation will never know most of their fellow-members, meet them, or even hear them, yet in their minds each lives the image of their communities" (Anderson, 1981). In this usage, and in mine, the imagined connotes the creative and compositional rather than the false or illusory, with national communities, in this example, assuming and interpellating subjects on the basis of the existence of a "deep, horizontal comradeship" (Anderson, 1981, p. 7), including inevitable differentiations from other, adjacent communities. It is this very creativity that makes the social imaginary difficult to observe as object, because it concerns the constant generation of worlds, the delineation of possibilities and the constitution of exclusions; because of this dynamic movement and because we are part of its generative labour, it remains elusive. Continually expanding, contracting, and redefining, the imaginary space is a changing space.

The diagram below (Figure 1) crudely illustrates the social imaginary as the overall horizon of a given society. The diagram should be seen as both cross-sectional (synchronic, but not static) and time-dependent (diachronic). At what point or time does one world, as it were, grade into another? It is suggested that such space/time demarcations or transitions (e.g., between the medieval "Kingdom of God" and its enemies—"heathen", "Lands of the Infidel", "anti-Christ"; or from one "era" or "epoch" to another, such as from a pre- to post-revolutionary

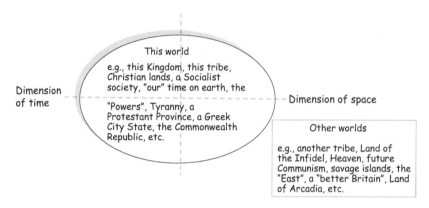

Figure 1. Social imaginary.

society, or from an austere-conservative time to an affluent-permissive period) is more like a fog than a precise boundary, regions within which certain beings and possibilities take form, become visible, or, alternatively, recede from sight. The monsters and deformed beings of early modern times are a good illustration of such places and the symbolism contained therein, playing an important role as a constitutive outside, "where maps run out" (Kearney, 2003, p. 1). Hence, something like "dark", linked to evil and images of purgatory, serves to articulate the light and glory of heaven—"an external reification of 'what-is-not' … offering itself as a template up against … 'what-is' … could be defined and measured" (Bildhauer & Mills, 2003, p. 56; Weegmann, 2008; Williams, D., 1996). In medieval iconography and hagiography, saints and monsters confront each other as though needing each other. It should not be assumed that excluded figures and elements are necessarily "far away" geographically, since they may just as likely reside deep within the body of the social, its inner demons, perhaps within the neighbour or wayfarer, who might be a leper, beggar, or witch. Frontiers, and the liminal creatures that populate them, are ultimately undecidable, with what is "inside" and what "outside" co-determined.

Between abjection and ideals

We have argued that social unconsciousness is the continual production of discursive worlds and imaginary spaces. This production neither stops nor covers all, with inevitable unclosable dislocations, contradictions, and untheorised regions; in the words of Derrida (1981, p. 94) "... spacing is the impossibility for an identity to be closed on itself ...". Although we cannot step outside it, we can look off-centre, as it were, to its margins and more obvious areas of incompleteness, in which its history and production can be glimpsed, towards those foggy social regions and occupants of the "foul lining of society" (Kristeva, 1982).

Kristeva's (1982) concept of abjection is useful, since if we look at what is ejected and jettisoned-off from the social body and "proper self", the meaning of that which is *central* to that social body and self are more easily discerned; the abject, in her definition, relates to "what disturbs identity, system, order. What does not respect borders, positions, rules" (p. 4). What is unconscious about social unconsciousness is in part that which is disavowed, repressed, isolated, rendered unthinkable. Dangerous forces and beings transgress and pollute order and yet their existence is itself a paradox, since what explains them? At one level they are a constituency of "impossible subjects" or marvels, which like monsters or the phenomenon of Evil are not quite meant to be, and at another, as we shall see in the discussion of witchcraft to follow, are all too "necessary" to assume, and much feared. Rather than absolutes, there are many faces of marginality and degrees of (in)visibility. In a German study of "defiled trades" and "dishonorable folk" (e.g., skinners, executioners, grave-diggers, barber-surgeons, bailiffs, etc.). Stuart (1999) investigates the existence of a visible, yet outcast subgroup, defined by occupation and family lineage, who were seen as source of social pollution, an underbelly to the respectable world of "honourable" professions and guilds and yet who were not subject to direct persecution. Such a world depended, amongst other conditions, upon categories of social pollution and hierarchical status, with distinctions between honourable and dishonourable. A similar point can be made with regard to many other "groups on the edge", not always entirely excluded, but sometimes tolerated as "lesser evils", "remnant religions", and so on, including Jews, beggars, and prostitutes; "In its medieval context, marginalisation is, paradoxically enough, a way of incorporating deviant groups in society, albeit in its outer spheres" (Bejczy, 1997, p. 375).

The abjected does not vanish, but as an absent presence serves as reminder and plays a demarcation function; as Butler (2000) puts it, the excluded, "return to haunt the politics predicated on their absence" (p. 11). As noted, in the Middle-Ages, "monsters" had many cultural and symbolic uses, demarcating spheres, bodies, and valued practices—such as Christians, humans, saints, rulers, male-ness, obedience—from their denigrated counterparts—such as non-Christians, demons, animals, rebels, subservient beings (Weegmann, 2008). Wittkower's (1942) intriguing essay notes how the sundry monsters and "marvels of the East" were in fact reformulations and revitali-sations of monsters described by the ancients, only second time around acquiring Christian, theological justification, such as the idea that they could not be *contra naturam* but were created by God, who had his own purpose for doing so; indeed, as we shall see, even the activities of witches were seen as being given permsission by God to "disburb the elements" (Kramer & Sprengler, 1486, p. 10). As "intimate strangers", monsters lived close-by, within, or else inhabited presently unknown regions that humans may not yet have contact with, beyond the Pillars of Hercules and so on. In this way, monsters were an army of imaginary others, figures within a discourse of deformity (Williams, D., 1996). The relation between the two realms, the monstrous and the orderly, the abject and the normal, is not "accidental", in the sense that anyone could simply opt out of seeing the world as it was customarily defined; they have some kind of meaningful relationship to each other—"medieval demonology created an explanatory resource for exploring the distinc-tions between possible ideals and their flawed, human expressions" (Bildhauer & Mills, 2003, p. 14).

A complementary approach, starting from an opposite pole to abjec-tion, is to consider social unconsciousness and the imaginary in terms of what a given society or group represents as being its *ideal* state. In other words, what regulative ideals "pull", and thus thematise, the social in a particular way? As Ricoeur (1984a) puts it, "… there exists the *imaginaire* of rupture, a discourse of 'utopia' which remains criti-cal of the powers that be out of fidelity to an 'elsewhere', to a society that is not-yet" (p. 138). Hence, the present life is complemented by a Golden Era or After Life, the Devil by God, the witch by the Virgin, the stake by the pedestal—contraries particularly apparent in societies dominated by the ubiquity of hierarchy (Amussen, 1985). Frequently, a mythic past and mythic future promise to join up, as in the discourses of "millennial" movements; for example, radicals of the English Civil War anticipated the final lifting of the oppressive "Norman Yoke", a return to an "earlier" period or an "outside" of time (the image of the Garden of Eden, the "free Anglo-Saxons", the time of the primitive and uncorrupted church), and the elimination of the mythology of the Monarch's "divine right" by the counter-mythology of the coming of Christ's Kingdom (Hill, 1972). Regulative ideals may include "utopias", an idea made famous, if rendered enigmatic, by the Catholic critic and statesman, Thomas More, whose *Utopia* (1515) was at once a "no place" and a "good place" (from the Greek *ou*, meaning "non-", *topos*, meaning "place", and possibly *eu*, meaning "good").

Although actual behaviour and practice falls short of regulative ideals, the former will be interpreted within terms constituted by the latter (e.g., in widely different languages of "sin", "human frailty", "ill-discipline", "selfishness", "vulnerability", and so on). People do not simply live "a life"; it is a life conceived and coloured in particular ways, with "ends of life" in view, explicitly or implicitly (Thomas, 2009). As "self-interpreting animals" (Taylor, 1985), humans inevitably recognise and "talk" to themselves within socially sanctioned categorical schemes, which they reproduce, reinforce, and fashion. Regulative ideals provide coherence and overarching symbols, their presence entering the heartlands of what is thinkable, doable, and ethical. Everyday moral codes guide action that is attainable, for example, gestures of respect between feudal groups, prescribed/proscribed behaviour amongst neighbours, attitudes towards strangers, the required discipline of living in a monastic order, table manners, behaviour considered desirable in the marketplace, trading etiquette. Regulative ideals constitute limit-points, supporting the ultimate interpretation of these everyday codes, for example, being a "devout Christian subject", an "honest trading man", and so on.

Flesh, sex, and gender in early modern times— examples from history

Neither sexuality nor gender has much prominence in Foulkes' writings and when they figure, he appears satisfied by a traditional, psychoanalytic model of their formation. He gives no suggestions as to how either might be seen in terms of social unconsciousness and history. Sexuality is an interesting topic in so far as, as soon as one starts to think about the personal and social meanings of human sexuality, "bodily nature" becomes hard, if not impossible, to describe outside of a discursive universe. The "body", which could include many aspects, such as comportment, preparations, decorations, visibility, and so on, has its own history (Foucault, 1978b), and indeed, what are considered "human attributes" vary enormously across cultures and times (Hirst & Woolley, 1981). Norms, training, and cultivation enter deep "into" the body, and whilst "flesh" is undeniable—all bodies bleed—notions such as "sins of the flesh", "crime against nature", or "unblemished", open up ethical-symbolic worlds that might inscribe human beings as "fallen bodies", inheritors of "original sin", "virginally pure", and so on (Elliot, 1999). In the medieval period, there was no equivalent to our word "sexuality", itself something of a nineteenth-century invention; indeed, it can be said that "sexual identity" had altogether different connotations and that, rather than "sex" being something that two people did, it was regarded as something that one person did to another (Dinshaw, 1999; Karras, 2005). The modern, free "western body" is no less than the product of complex significations, premised on our valuations of presentability, ideals of beauty, categories of "sexual liberation", technologised intervention and enhancement, norms of pleasure and gratification, significations that would utterly baffle those of another era, and indeed those of many another countries nowadays.

The two historical case examples to follow, concern representations of female nature in early modern Europe and are associated with the abject and the ideal; they are, respectively, (a) witchcraft beliefs and (b) Lutheran marriage ideals. These examples are of interest because they illuminate aspects of a social unconsciousness and imaginary radically different and, in most ways (but not every?), incommensurable with how we nowadays think about sexual and desirable, gendered relations.

Dangerous bodies, lustful women, witches

Femina comes from *Fe* and *Minus*, since she is ever weaker to hold and preserve the faith. (Kramer & Sprengler, 1486, p. 44)

Early European witchcraft belief and persecution has generated a vast scholarship. Quite how and why the Devil "burst forth" into human affairs, particularly from the thirteenth century onwards (witchcraft persecution belongs to a much later period), will never be fully understood (Boureuau, 2006). The Devil's physical presence in the world and ability to occupy and influence frail human bodies is of particular relevance, but the more that is known about witchcraft, the fewer the generalisations one can make. No singular mode of explanation of witchcraft will suffice and, in the understated terms of one distinguished historian of the field, "there are many reasons why" (Biggs, 1996, for a detailed survey of witchcraft; for social theories of witchcraft, see Scarre & Callow, 2001). Amongst the many complexities is the relationship of witchcraft to gender and/or sexuality. Despite stereotypes, not all witches were female (Levack, 1987, estimates seventy-five per cent female victims in most of Europe, with male victims in the majority in four more peripheral areas, and equally represented in Finland) or old or spinsters, although in some contexts the victims were overwhelming female and single (in England, up to ninety per cent were female), with part of the problem of interpretation being that there were very different waves, patterns (over a 300 year span), beliefs, countries, and regions involved. One formula, although not without its critics, is Larner's (1981, 1984) sober judgement that witchcraft (Larner was an expert on the Scottish witch context) was sex-*related* rather than sex-*specific*. As for the Devil, in spite of possessing chameleon form, there was no disputing the fact that he was male.

A famous and influential account, in Central Europe, was *Malleus Maleficarum* (literally "The Hammer of the [Female] Witches") by the German Dominicans, Heinrich Kramer and Jacob Sprengler, published in 1486. A guidebook for the educated, *Malleus* helped to consolidate a powerful, if learned, stereotype of the witch as subspecies of female, its ancient and theological surveys and didactic questions establishing the "reality" of feminine weakness and primary sinfulness. The book did not arise from nowhere and, in terms of its conditions of emergence and intertextuality ("authorisation"), it can be related to, say, concern in Germany about the non-implementation of Papal bulls and mounting pressures on the secular courts (Innocent VIII's 1484 frequently reprinted bull against witchcraft in particular; Middelfort, 1972). In some ways a derivative text, *Malleus* portrays women as excessive, backbiting, "over-tongued", superstitious, and treacherous—"evil of nature, painted with fair colours" (Kramer & Sprengler, 1486, p. 43). Kramer and Sprengler also quote good female models from the Bible, but these do not detract from an underlying vulnerability located in "female nature". Relating such characteristics to a defect in the "first woman", Kramer and Sprengler build to their conclusion that, "All witchcraft comes from carnal lust, which is in women insatiable" (p. 47).

Broedel (2003) notes the "founding", if tragic, value of *Malleus* in providing a model of the witch, even though it had contemporary critics who cited other sources or dismissed its morbid preoccupation with female sexuality; Biggs (1996) cautions against generalisation and the mixing up of rhetoric and justification with actual practice, in the case of this and other demonological guides. Yet the image of a disordered sexuality was resonant in many contexts and while medieval heresy may have been gender-neutral, witchcraft was an altogether different crime, a *crimen exceptum*. The emergent figure of the malevolent female witch differed markedly from medieval notions of the sorceress or wise women (Brauner, 1995). In Broedel's (2003) reading, *Malleus* sought to demonstrate that, "witchcraft, femininity and sexual sin form a tight constellation of interrelated ideas" (p. 178).

Constructions of the witch were born and disseminated in many forms, of which the scholarly text was just one. Others forms were woodcuts (Hans Baldung Grien's series are notable examples), sermon, teaching, the legal machinery of interrogation, and trial itself (again, with considerable variations throughout Europe), popular idiom, and linguistic convention. As Monter (1977) eloquently puts it, "The ingredients of the witch-maker's cauldron came from many different places" (p. 128). In an interesting analysis of gender hierarchies in the Renaissance, Classen (2005) considers belief about the "diabolic sensorium" of the witch, associated with nature's weakest member, woman. Amongst these are touch (the notion of the "evil eye"), slipperiness (e.g., the image of the spider), influencing from a distance (e.g., piercing of wax effigies), gluttony (the notion of an insatiable nature), evil odours (often associated with menstrual fluids), as well as (excessive) speech. Classen suggests that the latter was of two kinds—seductive or nagging—with nagging frequently linked to the wife, the subject of popular lore and many plays; "where men might use knives, women used words ..." (Larner, 1981, p. 86). Thomas (2009) notes the role of the early modern polarities of male/female and associated qualities of, say, "strong and weak", "rational and emotional", and so on. Let us briefly relate notions like these—the witch as personification of "bad" female sexuality—to the German and English contexts.

Roper's (1994, 2004) study of the German trials, uses a rich blend of sociological, psychoanalytic, and narrative formulations. Parts of the continent, such as Germany, entertained elaborate demonology and belief about the nature of the "pact" between witches and women; these beliefs included nocturnal meetings, flying objects and figures, and intercourse with the Devil, who appeared in endless disguise. Barbara Hohenberger (Roper, 2004), interrogated in 1590, confessed to having met a stranger who, preying on her status as a widow, courted her. He is an ordinary looking man, always wearing a feathered hat. Intercourse occurs and on the final occasion there is foul odour in the air. Intercourse effectively seals the devilish bargain, the pact. Roper notes how similar these German confession stories began to sound, with the Devil appearing in different, everyday guises, sometimes with charm, sometimes with force, and how typically he presents some kind of "solution" to a given woman's situation—for example, the wish to remarry in the case of Barbara, to overcome melancholy (often regarded as a sinful emotion), escape poverty, etc. In the narratives of the accused or condemned, it is easy to see how women used the language world of witchcraft to explain their everyday misfortune or dilemmas and how witchcraft could be fuelled by tensions between women (such as intergenerational), as well as from other sources.

In a particular emphasis on the maternal and post-partum period, Roper (1994) observes the role of wicked women who envy and target such a state, women such as lying-in maids, who "take over" an infant, or older, childless women who similarly harm mothers and infants. Tensions between women could be expressed in such fantasies, as well as those between men and women. Relating this partially to poverty and preoccupations around fertility, she contends that the ground was prepared for the powerful image of the "… death-dealing witch, attacking mothers, children and babies …" (p. 131). Fertility was overdetermined by all manner of fears and symbolism—barrenness, like crop failure, being a curse on the community as much as the individual person, older women or spiteful, younger ones, being associated with motives of vengeance. It is important to note that the other, major capital offence for women during this period was infanticide (stimulated mostly by poverty). Witches turned motherhood upside down, perverting its course and Roper emphasises the countervailing, demanding ideals to which women were held, ideals embodied, for Catholics, in the figure of Mary and, perhaps for Protestants, in women's destiny as obedient wife, etc. (more on this below). Motherhood is represented as ideal, but, "Idealisations of this strength and tenacity are likely to breed their own monsters" (Roper, 1994, p. 140).

If parts of the continent developed particularly sexualised, demonological accounts of seduction, intercourse, and enlistment by the Devil, England did not, apparently basing its witchcraft beliefs and persecutions more simply upon the notion of inflicting harm, *maleficia*—killings, harming others, destroying crops, spoiling food, etc. There seems to be more emphasis in England on the role of "imps" and the keeping of "familiars", though, as Sharpe (1996) says, from the East Anglian trials there was evidence of an increasing sexualisation of the relationship between humans, "witch marks", and such "animals". Sharpe (1996) refers to the use of an army of "women of credit" or "honest matrons", skilled in the detection of witches' marks (mostly a teat-like growth in the pudenda), from which "familiars" sucked. With the vast majority of victims being women, different connections to femaleness or sexuality operated. Purkiss (1996) offers a brilliant elucidation of this connection, to the realm of the domestic (the female domain)—house, hearth, body, and child. In considering the Essex trials, for which many documents have survived, Purkiss notes the connection of women to food and exchange in the rural economy, their responsibility for dairying and keeping house. In this regard, women's roles had a strongly symbolic dimension, as transformers of natural products, operating at those very boundaries where "nature and culture meet and are mediated" (Purkiss, 1996, p. 97). Acts of cultivation have a dark side, of which witchcraft is the ultimate perversion—the witch destroys order, meddles with, and pollutes, the community. Based on the amount of domestic detail quoted in these trials, Purkiss formulates the witch as the prime anti-mother, the figure who crosses the threshold of the ordinary household and community. The bodies of women are more "leaky", permeable, and therefore more problematic; "Just as the boundaries of the mother's body blend with her child, so the witch breaches the protective space around the body with a look, a gift, a touch, a word or a visit" (p. 125). A similar point is made by Elliot (1999, p. 56), in her account of women as perfect partners for the Devil, "ripe for uncanny insemination", symbolically, if not literally.

Anna Moats was judged guilty of witchcraft in 1645 in Suffolk, having confessed to courting evil spirits (imps) and encountering the Devil when cursing her husband and children. Reviewing this material, Jackson (1995) concentrates on the grain of domestic life—the rural, the intimacies of economy, with potential accusations around the bewitching of cattle, disputes over butter and milk, etc. She makes a convincing argument that those traditional feminine spaces and activities contain an abjected alternative, such as "feeding (poisoning), child-rearing (infanticide), healing (harming), birth (death)" (p. 71). In terms of the social figure of women more generally, Sharpe (1996) distinguishes references to grave, sober women—"a widdow of good reputation", as one tract puts it—standing in contrast to those women suspected of doing the "Divells work".

The witch symbolises danger, a danger above all others. She, when it is a she, like the heretics of earlier times, subverts the canopy that covers, and to some extent protects, normal human space. The covenant between God and humans, if one puts it in such terms, is undermined by the prospect of a malignant, alternative covenant between witch and Devil. Fertility, and all it encapsulates, is one, seemingly regular link. Is was not just a question of femaleness—equally, in peasant economies, the witch was also the prime anti-neighbour, who wrecks the peace, normal exchange, and wellbeing of the village or community; indeed, MacFarlane's (1972) classic study analyses witchcraft belief at the level of village anxiety and transactions in fascinating detail, emphasising the gradual decline in traditional (Catholic) attitudes of charity, borrowing, and communality.

Dutiful wives, ordained roles

"The Lord God has wanted three things made right again before the Last Day: the ministry of the Word, government, and marriage" (Luther, in Ozment, 1983, p. 381).

Elliot (2007) identifies a double attitude towards marriage, lasting over a number of centuries, as, on the one hand, over-implicated in flesh and, on the other, as hallowed institution. In parallel, women are, according to Elliot (1999), prone to true vision and revelation (cf. the female mystic tradition) as much as to superstition and hence temptation. By the time of the Reformation there was a vast scholarship and theology of marriage, as well as debates on the nature of the female ("querelle des femmes"), with one late seventeenth-century English preacher (John Sprint) proposing timely "reparation": "'tis but fair and just, that she, who hath been so greatly instrumental of so much Mischief and Misery to Man, should be actively engaged to please and comfort him" (quoted in Hester, 1992, p. 93).

Big questions, such as, "Was there a renaissance for women?", or "Was the Reformation good for women?" are difficult to answer, at least when posed in general terms, and Eales (1998) provides a succinct overview of the matter, referring to two kinds of broad historical narrative: on the one hand, a story of progress, of gradual emancipation of women from a feudal, medieval background and, on the other, a story of decline or regression, with a reassertion of patriarchal control, a "feminisation" of poverty with the advent of new urban economies, and so on. Ozment (1983) develops the former view, arguing that women did indeed find new allies and advocates, with humanist/Protestant critiques of the exaggerated clerical ideals of celibacy and the cloister, creating dramatic new, potentially positive spaces. That husband and wife eventually triumphed over monk and nun is, in his view, a major consequence of Reformation liberalisation. Many would concur and see in Protestant reforms the arrival of a more realist and "naturalised" concept of sexuality and its place within marriage (see Keeble's collection of contemporary documents/views, 1994). Roper (1989), however, in her studies of Augsburg, argues the reverse, suggesting a "conservative shift" with the Reformation, and that women became enclosed and oppressed within a newly confirmed claustrophobic family and moral system.

With the "progress story", one still has to account for waves of increased prosecution, if not widespread persecution, of women, whether it be the witches, the child-killers (infanticide), unruly women, or scolds (Underdown, 1985). Was a "crisis of order" mirrored by a crisis in gender relations, in the sixty years or so before the Civil War in England (Underdown, 1985)? Amussen (1985) supports this view, noting the emergence of new, strict versions of distinct, prescribed behaviour for women and men, wives and husbands. With an "anti-progress story", one equally has to account for the apparent rise, in spite of such persecutions and patriarchal control, of conditions for increased companionable and more equitable domestic relationships, paving the way also for a more privatised, freely contracted ideology of family life (Amussen, 1985; Stone, 1977).

Whatever else it did not do, the Reformation created new spaces and domains within which women could be effective and, no doubt, when one takes the longer view, both losses and gains are evident; hard to avoid, also, with a retrospective glance, is the tendency to see the "modern family" as hero, because of its eventual ascendancy (Houlbrooke, 2000; Sharpe, 1997). The reality on the ground was inevitably mixed, with family models based on the idea of a mini-commonwealth, with fathers representing the king, alongside many single female households (widows, sailors' wives, some poor women living together), punitive-shaming rituals directed against unruly women (e.g., the cucking stool, mocking rhymes), and women refusing to be underlings, being occasional leaders of food riots, empowered by membership of positive networks of female company, and so on (Capp, 1996).

What follows concentrates on Protestant, reformist ideals of womanhood in marriage in particular, not because of the definite existence of uniquely Protestant families, but because Protestants had so much to say and contribute in the shaping of new household ideologies, the marital state becoming, in theory at least, the regulative ideal for all virtuous Christians (Collinson, 2003). Not only this, but marriage and womanhood (indeed, also manhood, in a different way) were increasingly tied as related signifiers, "destinies", with a woman's presumed nature (e.g., her qualities of gentleness and yieldiness) well "suited" to its office.

Eales (1998) considers the influence of classical, Biblical, and medieval arguments concerning women, arguments that tend to slice the female world up in a particular way, "virgins, wives and widows, thus placing a central emphasis on the importance of marriage to their status" (p. 23). Eales acknowledges a problem: how can we know how influential was the abundance of scholarly, preacherly, or conduct writing on actual behaviour, any more than we can know the direct influence of *Malleus* or King James I's speculations on demonology on the actual persecution of witches? The ideal family, as represented by a plethora of Elizabethan and Stuart conduct books (values echoed and transmitted via clapbooks, ballads, fiction, and plays) may not have really existed, such texts being the self-justifying rhetoric of the new, marrying clerics. Perhaps this is the point, however, in that ideals are regulative principles influencing actual conduct, rather than its precise realisation.

Luther wrote extensively on marriage and, once he had overcome the monk in himself, became husband and father of six children. Collinson (2003) argues that, "Luther, above all theologians, knew that we live in our physicality and social relations, not in some segregated spirit zone" (p. 81). Luther believed marriage as institution was in need of reform, no less than the church itself, and complained that "marriage has fallen into awful disrepute". Not only this, but he questioned and challenged much contemporary anti-female popular prejudice or propaganda, double standards, as well as clerical corruption, and so on. Lutheran views on women and marriage are particularly interesting examples of the formulation of new regulative ideals that shifted the riverbed and river flow of social unconsciousness. Of the features he and other reformers most emphasised was promoting the estate of marriage, rescuing it not so much, or not only, from supposed Catholic denigration, but from being seen as inferior to the celibacy embodied in monastic life. In a pivotal "moment" of rearticulation, Luther defined marriage as *the* pre-eminent institution within which sexuality should be expressed, not only for the cultivation of honourable wives and daughters but for the ordering of male sexuality as well; in this way, the family becomes a positive "hospital" for lust, a suitable container, whilst monastic and priestly vows of chastity were condemned as impossible, undesirable, unnatural in the demands they placed on human beings (Karant-Nunn & Wiesner-Hanks, 2003); a naturalising of marriage (Leites, 1982). If society were truly to reflect Divine purpose, then marriage is God's chosen institution, households become "little convents", with marriage gaining reputation as demanding, spiritual vocation. Connectable to this were prevalent notions of a link or analogy between the structure of authority in society (e.g., comparisons of the king with father), and that within the well-constituted family.

Although some feminists have criticised this "rationalisation" and replacement, given ultimate expression by some Puritans (Hester, 1992), of (male) priest by (male) head of house, even of Pope displaced by State, Luther consciously sought a new paradigm of freedom and harmony between the sexes. For him, if Adam and Eve represented the first married couple, Adam (man) was not far behind Eve (woman) in terms of a propensity to sin. Strohl (2008) notes that Luther appears realistic, acknowledging the inevitability of struggle and fulfilment within marriage, justifying reasonable divorce, and acknowledging the need for reasonable agreement between parental wishes and those of potential couples—it is only the Devil who abhors harmony and wishes to come between husband and wife. In an interesting Renaissance notion of "gender complemtentarity", did the Reformation create (reinforce?) new polarities of influence- men as "public" and "political" figures, women as more "private", "domestic" beings, with women having "authority of the keys" (Brauner, 1995)? And was there a downside?; "the female assertiveness still tolerated in the Middle Ages gave way to silent submissiveness—at least ideally" (Brauner, 1995, p. 24).

How idealised was the Lutheran notion of marriage, as distinct from realistic, offering in principle a more charitable version of relationships and negotiation between couples? To Ozment (1983), the purpose of marriage was to stabilise individuals and society, "filling the land with homes and communities, laying foundations for household and government" (p. 8). Luther was certainly fulsome in his appreciation of the role of ambivalence within marriage, which if resolved helps end loneliness and temptation. One way of seeing these supposed ideals, is to regard them as articulating problems and solutions, helping form new hegemonic versions of good conduct, "pulling" individuals and communities in particular, desired directions, such as woman being man's "helpmeet" (Amussen, 1985).

Amongst emergent ideals of womanhood, contained within the excellence of the institution of marriage, were those of being docile, lovingly gentle, "restrained in feeling and submissive in action" (Leites, 1982, p. 389). Consider a few details of the courtship of German couple Lucas Behaim (1587–1648) and Anna Pfinzing, reconstructed from family records by Ozment (1999), from Nurnberg—a cultural centre (it was referred to as the "Venice of the North") and the first city to officially adopt the Reformation (1525).

Fresh from his "bachelor journeying", Lucas fell in love with twenty-one-year-old Anna. Their exchange of private vows a year before the public ones, represented a considerable risk, especially to the urban upper classes, for whom "greater discretion and discipline were expected" (Ozment, 1999, p. 14); private vows were often suspected as being a pretext for sexual intimacy and, when proved, such intimacy could lead to public shaming, fines, even imprisonment. The letters between them give an indication of how they managed longings and of the terms within which "cultivated" feminine and masculine qualities were regarded and interpellated. "Precious, virtuous, kindest, beloved, trusted Maiden bride ... apart from your company, I have, praise God, no other unfulfilled desire or need" (in Ozment, 1999, pp. 18–19). Fretting over lack of certitude, whilst also being convinced of their love, as sure as his devotion to God, Lucas seeks assurances from Anna, anxious in particular that she overcome her "maidenly modesty" and be bolder in her expression of feeling.

In a moment of weakness, whilst separated again, Lucas requests a gift that he soon realises might be seen as "coarse and shameless", "a portrait of your beautiful physical form, so that I might, from time to time, know true consolation and singular joy ..." (Ozment, 1999, p. 20). At times lusting, Lucas is tormented by his conscience and worried that his request might be read in purely carnal terms. He later admonishes himself, denying that he wanted the portrait for any "frivolous reason or passtime" (p. 29).

At a later point, as preparations for their marriage are underway, Anna moves to live with her pregnant sister. Lucas is delighted for Anna to be exposed to laudable "soronal service", which will serve her well in their future child-rearing. Their marriage proved successful and they had six children. Interestingly, in the light of the preceding discussion, there is reference to a less happy outcome, concerning a relative's illness and impotency, which is attributed to a witch (a common accusation at the time), the reverse of the godly female.

If the revolt-prone or wanton female, or the scold, are abjected figures, the demur but confident housekeeper and loyal housewife are the ideals. This did not exonerate husbands and there was cultural ambiguity between the degree to which a woman could act independently, guiding aberrant, wayward husbands, and her not being seen as a "woman on top" and thus usurping natural lines of authority. Similarly, if the drunkard, ridiculed, or cuckolded husband are abjected figures, the strong head and spiritually stable man is the ideal. Did such notions influence the evolution of sexuality itself? We have noted Luther's notorious insistence that man is naturally stronger, wiser, and that "natural womanhood" meant desiring of the states of marriage and motherhood, a desire that could reinforce women's sexual submissiveness. On the other hand, it could be argued that the Lutheran notion pulled women's sexuality away from its very association with "greater sin" and the unbounded carnality that has been noted in the discussion of witchcraft. Was this the story of another rearticulation, from women as inherently lustful/sinful to women representing "cultivated" (although it is equally assumed, natural) standards of modesty and gentleness?

Luther had much to say on witches as well as women, living in morbid fear of the former and justifying their persecution. Karant-Nunn (2003) attempts to capture something of the polarities within which he and other reformers might have thought about the two figures: "witches destroy, rather than sustain; they scold, curse or cast spells rather than be silent; they are lustful, independent and assertive, rather than chaste, pious and obedient" (p. 230). Yet the message is directed at both sexes, as the witch altered thresholds of shame in society, "frightening both man and woman" (Brauner, 1995).

Concepts of "social discipline" can help to conceptualise the operation of such ideas and the influence they had on actual conduct and subjective perception/experience. One big Reformation message, for example, was the need for couples to assume responsibility, to approach the tasks of marriage as serious ethical challenges, and, by implication, behave as though the home was the "cradle of citizenship". In this respect, with all its attendant hierarchies, the period promoted a version of "new" men as much as women (Collinson, 2003). All religious authorities wanted people to live in a proper and godly way, and "confessionalisation", in its varied forms (e.g., counter-reformist, Lutheran, Calvinist), promoted the external and internal social discipline to achieve such lives and to find within them the appropriate placing and meeting of human sexual desire.

Conclusion

The first part of this chapter explored social unconsciousness as discursive production and imaginary space. The sheer variation and indeterminate creativity of social imaginaries is balanced by their stability over time and the force of tradition. In complex societies one should really talk in terms of a number of overlapping social imaginaries, in the plural. There are productive contests, often stark contradictions, within social imaginaries between movements of "tradition" and "innovation", or to use the language of Husserlian phenomenology, between "sedimentation" and "reactivation" (Laclau, 1990; Ricoeur, 1984b). With "sedimentation" there is a layering or "forgetting" of earlier, "original" meanings, and with reactivation, an attempt to think again, anew. The distinction starts to merge, as not everything can be reactivated (assimilated) within a given culture—sometimes there is "no turning back"— and, equally, once new things are in place they often transmute into new traditions.

The case of early modern, European witchcraft, in all its diversity, offers fascinating insights into the formation of a social matrix that ordered the distribution of human kinds, the forces of the anti-Christ and the Kingdom of God. As abject beings at the margins of the social, the figure of "witches" condensed a veritable universe of discourse and power, which could not have been predicted from preceding eras, even if some many earlier discourses and symbols (e.g., of women's nature, heretical crimes, the ambivalence of magic) migrated and were rearticulated. Its eventual decline, like that of the category "devil", in the late seventeenth century (although it took until 1736 for the English

Witchcraft Act to be repealed; Bostridge, 1996), was equally hard to predict, except that its anchors within the social imaginary had long since loosened to the point of irrelevance and eventual unthinkability; it should be noted that, as Trevor-Roper (1978) puts it, "No mere scepticism, no mere 'rationalism' could have driven out the old cosmology. A rival faith was needed ..." (p. 110). By then, a very different kind of social world, with new symbols, myths and guiding ideals, was in ascendancy.

The analysis of changes in marital and gender ideals similarly illustrates the role of gradual, often subtle, changes in the composition of social unconsciousness. Some Lutheran innovations reactivated and reinscribed older values (e.g., surrounding the place of marriage in society, notions pertaining to the distribution of female/male duties; in the words of one authority, man's calling was to manage things "abroad, and women's with matters at home—'he without doors, she within'"; quoted in Thomas, 2009, p. 21), whilst creating new ones alongside. With relative secularisation, paradoxically alongside rearticulations of faith, there was increasing emphasis placed on new "disciplines" of self, and, for Puritans in particular, a "spiritualisation of the household" as the most basic unit of discipline. As we shall see in the discussion of the Reformation in the next chapter, this was a remarkable attempt to reforge lines of authority and spiritual responsibilities. As for the family-to-be, Stone (1977) has described critical changes from values and practices of "distance, deference and patriarchy" to "affective individualism", with a resultant intensification of affective bonding within the nuclear family.

Reforming subjectivity: personal, familial, and group implications of English reformation

Take any event, process, or fact and place it in history. Once done everything changes, since that event, process, or fact, gains the context of time, location, and movement. In other words, place something *in* history and it becomes possible to see it *as* history; history opens the door to contingency. All historical writing involves an interpretive dimension, since we can never be sure that we have comprehended the horizontal context in which the object of study occurred. The past is always there, but the activity of the present, including that of the historian, works upon it. Man is a symbolising creature. We cannot transcend the symbolic realm, and history is a discipline undertaken by those with particular foci and projects; further, the objects of historical study are *past* symbolic activities. History is the history of previous, meaningful being, and historians are themselves products of history (Burrow, 2007).

The Reformation, the subject of this chapter, is an interesting case in point, as it is a colligatory concept that joins up countless lesser changes into the retrospective, envisaged "movement", by which people redefined their worlds (Haigh, 1995). Is it though, part of a "continuum of history", or, "an extraordinary historical moment"? (Collinson, 2003); because the redefining was so extensive, the Reformation came to signify a vast watershed, with new confessional communities feeling invisibly united by images of their greater communion or brotherhood. If meaningful being is always underway, never settled, then an element of scepticism is inherent to the historian's craft. E. H. Carr, in *What is History?* (1987), gives the example of "the historian who has decided for his own reasons that Caesar's crossing of that petty stream, the Rubicon, is a fact of history, whereas the crossing of the Rubicon by millions of other people … interests nobody at all" (pp. 11–12). Carr thus concludes that the old dogma that "the facts speak for themselves" is untrue.

Norbert Elias proposed the discipline of "historical psychology" whereby "minds" and mentalities can be understood only if placed within the processes that shaped and defined them. In his view, human beings are interdependent rather than autonomous, existing within what Elias called *figurations*. Krieken (1998) explains that Elias stressed that the identity of human beings, "as unique individuals", existed only "within … networks or figurations" (p. 55). An early friend of group analysis, Elias noted similarities between the two disciplines, with the need to wander between the group level and the individual level, back and forth, "both having roots in the focus of one's attention" (Elias, 1997). Others (e.g., Mennell, 1997) have noted the family resemblance between the "figuration" of Elias and the "matrix" of Foulkes.[1]

Elias's (1978, 1982) two-volume major work explored the "civilising process" as it operated in medieval, absolutist, and bourgeois societies and the sociogenesis of the state. Volume one concentrates on the role of courtoisie, or court society, in transforming warrior society and producing far-reaching changes in levels of civility, mutual recognition, and pacification. Rules of conduct and practices such as manners, restraint, foresight, privacy, and shame were amongst the objects of his analysis. Like the *Annales* school of French historians, he acknowledges the slow, but cumulative nature of such changes in conduct and milieu, history in *longue durée*.[2] These are changes involving more than one generation and that, in the technical language of group analysis, involve recompositions of the "foundational matrix". Foundational or figurational change represents changes in the pattern of individual/group, figure/ground relations.

Elias tended to focus on elites (warriors, members of court society) rather than ordinary folk (Rosenwein, 2006). Neither did he pay much attention to the role of Christianity and church practice, preferring to concentrate on secular domains, particularly the court. This, however, was not the only, or even the most influential, realm in terms of the evolving subjectivities and rules of personal conduct (Hirst & Woolley, 1981). Smith (1991, p. 53) observes that "The age of the knight was also the age of the monk". Monasteries were, for example, equally complex institutions as courts, within which new relations of conscience, conformity, respect, and mutual surveillance operated. There was also the religion of everyday life; it is with these, albeit later, processes of Christianisation that this chapter is concerned and how religious practice powerfully influenced the "formation and maintenance" of human attributes (Hirst & Woolley, 1981). In Tudor England, Church and State were one and the Bible not simply a "religious text" but one integral to most spheres of cultural and intellectual life; Febvre (1973) argues that "early modern minds"—an unfortunately objectifying term perhaps— could not think beyond terms other than religious, with the Puritan revolution a radical reinterpretation which sought to inscribe the spirit of the Scriptures in men's hearts and minds. The story of the Reformation and early-modern religious struggles remains an inescapable, even if distant, component of the story of who we now are, in this region of the world.

Following a summary of the backdrop to these changes, I offer four intimate "case reflections" upon the back of historians, Puterbaugh (2000), Jones (2002), Underdown (1992), and Todd (1992), and others. The social theory used is the same as that outlined in the preceding chapter, and, in addition, I use Anderson's (1981) concept of "imagined communities". Protestant communities of various kinds, can be understood as imagined communities that assume the existence of a "deep, horizontal comradeship" (Anderson, 1981, p. 7), with inevitable differentiations from other, adjacent or competing communities. Rosenwein's (2006) concept of "emotional communities" is equally apposite, signifying as it does, in her study focused on communities in the early middle ages (guilds, monasteries, etc.), "groups in which people adhere to the same norms of emotional expression and value—or devalue—the same or related emotions" (p. 2). In other words, throughout history and cultures, there are not only great variations in emotional vocabularies available, but also in the expressive repertoire of groups. The emotions involved are not simply turned "on" or "off", constrained or expressed, but are formed within contingent acts of performance— discursive, institutional, and so on (Rosenwein, 2009). Hopefully, it is in the everydayness, the "playne meninge", of the examples cited, that much can be gleaned about the changing and relational nature of historical subjectivities, emotions, and communities.

The Protestantisation of the social

What is revealed during moments of great historical disruption, redefining the social ground with new images, myths, and values? How, when such changes are successful, does an "emergent form" become a "dominant form", recasting the whole meaning of social relations and transforming "structures of experience" (Williams, R., 1977)? During the Protestant Reformation, common-sense structures of experience were transformed and with it, the reinscription of the personal in relation to the public, the godly and the community. New standards of comportment, discourse, and conduct were established within the context of emergent "emotional" and "imagined communities"; of course, active opponents and countervailing emotional communities articulated different norms. In the hierarchical society that was Tudor and Stuart England, there were all sorts of "degrees or person", whose very classification created implications for conduct, interaction, and expectation (Wrightson, 1982). In this structure of dominance, new and denigrated subject positions emerged, forces such as "masterless men", the poor (although Protestant attitudes towards the poor and marginalised are ambiguous), scolds (disorderly women who abused their neighbours), dishonourable men, and the witch (mostly, if not entirely, women). Whilst one set of figures established themselves on the legitimate stage—"the Godly", "true believers", "puritans"[3], etc.—others flourished in the dark, threatening the very existence of the social (Catholics, recusants, forces of the anti-Christ, etc.). Although some of the anxieties about such groups were based on reactivated, sedimented ancient fears, new significations and symbolisations arose. Varied, illegitimate figures were powerful targets of concern and persecution by those whose job it was to maintain social order.

The Reformation in England took a different course to that on the continent, change initiated by Henry VIII's break with Rome (creating a form of Catholicism without the Pope?) and stabilised in some aspects by the Elizabeth settlement. The Church of England forged a middle-way between Catholicism and radical versions of Protestantism. Still, there were shifts and reversals, with a swing to Protestantism under Edward and the return to Rome under Mary. Post-Reformation life created new pressures and turmoil, leading ultimately to the polarisations of the Stuart and Civil War periods, settling, eventually, in new forms with the Restoration (for a comparison with the continental Reformation and Counter-reformation, sees Mandrou, 1979).

It is useful to delineate some of the constituents of this lengthy process:

- Henry VIII, for his own reasons, created a reform of religion that was neither Lutheran nor Roman. He secularised church property on a large scale, to benefit the Crown and proceeded to break the tie with the Rome. The Anglican Church emerged with the episcopate recognising Henry as supreme head of the Church of England.
- Traditional sources of authority and allegiance and medieval concepts of orthodoxy were weakening. There were many earlier "nonconformists" (although that very expression comes from a later period), such as Wycliffe, condemned after his death, who were recast as heroes of reform; Foxe dubbed Wycliffe the "morning star of the reformation" (Kenny, 1985).
- In a range of ways, belief moved away from the medieval hegemony of the Image, intercession of saints, ceremony, pilgrimages, and so on and recentred on interpretation of the Word. Changes in literacy, and the rise of vernacular languages, were of immense long-term significance to the Reformation; Anderson (1981) refers to "print capitalism". The democratisation of the Bible and Luther's idea of the "priesthood of all believers" stressed the individual conscience and displaced blind allegiance to traditional authority. In different ways, Luther and Calvin relocated the centre of authority from ecclesiastical institutions to the elect soul; "… anyone could understand God's word if he studies carefully enough and if the grace of God was with him" (Hill, 1972. p. 93). Hill (1997 and Thomas (1971) analyse many aspects of this complex process, including the spread of urban values and growing numbers of "masterless men", that, together with a privatisation of conscience and decline in magic, created new possibilities of subjectivity and anxiety.
- Printing and availability of texts cannot be emphasised enough in importance. Collinson (2003) refers to broad shifts from a culture of orality to one of print, but also the formation of new modes of discourse, address, and "plain speech", a scripture designed to "speak the language of the spinning woman or wayfaring man" (p. 37). Books

such as Foxe's *Book of Matryrs* (its popular title—its actual title being *Acts and Monuments*) circulated in numbers surpassed only by the Bible and helped to cement a new Protestant identity and mythology, written, as it was, in response to the persecutions of Mary I. Indeed, Foxe believed that printing was the product of divine intervention. Hence, Protestants and printers helped create a new culture, demonstrating that more people could be taught to read. In the words of a seventeenth-century commentator (quoted in Hill, 1972), the books that had once been the preserve of monasteries "were redeemed from bondage, obtained their enlargement, and freely walked around in the light" (p. 7).

A central consideration, then, is the transformation of a country of "good Catholics" into a Protestant nation, with innumerable, long-term implications for the conduct of social life and belief; a new "culture of discipline" emerged. Norman Jones (2002) puts it succinctly: "over the course of three generations the way the English worshipped, did business, governed themselves, and related to their place in the universe underwent a sea change" (p. 2). What is particularly valuable about Jones' research is that he draws upon the records of specific individuals and families during this period, providing an impression of personal meaning of such changes.

Dialogue of difference between son and mother

Although views differ as to the rate and mode of spread of Protestantism (Haigh, 1995), by the 1580s, Protestant persons had Catholic grandparents and sometimes parents, creating moral dilemmas in a culture that stressed family honour and obedience. Children, like wives, were seen as being in a state of tutelage, with their male superiors knowing more on all subjects. Yet the appeal to individual conscience and answerability to God only, could conflict with a traditional state of assumed patriarchal dependence. Youngsters, in rebellion and assertion, had been in the forefront of the Protestant changes in the 1530s—changes that were increasingly recouped by the establishment—but who, in years to come, would rebel further, and some would be attracted towards Puritanism and radicalism (and, paradoxically, for some, Catholicism, which became a symbol and source of resistance again in the 1590s). If heads of families could be challenged, then, by extension, so too could magistrates and monarchs. But how, in the light of this two-faith, complex denominational world, where Catholicism was publically stigmatised, were family contradictions of this sort negotiated?

Puterbaugh (2000) quotes the case of a "Zealous Protestant" son, who attempts to convert his "Devout Recusant" mother. It is based on Francis Savage's *A Conference*, published in 1600 and dedicated to Gervase Babbington, bishop of Worcester. Worcester was seat of Catholic resistance and Savage had had his own loyalties in writing it. "Zealous" did not have modern-day connotations of fanaticism, but signified a sense of sincerity or constancy. The word "recusant" signified anti-conformity or refusal to attend pubic worship and was a gesture/symbol within the social identity and practice of Catholics during this period. Churchgoing was a heated issue, with some Catholics, or other non-conformists, preferring segregation, even postures of irreligion, whilst others adopted outward conformity as "church papists". The concept of a "conference" or dialogue, in which participants and churchgoers engaged, challenged traditional dogmatism and received wisdom, although in this text it is clearly placed in the context of an assumed superiority of Protestant faith. It is an everyday dialogue, which, however, as far as Savage is concerned, resonates with a far bigger societal dialogue—that of the pre-existing formal Church and theological debates/disputations. In other words, this metanarrative is the informing context within which this minor, everyday dialogue between a son and his mother takes place, one that had already assured the triumph of Protestant doctrine.

The son in question is keen to engage his mother on religious observance, doing so within the "terms of duty or reverence" owed to her. But why, given the emphasis on filial obedience to the parents, is the son instructing his mother on religion and not the other way round? In the account, the son, returned from university to his home in the country, initiates a dialogue with his mother in matters about faith. Whilst respectful, he is questioning of her religious views and attachment to the "Old Faith", surprising her at the outset by claiming that it is *not* in fact Catholicism that is the Old Faith, but one "newly minted in culture"; it is really the Protestant faith that is the more ancient of the two, "certainly we planted no newe religion, but renewed the olde" (Puterbaugh, 2000, p. 430). She confesses surprise and is clearly not used to hearing arguments on behalf of what she would regard as Protestant heresy. The son skillfully listens whilst offering interpretations to fill the gaps and inconsistencies in his mother's position. There is a theme of restoring his mother to the new conformity, to public worship, and with it, to the rule of her husband, indeed, the state. He vigorously counters her fear that she is bound by her Catholic oaths and creates a space within which she might duly reassess her "erring conscience", advising her to "ponder with your selfe" and equipping her with various Protestant and Biblical reformulations. Their dialogue ends with the mother's quiet withdrawal and inner conversion. She is impressed by his heartfelt efforts and complains, retrospectively, that, "we on our side are greatly wronged, when we are forbidden to read your bookes, or to conferre with you" (Putterbaugh, 2000, p. 423). In gratitude, and in the context of her conversion, she exclaims, "thou hast raised out of mine bodie a teacher for me … he by thee has offered me a life concerning my soule, if I will receive it" (p. 422). A proscribed subject position, "Catholic", is potentially supplanted by another position, the "true believer" who is called into being on the basis of an appropriately "examined self".

This interaction was no mere impudence on the part of the son, but reflected the growth of a Protestantised culture that saw the past as inhabited by religious darkness and the spreading of the Word of the gospel as the central Christian responsibility. Far from occupying a compartment of life, the Bible was regarded as all-encompassing in significance (Collinson, 2003). Thus, the son partakes in a role, indeed duty, assigned to him by new cultural necessity, to restore her as a loving subject, an obedient wife, and a true Protestant. The affective tone of the dialogue is one of tenderness rather than rejection, even though the object of the dialogue is of grave, ultimate significance. Whilst some youngsters might have abandoned their families out of spiritual conviction, or been ejected for the same, more common and likely seems to have been some form of compromise and social disavowal of contradictory realities. The mother wrestles with her conscience, worried by the implicit invitation to break her oath with the Church of Rome. The son warns her of "tricks", "fond" arguments, and "intanglements" brought by previous generations and, armed with accompanying books and notebooks, strenuously argues the need for courage, to confront the "erring conscience" and, during crises of faith, to await for further revelation from God. Within a new casuistry and interpretive world of scripture, the son effectively offers a third space within which he can "hold" his mother's beliefs about this troublesome "new doctrine", although the notion of a "middle-ground" was not an accepted idea in the context of the times. This having been noted, there is another possibility, that the mother, with or without her son's connivance, adopts an outward sign of conformity whilst retaining Catholic belief, a position sometimes referred to as "statute protestantism" or "church papism". And whilst the son acknowledges that the state cannot "compel" religion, he continually appeals to her capacity for honest pondering and use of faith. In tackling her allegiance to baptism, for example, that ceremony of naming, he attempts to rearticulate the fixity of her world, freeing signifier from signified and leading her to an alternative.

The concept of the "conference" was an idea unfamiliar to his mother and new to the culture. According to this Protestant notion, although the sermon might be paramount, subsequent dialogue and conference gained importance as a means of dissemination and responding to a heterogeneous population. Through judgment, hearing, and questioning, there is the possibility of debate between divine truth and mortal knowledge. Thus, the conference could provide an interpersonal perspective, even though the state authorities were wary of its potential for fermenting discontent. Jones (2002) argues that, in creating "neutral private spaces, in which conformity and deviance in religion were accepted as individual choices, families developed strategies for coping that prevented disintegration whilst shaping group identity" (p. 35). There is a further level to this particular family dialogue, in so far as we learn that the son had been sent away for education. Perhaps at an earlier stage, he had, like the Prodigal Son, strayed or lacked appropriate religious guidance. This brings in the role of his father and the reference to university or books, standing as symbols for a rightful, Protestant education. Now it is the son's turn to bring the fruits of his learning to guide the older generation. Overlaid with this educated/ignorant polarity, is a rural/urban dynamic, whereby what is attained in the civilised cities should spread to poorer, benighted, less educated areas. This is consonant with a Protestant view of the Catholic as dull-witted members of an ignorant multitude; this was a time of intense projections and negative mirroring (Haigh, 1995; Marotti, 2005). For Protestants there was hope that "playne meninge" and lay interpretation could carry the word/Word, aimed especially at the poor and "unthinking" populace.

There is an issue of gender in all this, with a feminised, seductive image of Catholicism at large. The broad trend at the time, in so far as women were concerned, was the building of expectations and roles as to what constituted a "good" housewife, as contrasted with the alternatives. New urban ideals of femininity and womanly obedience arose, which can partly be analysed in terms of a disciplining of unruly women and an evolution of patriarchal norms (Brauner, 1995; Stone, 1977).[4] Hence, in the dialogue in question, the mother's recusancy is seen as the product of her weakness as a woman and isolation from proper instruction or authority. Contemporary concern with the prospect of "popish wives" and the rise of leading women recusants, lead to legalised discrimination in 1606; husbands could thereafter be denied civic appointment and promotion on the grounds of problematic marriages. Ironically, later, it was often Puritan wives who admonished their non-attending, straying, or idle husbands. In the dialogue in question, the son is worried that his mother's position sets her apart and potentially dishonours the family. The son invokes the memory of "simple women, maidens and girls" (Putterbaugh, 2000, p. 425), with a political implication of recusancy, pre-established in a culture that merged religious conformity with loyalty to state/ruler: "For if the Father cannot rule in his own household, the son asks, how might he be able to 'rule others abroad'?" (p. 425).

In the culmination of the story, the mother withdraws into her closet, "where all bewashing her selfe with tears, she braek out in this sort" (Putterbaugh, 2000, p. 429). We enter the domain of the conversion narrative, in which inner dialogue with God replaces dialogue with her son. Yet it is the preceding dialogue with her son that has made this possible, as too, perhaps, has his quoting of models of conversion from the Bible. The reference to closets and cabinets (also diaries and other forms of confession) during this period is emblematic of introspection and Protestantised self-examination.[5] In the climax of conversion, she exclaims, "I am caught, I am caught, o my God, if I will not damnably breake out of thy net again" (p. 429).

One way of reading the dialogue is simply to say that one "ideology" replaces another and that any implication for the respective subjectivities of the participants is merely an "effect". In this reading, subjectivity is regarded as a more or less continual space, "filled" by different contents, or a question of occupying different roles at different times. Another reading, however—one favoured here—is the argument that new subjectivities are partially born, formed, and maintained through the very constitution of discourse and dialogue, in which new subject-positions and articulations of identity become possible.

In this view, self-narration is not merely descriptive of the self, but that "self-narration ... is what raises our temporal existence out of the closets of memorial traces and routine and unthematic activity, constituting thereby a self as its implied subject" (Kerby, 1991, p. 109). The conference is inherently dialogical in the narrow sense of involving two people in discussion, but also in the wider sense of involving the voices, appeals, and interpellations of societal voices and positions; such wider voices are there even in the quiet spaces of contemplation or conversion, for even here, in supposed solitude, the mother is on a journey of becoming, dialogically connected to a dynamic of past/present, person/God, old self/new self, and so on (Webster, 1997). Thus, in general, by offering new models of comportment, male duty, womanly conduct, self-scrutiny, civility, relational obligation, and much more, reformed religious discourse enabled changes in the very make-up of persons, changes that had long-term and unforeseen consequences.

Family life during troubled times

Jones' (2002) research shows how family folklore was re-edited, comprising an early form, one might argue, of "political correctness". It is equally illustrative of the formation of collective memories and the redrafting of moral selves, comprehensible within a changing context of social relations. A technique developed at the social and familial level to deal with changing culture, was that of revising memory and history, a process that has even been likened to an "iconoclastic holocaust" (Collinson, 2003). Rather quickly, and prompted by a loss of material evidence at hand, the language and forms of "old Catholic" were forgotten and would have soon appeared alien to the young. The printed word and practices of the new Protestant faith created new vistas and material conditions of faith. Another example was the disappearance of the general ritual of making the sign of the cross, stamped out by officials and preachers (although it survived in certain limited church ceremonies, such as baptisms, much criticised by some of the later Puritans). What had once been an automatic response to danger became associated with superstition or "old wives' tales". The past was recast, aided by new forms of literature, conduct manuals, sermons, and "common sense". At one point, the son in the dialogue example, just discussed, refers to Foxe's *Acts and Monuments* as an illustration of the established superiority of the Protestant, this being part of an intertextual reality in which the Bible is supplemented by other works. The foundational significance of Foxe's *Book of Martyrs* has been mentioned, providing, as it did, a view of events leading up to Elizabeth I's succession, seeing reformation within the context of a providential history and glorious emergence from the "declining time of the church" or the time of the "antichrist". Hence the break with Rome and the passing of the old religion became part of a grand story of the purging and rebirth of the church. No mere commentary on the events of reformation, Foxe's text became an important and widely known part of it, creating new modes and Protestant precedents (O'Day, 1986). It is part of the very story of the make-up of England.

One of Jones' examples is of the Wentworth family, whose father is fond of remembering the family's history and providences. In particular, he enjoys telling his son how he came along, given that for a long time he and his wife had "only" four daughters in eleven years. He talks of the intervention of a female apparition who assures him of his health and longevity and that he should wash himself at the well of St. Anne of Buxton. According to the prediction he did so and begot a son. There was a problem with this version, in so far as it ran counter to the Protestant rejection of miracles and the intercession of saints, which the son's grandparents might well have believed in. Somewhere along the way, therefore, with the change-over of cultures in England, the father dropped the reference to the well and St. Anne, whilst still being able to celebrate the son's conception as a source of joy and gift of God. Jones discusses other examples of mutations of memory and lore in families, and the silences, reflecting the way Protestant family chronicles managed the reality of their Catholic ancestors; had condemnation reigned, rather than a more benign process of "overlooking", entire previous generations would have been consigned to evil; therefore, more Janus-faced responses were required, with pragmatic adaptations to allow the construction of viable-enough family story-lines.

On the other hand, families that remained loyal to the "old religion" were increasingly excluded from social life and viewed with suspicion. Excluded groups, such as Catholics, also realinged their history, so that ill-treatment or isolation might be emphasised by family folklore as a sign of virtue and honourable suffering. Interestingly, the same form of argument from "noble suffering" as it were, was used by Puritans in the next century to give a particular meaning to their ill-treatment. New markers of difference came into play, so that individuals and groups who had previously been mere neighbours, might now be seen, in some contexts, as dangerous. As the ground of heresy kept shifting, these were uncertain times, and "learning to hate", as Jones puts it, as well as the avoidance of conflict, was a requirement of the times. At the same time, for others, perhaps it is also a story of toleration and the cultivation of compromises. In the example of the conference between mother and son, we see a kind, but compelling, form of dialogue, containing potential splits in family life, although one effectively facilitated by the mother's apparent conversion. Individuals growing up in these times were embedded within new networks of imagined community, religious and civil, from which they borrowed and built their identities and which carried an irreversible weight in English society.

Jones (2002) considers how Tudor families dealt with slow societal changes as they impacted upon kinship, marriage, and honour; he writes, "The reformations that did occur happened across the length of lives, slowly, as people found ways to get along in families that were increasingly complex religiously" (p. 50). It is worth noting that by the 1640s, life expectancy was thirty-two and the majority of the population young. Stone (1977) has analysed this period as one of a reduction in traditional sources of authority and kinship identification and growing "affective individualism". He charts how the household, over time, tended to replace the church as agency of moral and spiritual authority. The spiritualisation of the household—replacing the church as the most important organisation—meant a whole range of questions about how to nourish family life and provide leadership. Puritans were subsequently highly concerned with child-rearing and the discipline of home life, since it would be children who would inherit and maintain the Godly society; "Puritans were abnormally concerned about children and their upbringing because it was only by mass conversion of the younger generation that they could hope to create of perpetuate the godly society to which they aspired" (Stone, 1977, p. 125). In newer forms of patriarchy (but, significantly, which also included a revaluation of maternity and female authority), it was the responsibility of fathers to maintain domestic devotion and discipline, as children could all too easily be seen as "young limbs of Satan" (Spurr, 1998).

Group change within a town: from Dorchester to Heaven

From the historical research available, it would seem that there was no simple expansionist, uniform change in the religious identity of English towns and places, the Protestant "culture of discipline" not always a popular alternative to Catholic traditionalism (Collinson, 2003). There are complicated issues of hierarchical versus horizontal spread and a town/countryside divide, with literacy being an important factor in the spread of Protestantism (Haigh (1995) informs us that in the late six-teenth century, tradesman were five times more likely to be literate than husbandmen and that exposure to regular preaching was more likely in the towns).

The county of Dorset saw the formation of strong Protestant enclaves, such as the port of Poole and the more modest trading town of Dorchester. Underdown's (1992) research on Dorchester follows the fortunes of its inhabitants, from the great fire that wreaked devasta-tion in 1613 (and a much smaller one in 1623), through to the Civil War and the Restoration. Of particular focus are the efforts articulated by its chief minister, John White, to transform an unremarkable, though rela-tively wealthy town into a leading, Puritan centre, building a reformed, godly community to match, on a tiny scale, Calvin's Geneva. The fire, an event pre-eminently open to eschatological interpretation, was a centring event, Protestants seeing it as a sign of God's displeasure and as prompt for the comprehensive reformation of the town.

White's arrival after 1613, and the message of his subsequent fol-lowers, did not meet with universal approval and Underdown uses the example of Matthew Chubb, wealthy town elder, and his circle, as sup-plying an alternative vision, with an older concept of neighourliness and social order based on traditional alliances and obligations. Chubb and his followers were suspicious of Puritans; "The conflict between Chubb and the reformers was one for the town's very soul: for its entire moral and spiritual character" (Underdown, 1992, p. 38). Although reli-gious life in Dorchester (there were three churches) was shared by Puri-tan and non-Puritan alike, it was the puritans who were more conscious and actively reflective of their identity; it was they, after all, who sought to rearticulate the social/spiritual realm and it was Chubb's world that was on the defensive.

In the context of an expanding town, reformers were concerned to address its social problems of welfare, discipline, and order in new ways, furthering their campaign for godliness and sobriety. Their col-lective sense of living not only in dangerous times, but, one might say, in ultimate times, was clear, the period seen as "perhaps the great-est turning point, of history: at the final stage of the eternal conflict between light and darkness, between good and evil, between Christ and anti-Christ" (Underdown, 1992, p. 53). This was conceived within a local, national, and even international context and it is important to link local struggle with wider religious struggle and state doctrine. Underdown details perceived threats to order, ranging from drunkenness to sexual promiscuity, bear-baiting to popular sports and swearing. These were hardly new problems, but in the view of the reformers were not only urgent targets for discipline but emblematic of drift towards vice and ungodliness. "Masterlessness" was a growing worry, a term attached to bands of drifting labourers, vagrants, or unruly, assertive females. In term of everyday language, Underdown notes the frequency with which words of insult such as "rogue", "knave", and "whore" were used; "by punishing swearing the authorities were trying to control the vocabulary as well as the religious, sexual and work habits of their neighbours (Underdown, 1992, p. 77). Hospital, school, and home, as well as church, were central sites of change, White's vision of charity was not so much a contradiction to that of Cobb, but a rearticulation of its basis and rationale.

As conditions worsened in England, the dividing lines of reform and anti-reform grew larger. The Calvinist saws signs of popery and Arminiansm (i.e., the disapproved-of doctrine of the Stuart Church, under Archbishop Laud) everywhere, in the town and beyond. Although most believed their mission was to stay put and ensure the town's Christian future, others set sail to America, intent on creating their vision elsewhere, a New England. Dorchester became, in civil war, an armed camp and site of many horrors, such as the execution of Catholic priest Hugh Green, whose head was kicked around like a football on the green. The Royalists took the town, staying until routed in 1644, and White, old and in temporary exile, returned two years later. In White's retrospective words, "God stepped in between us and our utter ruin" (Underdown, 1992, p. 209).

By the end of the Civil War decade and Restoration, the passions and extremes of republican and sectarian trends dissipated. But what had happened over the course of a few preceding decades illustrates the role of both charismatic individuals and their assemblage groups, who both represent and lead, in an inevitable mix of influence. Each person and each group, as it were, tries to imprint its version of history, either proactively in the case of reformers or defensively in the case of others, more content with older ways, each construing and acting upon different narrative constructions of events and their implications; there are differing emotional communities as well. Beyond the Restoration, Dorchester became friendly to non-conformists, a tribute perhaps to the combined efforts of the previous reformers. Underdown (1992 eloquently summarises the outcome: "the vision of a reformed, godly community which had inspired its leaders since the fire of 1613 gradually faded. The reason in part was generational: great causes are always likely to lose their vitality as the original leaders are supplanted by others who have grown up in a different moral climate" (p. 244).

Samuel Ward: Puritan diarist

Studying the creation and spread of new genres of writing, such as the self-revelatory diary, autobiography, and letters, helps us reconstrue subjectivities of earlier times. Not only this, but perhaps such "technologies" themselves have an influence on the formation of, and enunciation of, subjecthood. Greenblatt (1980) believes that during the Renaissance there was a trend towards "deliberate" self-exploration through writing, and that writing is itself a component expression of such "self-fashioning". Books could serve as exemplars of virtuous, or problematic, lives and Puritans had many "good books" to point the way towards the "practice of piety". The following example of Samuel Ward[6] derives from a rich tradition of Puritan spiritual diary keeping. Politically, it is also of interest since, having aligned himself amongst the moderate reformers, Ward finally suffered imprisonment at the hands of his former student, Oliver Cromwell, charged with not having supported the Parliament cause in the war. My account is dependent on Todd's (1992) explication of the dairy.

Late in Elizabeth's reign, a young Cambridge scholar of Christ and Emmanuel Colleges began a diary which was his attempt at self-examination. The institutional location was significant, Puritan colleges being noted for their commitment to the training of Protestant preachers. In them, Samuel Ward found inspiration in certain role models, notably Laurence Chaderton, the master of Emmanuel and "pope of Cambridge puritanism", who served as good example to Ward of the Christian life. The ideas of *example* and *imitation* had specific connotations for Puritans and reformism: Christ was seen as the ultimate example (*exemplum exemplorum*) and the mode of *imitatione Christi,* from Luther onwards, stressed the spirit rather than the outward deed in faith and religion. Berkovitch (1975) writes of the shifting ground of private identity from "institution to individual"; "the concept of *imitatio* makes every man his own church" (p. 11). In Ward's case, inspired by Chaderton and others, he resolves to become preacher and his diary increasingly deploys the notion of *preacher as model*.

The diary takes the form of a confession, with a turning around of, or remaking of self, indirectly influenced by a confessional tradition reaching back to St. Augustine (an important cultural model for Christians). Taylor (1989) comments on a "language of interiority" that St. Augustine created, of much significance to later reformist practices: "Do not go outward: return within yourself. In the inward man dwells truth" (p. 129). As for Ward, he was "… clearly intent on transforming his frivolous, fun-loving, proud self into a more somber, disciplined, pious character" (Todd, 1992, p. 242) and notes in his diary, "My purpose this day is taking a new course of life. … more diligently serving God" p. 242). One of his techniques is the listing of "sins", of which the most frequently confessed was pride, including ambition and pride in achievements both academic and spiritual. To the modern reader, this can be difficult to comprehend, given our cultural and psychotherapeutic valuations of "healthy" expressions of pride and achievement. But to Ward, pride, like greed, is one of those feelings most easily perverted into purposes of sin. Bercovitch (1975) in his analysis of the rhetorics of Puritan self-fashioning, draws attention to the appearance of negative *self*-compounds in Puritan writing associated with sin: *self-affection, self-confident, self-fullness, self-sufficiency*, and others. Even the mirror, much noted in its importance as an invention (being able to see oneself as a whole image as never before), was hardly neutral in its ramifications for Puritans, since looking at oneself in the mirror might encourage earthly diversions, self as the "great snare".

Ward's self-fashioning involved drawing discursive lines between himself and the enemy, both from without and from within. We have already touched upon the latter in the progress of the soul's journey, through the admission of sin to internal reconciliation. But, in Ward's wider "discursive construction of antagonism" (Laclau, personal communication) the figure and guises of the "anti-Christ" are everywhere. The anti-Christ is a force from within as well as without. Of course, this was a feature of the Puritanism of the day and illustrates how Puritans sought to hegemonise their picture of the world and its constituent, vital forces. Hence, the diary could be seen as an anti-Catholic text, with "popery" regarded as the ultimate threat to God's Word and Christ's Kingdom.

Ward's diary and confessions chronicle his voyage of repentance and "turning around". This is an essential and characteristic feature in the religious thinking of the day. In assuming the identity of preacher, the diaries constitute an interesting combination of attitudes, with Ward as both preacher *and* auditor, exhorter and penitent, often addressing himself in the second person. Todd (1992) summarises the wider Protestant theme woven into Ward's account of "human helplessness before the power of sin" and the "overriding aim as permanent conversion to an object reliance on what protestants called the grace of God for that transformation" (p. 258).

The diary is a fascinating insight into the Puritan process of self-definition and points to the centrality of the person relating to biblical texts, of identifying in communal rather than individualistic terms (particular fellowships, those emotional and imagined communities of the godly), and the need for constant watchfulness concerning the forces of the anti-Christ, either in Cambridge, further afield, but, moreover, deep within one's own mind. The diary reads as "a dialogue, between individual and God, conscience and actor, reader and text, the self and himself" (Todd, 1992, p. 241).

Ward's diary gives contemporary readers a glimpse into how a given Puritan individual saw the world and himself within it. Of course, this could not be the product of the individual alone, since Ward, like anyone else, was preconstructed by the times and discursive/symbolic possibilities that surrounded him. Puritan values supplied, as it were, many of the elements or sources of discursivity and identity: a view of true belief, the nature of sin and grace, the nature of threats to "good life", a notion of what "looking inwards" means and what one might find there. A version of good and virtue, or moral sources, goes hand in hand with construction of self, with "flesh" and "spirit" defining contrary impulses within man (Porter, 2003; Taylor, 1989). Beyond the contingencies of his family life, education, and other influences, Ward still choose *one* identity amongst other possibilities, fashioning himself in a particular way. In the world of Protestantism at the time, even though certain patterns and practices were available (including the self-disclosing moral diary or journal), they could not *determine* what Ward made of himself. There still is a process of self-interpretation, a response to potential conflicts of interpellation or calling by competing communities (Pecheux, 1982). He could, after all, have become a radical sceptic or, had he turned from religious preoccupations, an indifferent libertine; or any number of alternatives within the horizon set by the social, discursive world at that time. Group membership and identity is integral to the process, as Puritans were not isolated figures; they were sustained by appropriate emotional fellowships or communities. What Jones (2002) points out with respect to an earlier period of the Reformation, has equal relevance to the seventeenth-century context, in that there was always a tension between institutional responses and individual choices: "No single institution represents or rules an individual. Personal choices are always possible" (p. 5).

It is the ensemble of articulations and interpellations which endow a particular ideology its relative unity and consistency (Laclau & Mouffe, 1985). Communities are glued by the shared elements, assumed and imagined, that unite them. The "individual" Puritan lies at the confluence—like Foulkes's "nodal point"—of a variety of discourses that call upon him as much as he calls upon them, with the process by which these elements bond representing articulations, outcomes of efforts to fix meaning in particular ways.

Conclusion

It is generally recognised that both Renaissance and Reformation produced changes in the concept of self, relations, and affective life. On the one hand, Renaissance ideals encouraged a self-styled individuality, in the words of Donne, "every man alone thinks he hath got To be a phoenix, and that then can be None of that kind of which he is, but he" (in Shawcross, 1967). At the same time, Reformation ideals sought to embed forms of inward inquiry that paradoxically de-emphasised "self". In the new interpenetrations between the sacred and the profane, personal adhesion and commitment were of central importance, components of what Taylor (1989) calls "the affirmation of ordinary life". Not built in thin air, changes in selfhood, self/community relations, require a host of discourses, observances, cultural practices, and disciplines, from the household to the court, the church to the market-place.

In the four examples, it is suggested we can observe something of the complex interlocking of large-scale and small-scale changes, evolving norms and practices of self-reflexivity, with the development of persons describing themselves in new ways—even if ever so slightly— and modalities. One could talk in terms of a co-creation of subjectivities within a variety of "imagined" and "emotional" communities, each vying for their version of the world to be the successful one.

Times of significant change entail conflicts between different versions of the world, between old and new, central and marginal. Taylor (1989) comments that the rise of Protestant-based senses of self-possession, speeded up the displacement of traditional authority and loyalty to "inherited communities". But, with inevitable conflicts of interpretations, individuals or groups may identify, counter-identify (i.e., risk becoming a "bad subject", from the view-point of the dominant group), or dis-identify (i.e., displace or try to transform dominant elements). Opposition is not "pure", but depends on the alternative systems of interpellation and meaning that are available.

The areas examined in this chapter, tell us something about the make-up of England, the centrality of religion, and the means by which individuals, families, and groups accounted for the changes they saw around them; not simply examples of changing beliefs, but the veritable enlargement and diversification of subjectivities and configurations of group/individual, family/culture. Some refer to England's "Long Reformation", as effects of religious change reverberated down the centuries, with unforeseen consequences (Collinson, 2003). The edges and defining zones of the new networks and communities were of grave importance, in, for example, defining whether you might be part of the Godly community, the Elect perhaps, or "with" other, more sinister forces. Some identities were positioned as malignant, casting even whole communities amongst the forces of the anti-Christ (those put to death for crimes related to suspect religion, though not including victims of witchcraft, from the reigns of Henry to Elizabeth, numbered around 600). This defining process took place at many levels, including the household; Jones (2002) examples a Puritan father who gives thanks that his children were not born of "popish, pagan or Turkish" parents.

One could explore the post-Reformation in terms of acquired prejudices and racisms, but also, equally important, of increasing toleration (Hill, 1990, 1997). For example, out of the ashes of religious "enthusiasms", a more secularised society emerged, with Puritans gradually abandoning their struggle to change the English church from within, by the struggle for freedom outside it; non-conformity was institutionalised. With a multiplicity of worlds on Earth, why not also in the heavens? The once feared "sin of schism" decreased, differences and separations better contained, albeit it within the framework of the Anglican ascendancy (Spurr, 1998).

In turn, but in some respects only, religious tolerance paved the way for other forms of civic tolerance. The traces of these times are with us still, even though how we build our identities and conceive of our virtues, anxieties, and pleasures are unrecognisably different; in most ways, we are different kinds of subjects to our predecessors. But given our different notions of mental life, affectivity, and rationality, it is easy to forget the fact that we too are on a train and construct our landscapes—psychic and cultural—as we journey. In short, the project of "historical psychology" is one that does not stop at the doors of the present.

CHAPTER SIX

An exclusionary matrix: degenerates, addicts, homosexuals

The concept of "matrix" is central to group analysis, signifying, as it does, those supposed invisible but highly effective connections which bond persons, "a psychic network of communication which is the property of the group and is not only interpersonal but transpersonal" (Foulkes, 1968, p. 182). Foulkes extends the idea of the matrix to the "mother-soil" of the social unconscious, in which people are said to "share a fundamental, mental matrix (foundation matrix)" (Foulkes, 1973, p. 228). Two aspects of his views are of relevance to the current chapter; first, that the matrix is (usually) conceived in a positive manner, and, second, that it emphasises that which is shared and disemphasises those excluded and unincorporated elements who exist on another side, as it were, who stand on uncommon ground and who are thus seen as threats to the symbolic social body.

This chapter explores this "other side", that of a negative matrix and site of non-incorporation. It focuses on the way the nineteenth-century culture conceived of certain types of deviant persons and groups. Importantly, there is a footnote here concerning correlations between group theories and some actual groups that are to be found in this end-of-the-nineteenth-century cultural mix; the coincidence of the two helped to identify and imagine several feared groups, "dangerous classes" (e.g., immigrants, anarchists, women's activists), who, from the dominant viewpoint, represented monstrous possibilities within society (Barrows, 1981; Weegmann, 2008).

An exclusionary matrix

Mills (2005) coins the term *exclusionary matrix* to signify the production of "a dangerous, abject region that circumscribes the identities of ideas, institutions and selves" (p. 7). Although scapegoatism accompanies exclusion, the exclusionary matrix often involves more than one suspect category, suggesting overlapping subjects who co-occur or supersede each other over time, with a metonymic sliding of associations between them. More importantly, it is not just that certain projections are put upon pre-existing groups and identities, but that discourses, rules, and narratives help to constitute the very objects that they derogate or malign; from this point of view, the notion of "construction" is a more fertile one than that of "projection" alone.

An example of one such configuration, from early modern Europe, is that of Jews, heretics, and lepers. Moore's (1987) classic account of the formation of a persecuting society, mapped the evolution of such exclusions and negative attributions from the thirteenth century onwards. Paradoxically, such subjects disturb central, normative identity whilst at the same time affirming it. As super-excluded figures, these groups were objects of discourse and law, subject to edict and management, and although they were not regarded as incomprehensible subjects, they nevertheless represented a dangerous or perverse "outside" of order, a remnant or a warning to the community of the faithful. Thus, Jews (physically excluded from Britain in 1291) increasingly represented the enemies of Christ. Valuably, Bauman (1998) has suggested the term "allosemitism" in premodern contexts, meaning the setting aside of Jews and the consignment of different concepts to apply to them, practices which whilst non-committal in theory, contained the seeds of hatred as well as more positive attitudes towards them. Lepers were regarded as unclean representatives of the living dead and thus subject to laws of segregation; according to Foucault (1965), the imaginal, if not the actual physical, spaces occupied by leprosy were later filled by others (the mad) on the margins of communities. Through complex transformations of dissent into heresy, the same period witnessed a dramatic demonisation of heretics. Moore (1987) contends that, "the disparate, fragmented, inarticulate heresies of the 11th and early 12th centuries were converted from their untidy, and generally insignificant selves into fragments of a larger picture—the picture of a monster by which their adversaries believed themselves to be threatened" (p. 72). Amongst the overlapping strands connecting the three groups were attributions of malevolence and death, inversion of the natural order, spiritual darkness, sexual debauchery, and vileness. This does not exhaust the negative matrix, since other contenders (e.g., homosexuals, female prostitutes, and, at least in some contexts, Muslims) had contemporary, overlapping associations with the same set of assumed dangers.

Borrowing ideas from social anthropology, I refer to *core dangers* as constituting a focus of social anxiety; what lies close to or beyond acceptable boundaries is met with horror and disquiet. "Groups" and "grids" coincide in a work of articulation, groups offering a boundary around communities, on the horizontal axis, and grids (rules, regulations), operating on the vertical axis (Douglas, 1970). Hence, dangerous forces live around boundary lines, transgress order, and threaten to weave their way inside, hence the common association to pollution or corruption (Douglas, 1966); if unchecked, such pollutions could lead to a "permeation of society and the individual by the unseen and unwholesome" (Foxcroft, 2007, p. 11). The human body has often been used as a metaphor for social and governmental relations (e.g., the "head of state" idea), and this is no less true of the nineteenth century; in that century, the very health and order of the "social body" was at stake, threatened by new sources of disorder.

The strong hold and slow evolution of core dangers point to a process of sedimentation, meaning the silting and overlaying of cultural elements; as when Foulkes and Anthony (1957) claimed that "words are old and so carry layers of meaning". What was once deposited in a given culture can become reoccupied through later social mutations. Although reverse and alternative discourses are possible, if not inevitable, they face the discursive weight of history, the power of established discourses and institutional conditions, defining who can speak, from which position and about what. On the other hand, as will be hinted, from positions of marginality and attributions of abjection, new sources of discourse and identity can arise, which help reform that which is considered acceptable and valued.

The notion of degeneracy was central to a great deal of nineteenth-century culture, its portmanteau nature allowing it to be deployed in relation to the natural sciences, criminology, sociology, social debates, literature, and images of the crowd. Such concepts played an important role in both the new science of the "mass" or "collective" and within the emergent science of the individual, that of psychology (Rose, 1985). If degeneracy formed the "ground", as it were, the "figure" of the degenerate was occupied by various human types who came to embody it, including criminals, alcoholics, perverts, primitives, and so on (Neve, 1997). By the close of the nineteenth century, addicts and homosexuals were part of this cast of characters and became objects of a searing psychiatric and criminal gaze. I argue that alcoholics, addicts, and homosexuals, amongst others, populated a significant exclusionary matrix, linked together in many ways because of the supposed dangers they represented to society, to its health and defence. Such beings and errant bodies were indeed inhabitants at the very margins of society, groups on the edge, whose very presence was a threat to it.

Foucault's work is useful background to this historical excursion, particularly his analysis of a new regulatory "biopolitics" of the population and the rise of a "disciplinary society" (1977, 1978a). In his words, "Nineteenth-century psychiatry was a medical science as much for the societal body as for the individual soul" (Foucault, 1978a, p. 8). And, as Gilbert (2007) points out, the figure of the "healthy body" had considerable prominence in a range of Victorian concerns, including debates on the franchise, sanitary and housing publications, and in novels: "Throughout the mid-century, evolving discussions of the healthy body and its tastes would undergird debates about individuality, the social body, and fitness for citizenship" (p. 6).

Degenerates and dangerous classes

The precise origin of the idea of degeneracy in nineteenth-century culture and psychiatry is difficult to pinpoint, although Morel is usually quoted as father of the notion. Degeneracy concepts acquired a general presence and resonance in the culture, reaching a climax around the 1890s and serving as a generative metaphor around which a whole language was constructed, and from which certain personages, categories, and worries were defined as objects of concern and intervention. In Walter's (1956) survey, the term, as applied to human life, was "an important framework for explanations dealing with psychiatry, sociology, criminology and eugenics" (p. 422). Predictive of a range of possible "deteriorations" and productive of a variety of dangerous classes, these concepts prompted extensive intellectual as well as imaginative labour, as with the late Gothic novelists (Greensdale, 1994; Morris, 1994). Theorists of degeneracy were excited by the discovery of what they thought was a tangible, semi-zoological "reality", the visibility of particular "types" of persons and the signs and stigmata that betrayed them; amongst others, *homo criminalis* was born. This created fear and fascination, since deviant bodies were felt to be close-at-hand and were potentially common, not rare. Whilst the influence of degeneration psychiatry and older, heredity-neurological models faded with World War One, degeneration had an after-history, as in the case of eugenics societies (Rose, 1985). During the War, it was easier to project degeneracy onto the enemy and to spare one's own nation, but notions of tainted heredity was no longer a viable explanation for the mass breakdown of men both on the battle-field and away from it (Pick, 1989).

French psychiatrist Philippe Morel summed up the key features of degeneracy: "hereditary transmission, and increasing severity in successive generations leading to extirpation of affected individuals, families or groups" (Lewes, 1974, p. 134). Like a diseased tree, human life too could be deformed. One of Morel's central concerns was cretinism, analysed with a mix of theoretical speculation and Catholic moralism. Degeneration fitted well with contemporary evolutionary theory, promising to explain a range of phenomena, such as atavism (from the Latin *atavus*, ancestor), regression, and decline. Morel's version of evolution posed the gloomy proposition that degeneration would spread, manifesting itself in a whole series of morbid transformations that would be passed down the generations. Degeneration was the shadow side of a period, "so often identified as the quintessential age of evolution, progress, optimism, reform or improvement" (Pick, 1989, p. 2). The notion provided an effective backdrop to sickness/health models emergent in a psychiatry, which was busy carving out its territory, naming and mapping disturbances and identifying departures from the norm, with its -manias, -phobias, -philias, and -isms.

Meanwhile, in Italy, Lombroso's founding of "criminal anthropology" exploited the idea in a similar manner, focusing, as it did, on the potential for savagery in society, atavism, superstition, and so on. Lombroso's famous "faces of criminality" and "criminal composites" used the new technology of photography and device of statistics to demonstrate its "findings" whilst Foucault (1978a) reminds us that criminal psychiatry was then preoccupied by the "pathology of the monstrous". This new criminal anthropology attempted to isolate criminal man, or the "born criminal", from his worthy alternatives and as a science was devoted to the defence of modernity from the threat of "backwardness".[1] Lombroso's version of evolution was different in emphasis to Morel's, in so far as he identified with the prospect of *regeneration*, even if the criminal class was seen as a recalcitrant force and a throwback to an earlier stage. Whilst British psychiatry was sceptical of some of these continental speculations, it, too, was establishing its authority and theorising anew those populations that inhabited the asylums, threatened decency, or who came together in riotous assembly. Maudsley used his own version of degeneration and crude "psychiatric Darwinism" to bolster a class élitism and anti-feminism, arguing, for example, against further extensions of women's rights on the grounds that it would undermine the natural productivity of society (Nye, 1993; Showalter, 1986).

As Morel and others indicated, degeneration was not solely or even predominantly an individual matter, but afflicted families and even nations. Hence, the tracing of pathology and its social consequences down the generations was considered important. In Foucault's (1978a) terms, addressing criminology, degeneration touches upon the presence of a "dangerous element ... in the social body" that unless rooted out would work its invidious effects; "dangerous classes", criminal groups (indeed, criminals as constituting a class or nation in themselves), and lower class pathology were the objects of such worries (Carlson, 2001). Racist doctrines thrived on the idea, raising alarm around the notion of decadence and possible national and "race suicide".[2] The emphasis on social pathology and defence is a field of inquiry in itself, articulated by the pioneers of crowd psychology as well as by criminologists (e.g., Le Bon, Tarde, and others): "As they described the crowd's savage, instinctual behaviour, they encapsulated many of the fears of their well-to-do contemporaries ... Their crowds loomed as violent, bestial, insane, capricious beings whose comportment resembled that of the mentally ill, women, alcoholics, or savages" (Burrows, 1981, p. 5).[3] An element that links the theoretical speculations of Le Bon to the literature of, say, Zola is the idea of groups bent on revenge and mindless destruction. Zola's novel *Germinal* portrays violent contagion, the overthrow of male power, with the spectre of communism and anarchism never very far away. Given its turbulent history, military defeat, and the upheavals of the Third Republic, it is no surprise that crowd psychology blossomed in France.

Closely related to fears of crowds, was the imagery of the "city" and modernity, described in the English context by Steadman Jones in *Outcast London* (1971). Fears located in what he calls the urban "residuum" were relevant to the construction of the "alien", a term which continues to connote danger and civic illegitimacy. Although Edward Said's *Orientalism* explores representations of the East as backward and exotic, he touches on the link between external Others and their internal counterparts: "The Oriental was thus linked to elements in Western society (delinquents, the insane, women, the poor) having in common an identity best described as lamentably alien" (Said, 1978, p. 207). The city might have imperial connotations but equally contained the possibility that degenerate elements might subvert civilisation from within.

Pick (1989) offers a brilliant commentary on the concept of degeneracy, exploring the plurality of connotations surrounding the notion, mostly lost today. He analyses the continual movements in science, literature, and the press between the supposed "individual species" and the collective manifestations of degeneracy. Core dangers involve a dialectic of fear and reassurance: "Degeneration involved at once a scenario of racial decline and an explanation of 'otherness', securing the identity of, variously, the scientist, (white) men, bourgeoisie against superstition, fiction, masses ..." (Pick, 1989, p. 230).

Let us consider some of the personages who populated the field of degeneracy.

Alcoholics and addicts

Whilst excessive drinking and its consequences were concerns since time immemorial, the nineteenth century invented "alcoholism" as a medical condition.[4] As has been noted, alcoholism was prominent amongst the list of the "curses of civilisation", with intemperance regarded as a general social evil that, if not contained or eradicated, might lead to revolt and unruliness by whole subsections of the population (Bynum, 1984; Donnelly, 1983). Morel, and others, drew scientific attention to alcoholism, with his emphasis on the role of external agents, intoxicants, in the degenerative process (Carlson, 1985); it remained unclear however, how much alcoholism was regarded as the product of degeneration or its cause. Intemperance sapped the social body and, associated with the logic of degeneracy, was a particularly powerful emblem of malaise. Addiction, conceived of as excess and illness, with a border on vice, was thus highly susceptible to symbolic embellishment in society (Foxcroft, 2007; Zieger, 2008). Indeed, Barrows (1981) argues that, "seldom has any disease been invested with an emotional resonance as terrifying and well publicised as was alcoholism in the late 19th century" (p. 71). One doctor, commenting on the Paris Commune, even diagnosed the whole event as the result of a "fit of alcoholic pyromania" (Sournia, 1990).

Alcoholism and habitual drunkenness, notwithstanding their actual consequences in society, were powerful metaphors of irrational behaviour. Alcoholism signified not only a loss of control by the individual of his capacities but more worrying, the loosing of controls by and over dangerous classes; violence, like drink, could overflow. Hence it was a small step to see alcoholic spirits (in particular, "hard", distilled spirits, although this was often extended to include all alcohol, especially for the working class) as the tangible source of social evil, exemplar *par excellence* of noxious, degenerative elements. Linking this to crowd psychology, Barrows (1981) argues, "The picture of alcoholism was terrifying … and in comparing mobs to drunkards, crowd psychologists again provoked the spectre of race suicide, hereditary insanity and unmitigated violence" (p. 61).

Victorian society was saturated by drug use. Alcohol use was widespread, peaking in the 1870s. Likewise opium use, taken not only by distinguished writers and the wealthy, but by the populace as a whole, in manifold preparations and tinctures. The conditions which lead to conceptualising substance use as "addiction" rather than as mere "excess", is a complicated historical topic. How was it, for example, that from being regarded as a way of life, albeit a sinful choice or an eccentric penchant, drug and alcohol misuse became a morally dangerous site of disease, christened by the appearance of the "inebriate" and the "addict" as social and personal identities? How did the shift occur, from locating the sources of addiction within intoxicating agents per se, to finding it within the suspect, individual body? And how did this new gaze refigure addiction as loss of control rather than as wayward choice? (Levine, 1978). Emergent medical taxonomies of disorder created new names for new phenomena: "morphinists", "morphinomaniacs" (distinguished from the former by their lack of interest in being cured (Crothers, 1902)), "drug habitués", "narcomaniacs", "cocainism", cocainomaniacs", and so on. It is one of the supreme paradoxes of our historical relationship with drugs, that substances that were once exalted as medicines and cure-alls, such as alcohol (the "good creature of God", in Puritan lore), opium, morphine, and cocaine (the latter trumpeted by Freud during the 1880s), ended up viewed as menaces (Berridge & Edwards, 1981; Jay, 2000). However, whilst the temperance movements and reformists regularly blamed alcohol—"demon drink"—for the nation's insanity, it must be underlined that medical and popular views remained mixed, with many doctors reserving a positive attitude towards alcohol, which was regarded as a potential medicine, restorative, and pain-killer. Opium preparations were rationalised and marketed as "mother's helper", and the like, whilst a growing number of injecting morphine users (many female), were introduced to the drug and procedure by enthusiastic medics. In America, concern over narcotics arose much later in the century, somewhat eclipsing earlier temperance concerns and associated mass publicity concerning heavy and habitual drinking.

Those who have researched the history of addiction as social construct have traced its complex surfacings in discourse—popular, scientific, and administrative—concerning notions of uncontrollable habit, vice, and pathological consumption, and coinciding with the early professionlisation of the field (White, 1998; Zeiger, 2008). Newer disease concepts of addiction, as favoured, for example, by physicians writing in the distinguished *Journal of Inebriety* (1876–1914), challenged simplistic moralistic positions, and were infused with medical optimism concerning cures, remedies, and the potential for the reform of morbid habits through specialised asylums and inebriate homes (Weiner & White, 2007). In public policy associated with inebriates, however, there was a continual mixing of the moral and medical registers, with fears of licentiousness and degeneracy never far away (Berridge & Edwards, 1981).

Zieger (2008), drawing on novels and literary representation of the addict, argues that addiction was "invented" (which is not the same as claiming that it did not exist) and can only be understood within a broad context of the cultural forces of society. In her view, it is not coincidental that addiction, which, after all, is a story of unmaking and self-loss, emerged during the fertile period of bourgeois self-making, with its ethics of improvement and social mobility. Alongside this were other social changes, including the growth in consumerism, reform movements, imperial expansion, and a widening public sphere. "Addiction", she writes, "with its incoherent subjects, chronic repetitions ... presents its own distinct blur in the side of rational Enlightenment modernity and progress" (Zieger, p. 10). In the American context, Levine (1978) argues a not dissimilar case, that cultural shifts in definition, from those who simply drank to excess to the identification of the diseased and afflicted individual, was brought about partly through new social emphases on self-reliance and responsibility. This was, itself, linked to the requirements of the new republic, where there had been a weakening of traditional support networks for the nuclear family. The early inebriate asylums and homes, confident of their claims to cure, were institutions set up to "restore the power of self-discipline to those who has somehow lost it" (Levine, 1979, p. 498). One can thus begin to appreciate the links that formed between the troublesome individual addict and the breakdown in order and social discipline that might ensue through contagion; if individuals lost control, then so, too, might groups, which could then threaten the very fabric of society.[5] The various Public Health Acts of the 1860s onwards, in Britain, galvanised an idea of sanitary protection, a concept eminently expandable to these other pollutants and threats.

Within this matrix, involving regulative ideals of (white) liberal, male selfhood and self-discipline, a new "suspicion of habit" arose (Zieger, personal communication). Addiction and its metaphors had travel value, endowing "other horrors" and unnamed desires with added meaning (Zieger, 2008). Addicts could symbolise a loss of (masculine?) control, the perversion of pleasure constituting a particular fulcrum of concern. Into the mix went a variety of concerns: class-based (whether those of drunkenness amongst "lower classes", or, indeed, of the "higher degenerates" whom some believed were more prone to neurasthenia and related illnesses of urbanisation); military (in times often preoccupied by "national efficiency" and population fitness); eugenic (the desire to curb "feeble-mindedness" and threats to moral fibre); or, and this is another aspect of unfitness, gender-based, with some believing that women were particularly liable to morphine use, via the hypodermic needle, due to supposed feminine vulnerabilities, hysteria, and mendacity (Zieger, 2005). Indeed, according to Skelly (2010) those in the nineteenth century most opposed to feminism, "invoked the plight of the female habitual drunkard in order to portray women as lacking the kind of will power and self-control necessary for self-representation and self-possession" (p. 502).

A further dimension in the formation of this exclusionary matrix, is that of nation-linked-to-race. In a metonymic sliding of associations, it can be argued, fears surrounding external agents taking over individual bodies and lives, produced and magnified the notion of "foreign body". Was it seen as the case, for example, that addicts had violated natural/unnatural distinctions and succumbed to a deviant, alien desire? "Addicts were 'unfit', whose appearance in many areas presaged, it was thought, national decline" (Berridge & Edwards, 1981, p. 157). In other words, foreign substances and foreign *others* were linked, with the changing position of opium, from everyday remedy to dangerous substance, being an apposite example, standing as it did as an imperial signifier for the British. Indeed, valuable research is emerging about the complex link between colonialism, opium, and images of the English nation as a potential victim of others, particularly the Chinese and other degenerate nations (Schmitt, 2002). The mystical, the exotic, and the dangerous merged, with Foxcroft (2007), and other historians, suggesting a semiotic synthesis within culture between China and "Darkest England", famously typified in Dickens' last, unfinished novel, *The Mystery of Edwin Drood.* Consider the imagery of the opium den in that novel, site of abjection, a moral slum; of its various visitors, one "haggard woman" is said to have "opium-smoked herself into a strange likeness of the Chinaman" (Dickens, 2009, p. 4). Powerfully, Foxcroft (2007) observes, "The portrait of opium dens and opium addicts that appeared in novels, newspaper articles, magazines and journals presented the reader with the same lost figures, the same sulphorous and wizened figures of smokers and the same poisonous, sickly atmospheres" (p. 75). As for America, Szasz (1973) analyses the "Yellow Peril", and how Orientals became "model scapegoats"; images of "negro coke fiends", and variations upon that theme, were also a feature of that legacy.

Homosexuals

Sexual anxiety and projections are a common, even universal, feature of societal "core dangers". Quite why this is so is open to speculation, but one can claim that such anxieties powerfully feed upon, and create images of, transgression and corrosion, positing a dangerous body/activity/Other who personifies the threat. It is telling that, for example, the social purity movements of the nineteenth century placed so much emphasis on sexual impropriety, prostitution, and disease. Images of unruly sexual contagion have been referred to in connection with the crowd and hinted at in the different kind of "unbounded pleasure" inferred in relation to the addict. At a general level, sexuality was eminently linkable to the logic of degeneration and its biopolitical domains of population, pathology, and heredity; Gilman (Chamberlain & Gilman, 1985) claims that "No realm of human experience is so closely tied to the concept of degeneration as that of sexuality" (p. 191). An erosion, or even seizure, of power by this Other was the worst prospect for society. "Homosexuals" (I use the term for shorthand, although it covers a number of others in the nineteenth-century vocabulary of deviance)[6] were considered by some to represent the ultimate spectre of degeneration, with same-sex desire constituting those "dark places" (itself, a Gothic, potentially racial, image) of the psychic and social worlds. So positioned, between criminality, decadence, and fear, it was peculiarly difficult for such subjects to answer back or to gain a voice; "Any actual or political challenge from such marked-out groups was neutralised by the charge of degeneracy" (Greensdale, 1994, p. 18). Whilst I limit my discussion chiefly to sexology and its implications, medicine was by no means the only plane within which the "problem" and "danger" of same-sex desire was highlighted.

The nineteenth-century science of sexology was integral to the carving up of the new territory of psychiatry. Although it is easy now to regard *psychopathia sexualis* as an obsolete science, it had widespread influence, including the formation of psychoanalysis (Freud borrowed extensively from it, whilst transforming its terms) and on many taken-for-granted post-Victorian representations of sexuality (Bland & Doan, 1998). In an over-dramatic yet interesting claim, Foucault (1979b) argues that medicine effectively "invented" the homosexual (he cites 1870 as its birth date), in so far it was only from this moment in time, supposedly, that "homosexual became a personage, a past, a case history, a life form and a morphology, with an indiscreet anatomy and possibly a mysterious physiology ... The sodomite had been a temporary aberration; the homosexual was now a species" (p. 43). In his view, sexology represented a generative way of specifying individuals, classifying natures, and identifying disorders, the realm of "perversions". Similarly, Reed (2001) traces the move from "acts to natures", "sodomites to homosexuals", and the significance of the gathering of new kinds of "evidence" in psychiatry and sexology, including the use of the deviant "case study" as exemplar and iconographic devices (e.g., photographs) as identifiers of "types".

Sexology classified bodies, defining the true nature of feminine and masculine beings and, by complement, identified those beings who veered off into inversion or deviation; "Healthy subjects—structurally equivalent and behaviourally similar—would behave rationally and appropriately" (Gilbert, 2007, p. 6). In this regard, sexology is relatable to the processes of "normalising judgment" and "hierarchical observation" identified by Foucault (1977) in his notion of the "disciplinary society". As for nineteenth-century and *fin de siecle* anxiety, Showalter (1990) describes the panoply of fears that ran through England, especially those that threatened cherished belief in the separate spheres and proper places of men and women. Was England in danger of becoming feminised from within and losing its virility? Showalter draws connections between fears of sexual erosion and those related to class challenges and racial "mixing"; likewise, Somerville (1994) emphasises the racial dimension in segregated America, with the twin pathologisation of the non-white body and the non-heterosexual body.

Why was the figure of the homosexual, or invert, so central to the nosological project of sexology? And how did concerns about relationships between and within the sexes take on the importance that they did? These are large questions. In France, birthplace of degeneracy theory, Nye (1989) notes that by 1900, homosexuality was considered a grave threat to the nation and this in spite of the fact that, unlike in the England of the time, homosexuality between men was not illegal under the French penal code. It was assumed that effeminacy in men (including, but not exhausted by, homosexuality), reproductive sterility, and fears around the emancipation of women, presaged doom. Nye argues that as medical ideas around the human sexual economy were tied in to the capacity to engender, reproductive ideals and family were enshrined as central, unquestioned principles. Sexual energy was a finite resource and so perversion signified an excess, misuse of, or deficiency in, sexual expenditure. Nye (1989) contends that "rising rates of alcoholism, insanity, crime, syphilis and other organic and social pathologies bred widespread fears amongst critics of culture and the political elite that *La Grande* nation was in a state of irreversible biological decline" (p. 36).

Masculinity, as assertion or perversion, was both a source of such problems and a part of the solution to them. It can be suggested that sexology provided a measure of reassurance, in so far as medical and psychiatric science added weight to prevalent definitions of normality and traditional masculine identity. In other words, sexology offered a discursive resource through which sexual selfhood and biomedical reality was defined and assured. Sedgwick (1994) emphasises the hardening of homo/heterosexual definitions, with the latter dependent for its own definition on its derogated other: homosexuality. Her case is that in such "world-mapping", everyone became assignable to a binarised identity, an exclusive homo- or a hetero-sexuality, although her view is not without qualification (Brickell, 2006, analyses the complexities of sexology). The binary of sexual identity was nevertheless congruent overall with the medical bipolarity: normal and pathological (Nye, 1989).

In England, masculinity also faced a crisis, perhaps expressed differently to in France. One response was increasing male solidarity, as exampled in the formation of male clubs and societies—working class and middle class—although greater homo-sociality was paradoxical in its effects. Brady's (2005) research argues that there were no real models of sexuality between men and that "independent, uxorious masculine social status was the benchmark of social inclusion" (p. 221). Weeks (1977) notes a deepening hostility towards homosexuality in the same period, with "male lust" seen as a breeding ground for prostitution and homosexuality and that homosexuality had supplanted masturbation as the chief vice in society. One can readily appreciate how emergent sexualities, and the dangerous identities they suggested, were a powerful threat to the sanctity of procreation and the family, leading to increasing efforts to reimpose natural and unnatural distinctions into human behaviour. Having a long prehistory in the social unconscious, such distinctions, and the corresponding "crimes against nature" that accompany them, were not difficult to resuscitate.

Fears associated with decadence, indecency, and homosexuality came together, spatialised in the new urban centres and city. Walkowitz's (1992) research identifies the city as the maelstrom or labyrinth within which new narratives of sexual danger arose. Cook (2003) notes that the city (his subject is London) was seen in two contrasting ways, either as imperial, cosmopolitan, and lively metropolis or as decadent, degenerate, marred by poverty or immorality. Different districts or segments could typify these contrasts, such as a serious and grand financial district and a feminised, more sexualised West End.

Modern cities could suffer the same fate as imperial Rome and classical Greek society. In his chapter "A grossly indecent city", Cook examines press responses to homosexual scandals and fears, with an increasing journalistic emphasis on the importance of detecting and uncovering vice. The figure of the homosexual, leading a double-life, was one of the personages to be exposed: "This idea of concealed lives and the need to render them visible was crucial to the maintenance of sexual order, since it brought with it a regime of watchfulness and vigilance" (Cook, 2003, pp. 63–64). Homosexuality was both threat and symptom of a wider malaise, with Cook tracing some of the euphemisms used to describe it—"the hideous crime", "something objectionable", "a certain offence", and so on. The term "morbid" signified inversion, in a culture that stressed "manly assertion" and healthy bodies above all (Greensdale, 1994).

The final point to be made about this ambiguous naming in the press and courts, and the collation of "cases" by the sexologists, is that for some it provided the means by which the excluded could self-identify a desire which had not previously been named or recognised. In other words, some of the indirect references in the public domain had an opposite effect to that intended, in allowing a homosexual subculture to gain confidence in its own undeniable presence. Likewise, whatever the more reactionary aspects of sexology, the discourse of depiction and typology created new narrative and physical spaces within which "inverts" could stand up and naturalise themselves and, indeed, create the possibility of "reverse discourses" modeled on the very cases that were presented (Foucault, 1978b; Reed, 2001; Weeks, 1977).

Conclusion

Concepts of degeneracy permeated nineteenth-century "common sense", traversing different discourses and times, and entering into the very constitution of the social imaginary with its rich constellation of public dangers (Arata, 1996). In a real sense, degeneracy was "the condition of conditions, the ultimate signifier of pathology" (Pick, 1989, p. 8). As we have seen, several personages populated the field of degeneracy, including criminals, vagrants, addicts, perverts, prostitutes, and one or two "other monsters" (Pasquino, 1980). Some degenerates survived, or had an afterlife, into the next century, following the effective demise of the background concept of degeneration.

We have considered alcoholics, addicts, and homosexuals, where some of the overlapping chains between such suspect subjects seem clear—associations to vice, concealed lives, and the corrosions that each sow. Both represented a danger of "habit", deviations from the natural and non-productive, non-procreative wastage, a "solitary vice".

The visible, multiform presence of degeneracy—through types of person and physical stigmata—combined with its invisible effects, as its processes worked silently through the fibres and connective tissues of society. This visible, visual element is important, for as Skelly (2010) argues, "The visual culture of addiction points again and again to the desire for the legible addicted body, which parallels the desire for the legible homosexual body" (p. 171). Yet the hidden aspect is also important in the generation of social dangers and concerns. Hence, the visible/invisible, present/not-quite-present quality created potent fears, with degeneracy both nowhere and everywhere, with the "mother soil" of social life at risk of fatal contamination. The threat to the social body, to customary ways of life, was judged to be considerable; "Between culture and anarchy, safely and atavistic violence, there was only a 'very thin and precarious partition'" (Pick, 1989, p. 223).

The fascinating field of degeneracy is explored in the next chapter through the medium of the novel, in which degeneracy infiltrates the domestic sphere, hitherto the very interior of safety.

CHAPTER SEVEN

A modern monster? *The Strange Case of Dr Jekyll and Mr Hyde*

G othic fiction emerged as a popular genre in British fiction in the period 1760–1820. It had revivals and a late life, although the stage at which Gothic veers off into detective fiction, horror, or science fiction is a blurred one. Contrasting with its ordered, Classical alternative and predecessor, Gothic is associated with new forms and content, including mythical or semi-mythical settings, social transgression, hyperbolic sensualism, sensationalism, and disturbing disjuncture of narrative where no one is sure of what they are seeing or feeling; even the narrators are victim. The readership is participant to the effects, kept in suspense, rendered unsure, fearful (Hurley, 2002; Punter, 1996a).

Traditionally, "Gothic" concerned questions of history and geography, deriving from the Goths who plagued the Roman Empire. The term revived old, and acquired new, derogatory meanings, linking the Germanic tribes to the medieval world. Although the Goths had disappeared, the presence of unenlightened groups had not; nor had the potential for new "dark ages". New binaries replaced those of old, such as Northern/Southern, medieval/modern, light/dark, Protestant/Catholic, and the like (Mighall, 1999). The past could carry into the present and, moreover, could return it violently from whence it had come. Man himself was subject to reversals and horrific transformation, undermining the assumption of inevitable progress or constancy; images of metamorphosis, transcendence, and fragmentation enticed and threatened humanity at one and the same time (Hurley, 1996). As industrialisation spread, the early symbols of Gothic space, the castles, ruins, and abbeys, were replaced by the city, with its subregions of the slum, centres of vice and the opium den. Brennan (1997) captures many of the abiding principles of Gothic, when he states that it entails a "re-evaluation of the subjective and the sublime", the presence of terror and confusion, boundary-crossing and play upon liminal states as well as an emphasis on the "aesthetics of the dream and nightmare". Partly coming to his mind during a dream,[1] Robert Louis Stevenson's *The Strange Case of Dr Jekyll and Mr Hyde* (1886) is a one of the best known examples of late Gothic fiction, containing many of these elements in an explicit, if highly condensed form.

Stevenson spent years searching for a literary vehicle that might embody his "strong sense of man's double being" (Stevenson, 1888). As for his background, several aspects might help to explain this, including a strict Calvinist upbringing with its emphasis on sin, the chosen and the condemned, his long physical confinements due to ill-health, his awareness of Edinburgh as a class-divided city, his rebellions against middle-class respectability and feelings of guilt. His first attempt to write on the theme of duplicity and the "double" resulted in a play with W. E. Henley, *Deacon Brodia* or *The Double Life: A Melodrama*, about a publicly respected figure, a pillar of the establishment and (by night) a compulsive thief. In the confines of his hated, Bournemouth existence, where he had moved for reasons of health and, "trapped like a weevil in a biscuit", he drafted the novel in a matter of days. He had found the perfect vehicle. *The Strange Case of Dr Jekyll and Mr Hyde* was born (Callow, 2001).

This chapter develops a thread started in the previous one, but uses a literary text as its object. It is hoped that from the analysis presented, more can be learned about the constitution of a nineteenth-century exclusionary matrix and how the literary/aesthetic domain reflects and adds to social unconsciousness, in its figures, preoccupations, and articulations.

Monstrosity: "to think of this creature ..."

Monsters do more than scare, and monstrosity is more than an arbitrary occurrence. Monsters incorporate "fear, desire, anxiety and fantasy, giving them a life an uncanny independence" (Cohen, 1996, p. 4). Further, although the monster occupies a site of disturbed and deformed meaning, it is meaning nevertheless; in etymology, the monster "shows", "reveals", and "warns" (from the Latin *monstrare*, to demonstrate and *monere*, to warn; Cohen, 1996, and Punter and Byron, 2006). Appearing unbidden, the monster evokes the fear of something close by, yet not quite there or identifiable.

Monstrosity, then, signifies distortion, horror, and aversion, constituents of what Punter (1996a) calls the "dialectic of persecution" in Gothic literature. Enter vampires, ghosts, and werewolves. But what of the monstrosity within/of man, his "animal" side or "non-human/supra-human" dimension? Drawing on Kristeva's (1982) work, Hurley (1996) offers the term "abhuman" to describe it: "The abhuman is not-quite-human, a subject characterized by its morphic variability, continually in danger of becoming not-itself, becoming other" (p. 4). Similarly, Davidson (1995) draws on Butler's (1993, p. xi) image of bodies "unthinkable, abject, unlivable". In this respect, argues Davidson, an abject body is the fitting vehicle onto and into which contemporary concerns about degeneration or perversion travel. The moral and the physiological coincide. Enter Mr Hyde.

Commentators have pointed out the difficulties that the novel's principle narrators have in describing Hyde. Enfield is the first to try, referring to "a little man who was stumping along" and who callously tramples over the child, in Hyde's fist instance of violence (Stevenson, 1886, p. 31). Hyde gives Enfield a look "so ugly that it brought out the sweat in me like running" (ibid.). Utterson presses Enfield for further visual testimony, but Enfield struggles: "He is not easy to describe. There is something wrong with his appearance; something displeasing, something downright detestable" (p. 24). This ambiguity, the not-quite-describable quality (the "presentment of a fiend", p. 36) never resolves. In Utterson's first encounter, the lawyer asks to see his face: "Mr Hyde was pale and dwarfish; he gave the impression of deformity without any nameable malformation, he had a displeasing smile ..." (p. 40), and it is his very elusiveness to visual representation that allows suspense and fear to mount.

Stevenson draws upon contemporary models of degeneration, amongst which were representations of "criminal man", suggesting the influence of, if not Lombroso, then other English writers on physiognomy and the poor. Atavism, criminality, and lowly social origin are frequently merged in such discourses (Arata, 1996). The primitive ancestor lurks beneath the skin of John Bull (Smith, 2004). Significantly, people are repulsed by Hyde, "the man seems hardly human. Something troglodytic, shall we say?" (Stevenson, 1886, p. 40) Consistent with these discourses, Hyde stands for an earlier human stage and, indeed, is referred to like an "ape" or "creature". Jekyll's butler expresses repulsion, whilst defending the order of the household as it should be—"That thing was not my master" (p. 66).

More terrifying then than the monster "out there", is the one who inhabits, secretly or insidiously, a cherished order and system of values. So, in spite of the externalisation of Hyde the creature, in reality he springs forth from Jekyll. Jekyll is an upstanding gentleman, or so he seems, but as the story unfolds, Hyde is not simply his monster double, for part of the novelty and complexity of the story, is the play upon the strange liaison between the two, with the suggestion of an almost father-son, or tutelage-like relationship. Thus, Hyde does not live in a hovel, but in refined lodgings and Jekyll express keen interest in his fate. Utterson is keenly aware of an enigmatic bond and comes to regard Hyde as Jekyll's "protégé". Might there be something else that is monstrously unthinkable about the nature of this bond/age?

Sexualities

The plurality of the story's three narratives—Utterson's, Lanyon's, and Jekyll's—mirrors an inherent not-knowing what exactly is occurring. The two-in-one or one-in-two subject at the centre—Jekyll/Hyde, Hyde/Jekyll, Hyde within Jekyll, decomposing and recomposing—undermines the idea of a stable self, the very "fortress of identity". In fact, various models of identity, conduct, and order are exposed in the novel to their own antinomies. Haggerty (2006) refers to the importance of "social-sexual transgressions" in Gothic fiction and suggests that these implicate disordered identity as much as disordered desire. What in particular is the model of masculine propriety that is suggested yet simultaneously threatened in Stevenson's novel?

Jekyll and Hyde is about men: reputable men, undemonstrative men, sober men, as well as everyday or background men, in fact, "all sorts and conditions of men" (Stevenson, 1886, p. 40). Henry Jekyll's self-statement is clear about this male identification, in which he claims to be "fond of the respect of the wise and good among my fellow men" (p. 81). There are a number of indexes of the masculine ideal, such as a fondness for the healthy outdoors, as contrasted with the threat of idleness or solitary, indoor life and an ability to pull oneself together when the need arises, as contrasted with a womanly falling apart. And yet it is a faltering ideal, associated with its opposites—the morbid, the solitary, indulgence in that which is undignified, and, because of this, secretive. Jekyll summarises his proclivity thus: "Many a man would have blazoned such irregularities as I was guilty of: but from the high views that I had set before me I regarded and hid them with an almost morbid sense of shame" (p. 81).

Numerous critics (Davidson, 1995; Greensdale, 1994; Hurley, 1996) have contrasted this productive play between the upright—masculinity as moral toughness, pluck, and physical grace—and the unwholesome and perverse. If perversion, shame, and nausea are linked, then what if it is another deviation, not named but lurking, between the lines, that is at stake? The question to be raised is, when does bachelor homo-*sociality* veer into the region of the homo-*erotic* or homo-*sexual*? Sedgwick (1985) believes that it is in this very veering off, those "loose-ends" and "cross-ends" of identity, that the Gothic novel works its biggest punch. In her penetrating analysis of Gothic horror, she refers to the allure of the "other sides" to men and the trope of the unspeakable. In *Jekyll and Hyde,* this is contained in the motif of blackmail, as threat or motivation, which is Utterson's first, indeed, major theory. For Sedgwick, drugs, double-lives, and blackmail serve as camouflage for homosexuality (the Labouchere Amendment of 1886 was known as the 'blackmailer's charter').

Elaine Showalter (1990) makes the strongest case for an interpretation that links the double lives of homosexual men, the Gothic novel with its literary doubles, and end-of-the-century anxiety about sexual anarchy. This coincides with the growth of Clubland or bachelor identity and the reinforcement of social and spatial boundaries between the sexes; *Jekyll and Hyde,* she contends, "can be most persuasively read as a fable of fin-de-siecle homosexual panic, the discovery and resistance of the homosexual self" (p. 197). Is it that the supposedly celibate Henry Jekyll is protecting a forbidden mate, presented as his malignant double, Edward Hyde? Showlater highlights the continual ambiguities of the text, as it refers to doubles and "strange preferences"; other images, such as the odd, left-slanting signature of Hyde or his hairy-knuckle hand may signify this possibility (left-handedness representing homosexuality, the hand representing man's indiscriminate, animal desires).

Consider, also, the mysterious backdoor, "equipped", says Stevenson, "with neither bell nor knocker" (p. 30), which could, in this analysis, be read as a denigrated, non-female body. Davidson (1995) offers a similar analysis of this ambiguity, suggesting that "Hyde might be read as an interpolation at the narrative level of the traditional rhetorical strategies by which homosexuality was designated, strategies that are of inexplicit and oblique representation" (p. 25). The repugnance surrounding Hyde marks him off from respectable bourgeois bachelors, so that "homosexuality may be distanced from the notionally heterosexual fraternity" (p. 36).

Showalter (1990) also suggests that the suicide that ends Jekyll's life is consistent with a form of gay Gothic: "To learn Jekyll-Hyde secret leads to death … While Jekyll tries to convince himself that his own desire is merely an addiction, a bad habit that he can overcome whenever he wants, he gradually comes to understand that Hyde is indeed part of him" (p. 113). Thus, Jekyll's suicide, or self-destruction, is resonant with other tragic outcomes, such as murder, madness, and disease, associated with the nineteenth-century homosexual person/literary character.

Showalter's persuasive arguments aside, there is a tension between regarding the lose- and cross-ends of identity as the areas within which understanding lies, and the wish to diagnose *a* solution. If it is true that a strategy of "camouflage" is in operation, why stop at this one foundation point? (Haggerty, 2006). Hurley (1996) helpfully reminds us that, as far as a theme of sexual identity is concerned, Hyde can represent several things: (a) a terror of femininity within men (see the discussion of hysteria below); (b) forbidden homosexual desire; and (c) a dangerous male, heterosexual lust (also discussed below). Robb (2003) suggests that Stevenson used homosexual references simply in order to create "an atmosphere of unspeakable and mysterious depravity" (p. 224), without intending any character to *be* homosexual. The sexual/nonsexual issue is itself interesting. Stevenson himself balked at a sexual interpretation, not wanting Hyde to be seen, as he soon was, on the stage, as "mere voluptuary" (Callow, 2001). But this is the story of the story, and brings in Stevenson's professed anxiety about the popularisation of his work and the commercialisation of the "professional" author. Once the novella was out, much like the ineluctable process it depicts, it took on a life of its own.

Mentalities

The rich, anxiety-provoking theme of the double and of subconscious life, made Stevenson's novel eminently open to subsequent, psychoanalytic speculations and usage.[2] Whilst Freud did not refer to Stevenson's novel (published under ten years before the *Studies in Hysteria*), it is clear that *Jekyll and Hyde* belongs to the genre of the "depth psychological" novel and shares, or anticipates, with psychoanalysis, a compelling insistence on the duality of human nature and the role of the "underworld" and "unknown mind". That emphasis was already established in Victorian literature. Saposnik (1974) considers the location of Stevenson's work within a culture haunted by a picture of man's inescapable divisions, as does Miyoshi (1969), who explores the Gothic and romantic expressions of this in Victorian literature. What were these connections with the pre-psychoanalytic psychiatry of the era?

By the 1820s and beyond, a number of terms coalesced that spoke to a mind divided, which potentially signified a new form of moral insanity. These included *double consciousness* and *double conscience,* although *double personality* became a standard after the mid 1870s (Hacking, 1991). Fertile sources for such images were the study of and the depictions of mesmerism, somnambulism, spiritism, and trance states. Given the Victorian emphasis on will, self-possession, and masculine self-mastery, the idea of a mind divided was threatening, with its prospect of internal revolts and even usurpations. Another factor influencing such notions was the localisation of brain function and interest in the double hemispheres of the brain. The possibility of unintended, dispersed actions, organically in-built, was morally alarming. The sleepwalker, for example, could act in an irresponsible manner and the "host" personality be upstaged.

In a fascinating journey from the clinic to the courtroom, Eigen (2003) explores cases when "impaired consciousness", "lesions of the will", the "brain turning", and simply being "out of one's wits" coincided with criminal acts and thereby posed complex medico-legal questions of criminal responsibility. A further twist in the tale is that of how concepts of the unconscious changed, from being repository of forgotten knowledge to a seething storehouse of resentments and hostilities. Meanwhile, across the channel, Pierre Janet was penning his new psychological framework for describing multiple personality, hysteria, and somnambulistic states. Highlighting the role of psychogenic trauma,

Janet coined the term "dissociation" at a similar time as the publication of Stevenson's novel (LeBlanc, 2001).

Jekyll and Hyde poses a curious, mental issue: is it repression, dissociation, degeneration, or some form of madness that governs the processes that unfold? Brennan's (1997) Jungian analysis deploys the notion of man's shadow side and argues that for the most part Jekyll does, in part, perceive and admit to his other side: "when I looked upon that ugly idol in the glass, I was conscious of no repugnance, rather of a leap of welcome. This, too, was myself" (Stevenson, 1886, p. 84). And yet he, too, recoils, and it is after times of retreat, when he tries to be rid of Hyde, that there is a catastrophic return of the repressed; indeed, Hyde's powers increase with the growing sickliness of Jekyll. By contrast, Brennan suggests that Enfield and Lanyon are completely incapable of seeing their shadow natures and thus project it onto the figure of the despised Hyde. Lanyon himself disintegrates, whereas Utterson is credited for being the more integrated character in the story, with his indefatigable quest to know and to put the stands of the story together.

There are many readings of the story as cautionary tale, as critique of bourgeois respectability. Hyde's vices, at the very least, reflect the activities of a moneyed individual; indeed, his Soho den resembles the "retreat of a cultured gentleman", not a rogue (Arata, 1996). The book raises the possibility that it is the normative, if alienated, world of the middle-class professional male that creates its own demons (Smith, A. 2004). In the strange alliance and protectionism between Jekyll and Hyde, more is at stake than just the transformation of one into the other. In spite of the thrilling possibility of "housing each in separate identities" and of the "separation of these elements" in some form of co-existence, certain convergences occur. Arata (1996) pushes the consequences of this to the full: "It is one thing to say that Hyde acts out the aggressive fantasies of the repressed Victorian men, another altogether to say that he comes eventually to embody the very repressions Jekyll struggles to throw off. Yet this is in fact a prime source of horror in the tale: not that the professional man is transformed into an atavistic criminal, but that the atavist learns to pass as a gentleman" (p. 39).

The link between story and quasi-medical diagnosis is evoked by the use of that medico-legal term, "case". At one level, the narratives could read as dossiers by witnesses. Mighall (1999) points out that the narratives represent the worlds of law and medicine and that, whereas Utterson, the lawyer, uses the evidence of his sight as main instrument in his detection, Lanyon, the physician, speculates on a suitable diagnosis of Jekyll. The novel starts with the shock of Hyde's first instance of violence, the trampling of the young girl. In the first description of Hyde and in the account of his action, the implication is one of moral turpitude. We learn that the reputable Utterson has a vicarious interest in, or at least a tendency to become associated with, the lives of "going-down men". Seeing Hyde as 'fiend" is the most straightforward response. Hyde's violence turns murderous, and in a scene of notable professional hierarchy, Utterson discusses an example of Hyde's handwriting with his head clerk, Mr Guest. Guest jumps to the obvious conclusion, that "The man, of course, was mad" (Stevenson, 1886, p. 54). Utterson asserts his authority, whilst introducing ambiguity: "No, sir. Not mad; but it is an odd hand" (ibid.).

Utterson's narrative is the dominant one. Standing for the impeccable gentleman, he notes Jekyll's morbid seclusions and other "irregularities". As an instance of manly self-possession, he tells the footman Bradshaw to pull himself together, as he gathers evidence from the various servants. Jekyll's manservant, Poole, reports noises he has heard from the doctor's chamber, including a "lighter foot" than the "heavy creaking tread" of Jekyll, and sounds of weeping. Utterson presses him to reveal more. It was "Weeping like a woman or a lost soul", says the butler, who adds that he could have wept too (p. 69). Thus the simple insanity case is undermined and the novel introduces an alternative, that of hysteria, or at least the "wrestling against the approaches of hysteria", including hysterical reactions or contagions in those who witness the scene. We face the undignified prospect of men who cannot compose themselves. The elision of womanly behaviour, smallness of body, light-footedness, and weeping with disintegrating men brings us to the arena of *male* hysteria. Men are losing grip and self-disciplined, masculine selfhood is under threat. It seems no accident that the novel appears during a growth time in the professional industry of hysteria.

So far then, we have a menu of choices: do we see moral depravity, pure and simple, the ill-fortune of "going-down men", is it a more serious moral insanity, or is it some form of hysteria, where men turn into women? There is another option, dovetailing with moral insanity—that of lustful murderousness. Linking Gothic literature to the contemporary science of *psychopathia sexualis*, Heath (1986) points out that what the latter studies "is the *pathology* of the sexual and a significant area of attention is the *criminal*-sexual. The animal in man comes, in extreme, to the surface in what Krafft-Ebbing calls 'Lust-Murder'" (p. 103). Male sexuality can contain all that is undesirable as well as representing the norm. Stevenson's novel sold dramatically, 40,000 copies in Britain in the first six months alone. Produced as a "shilling shocker", it was rapidly read, performed, and translated. Walkowitz (1992) observes how, in an interesting blending of the imaginative and the actual, through the newspapers and broadsheets, it was linked in the public mind to the contemporary Ripper crimes in the East End. A real Mr Hyde had arrived.

Chemical uses

Elsewhere (Weegmann, 2005b), I considered *Jekyll and Hyde* in terms of what it might tell us about the fraught state of the drug addict, as he attempts to manage his mind and/or change the way he feels. The movement from Jekyll to Hyde is an induced one, involving the ingestion of a chemical. We have a glimpse of Jekyll's general motive for using the chemical when he considers the power attached to it, to be "relieved of all that was unbearable" (Stevenson, 1886, p. 70), but it is a dizzying power that leads to unpredicted effects. The weird potion that he creates, thrills and frightens him and after various drug-induced transformations into the sinister Mr Hyde and back again, Jekyll admits a gradual loss of hold over his "original and better self"; with increasing dependence on the potion, and physical tolerance, he realises that he risks suicide or death. There is intense moral agony as Jekyll "sees" what is happening, without having the power or inclination to pull back.

Stevenson used substances, including laudanum (a combination of opium and alcohol), cocaine-wine, and, for reason of health, strong cough linctus, likely opium-based. Later in life he used cocaine, but did not become an addict (Callow, 2001; Rankin, 1987). What is of interest, beyond his personal use, is the changing context within which widespread Victorian drug use became problematised, particularly for the working class. What if the novel's drug use is to be read for what it is, as opposed to a camouflage about something else? Can one then read *Jekyll and Hyde* in terms of a warning about decadence, of which unbridled drug use was a sign or a cause? Related to this, is it readable in terms of temperance, restraint and its breakdowns, with a mysterious drug as the "transforming draught" that signifies such danger? (Butler, 2006).

The 1860s saw considerable campaigning by the medical and pharmacist professions, concerned with their own turf struggles and the unrestricted availability of opium (Berridge & Edwards, 1981). The invention of the hypodermic needle, a new kind of self-administration, was trumpeted by its advocates as a technological miracle, potentially as important as gaslight or the railway. However, as the iatrogenic problems of syringes became apparent, new questions arose about thier risks and about the role of doctors in generating their own business; "Doctors needed to exchange this image of charlatanism for one of professional competence and expertise; the needle had seemed like a perfect way to modernize their knowledge and enhance their cultural authority. Now, however, it was threatening both" (Zieger, 2005). Not only this, but doctors, too, were susceptible to developing morphine habits. The use and availability of poisons, nostrums, preparations, and chemicals of many kinds created increasing concern, culminating in the 1868 Pharmacy Act. The Act included products such as opium and laudanum but excluded patent medicines, leaving a gap. In the 1880s a new campaign sought to control patent medicines as well, such as the morphine-based *J. Collis Browne's Mixture*.

Dr Jekyll, M.D., is a man of repute, in a world where status and profession matter. He is not the only M.D.; so too is his estranged friend, Dr Lanyon. Reinforcing Dr Lanyon's eminence, Utterson informs us that he lives in Cavendish Square, "that citadel of medicine". We learn that the cause of their estrangement lies in medical differences, Lanyon believing that Jekyll's pursuit of a "transcendental medicine" amounts to "scientific balderdash", whilst Jekyll regards Lanyon as a "hide-bound pedant". Does Jekyll in this respect, become a merged figure of physician/scientist, opening the doors to forbidden and ruinous knowledge? The projections flow. All the same, Jekyll reassures Utterson that his adversary remains "an excellent fellow". It seems possible that in this world of gentlemanly professionalism and difference, a "good doctor", even if an uptight and non-experimental one, contrasts with a "bad doctor", who frees himself from constraint and meddles in a game of chemical chance. We are informed that Jekyll bought his house from a "celebrated surgeon", but that his own tastes are more "chemical than anatomical" (Stevenson, 1886, p. 51). The doctor takes his chemical experiments into dangerous territory, with the "lab" as his operating site. Jekyll rationalises his "transcendental medicine", in a way that harks back to the Romantic image of drug use as offering inspirations and altered mental states. What is denied is the

"Gothic" reality of a drug use that threatens integrity and fragments the self. As experimenter, even without the horrific transformations that ensue, Jekyll risks the charge of straying from his profession base into charlatanism or worse.

The textual shifts and narrative uncertainties in the story mimic the loss of control that occurs as a result of Jekyll's "addiction". He not only rationalises his experiments, but attempts to reassure himself and others, reasserting control. This is partly prompted by the concerns of his interlocutor, Utterson, who sees and does not see, knows and does not know what is happening to his esteemed friend. If "Hyde" symbolises the drug and not only the alter-person, the dialogue takes on a new meaning. Utterson offers his assistance, to which Jekyll states, "the moment I chose I can be rid of Mr Hyde" (p. 44). Utterson appears convinced, responding, "I have no doubt you are perfectly right" (p. 44). Although holding back, Jekyll says, using the "we" of an implicit agreement, "we have touched upon this business, and for the last time, I hope" (p. 44). The "I hope" betrays a wish and an uncertainty. After a worsening situation, Utterson once more tries to gain access into what is happening between Jeykll and Hyde/drugs, only to face an even greater rebuttal of anxiety—"I am quite done with him" (p. 52).

One could read the next sequence of the story in terms of a relapse with a vengeance, in so far as Jekyll retreats from contact ("isolates", to use a psychological term), even from Utterson. Disquieted by Jekyll's withdrawal, Utterson refers to his residence as being "that house of voluntary bondage" and to his erstwhile friend as an "inscrutable recluse" (p. 59). Jekyll is fixated at his cabinet in the laboratory. There is worse still. Manservant Poole reports to Utterson that his master's demands are ever more desperate: "Well sir, everyday, ay, and twice and thrice in the same day, there have been orders and complaints, and I have been sent flying to all the wholesale chemists in town" (p. 65). When Poole brings the "stuff" back, it is often rejected as not being pure enough.

The seduction/fear cycle of addiction is powerfully expressed in Jekyll's concluding narrative, where he notes the changing sensations and giddying feeling that ingesting the chemical produces. Initially, there is a description of novelty, something "incredibly sweet" (p. 83), but shortly "disordered sensual images" and a "heady recklessness" that proves compelling (p. 83). There is a compulsion to repeat. Although he faces certain cross-road decision points, Jekyll does not, or cannot, pull back, and all containment breaks down. The sense of a psychic/physical take-over by the drug is dramatic, and, capturing his dire situation, Jekyll complains and resigns in the same breath. The take-over is complete.

Order, space, place

Consider the following passages;

> A fortnight later, by excellent good fortune, the doctor gave one of his pleasant dinners ... all intelligent, reputable men, and all judges of good wine; and Mr Utterson contrived that the remained behind after the others had departed. Hosts loved to detain the dry lawyer ... sobering their minds in the man's rich silence, after the expense and strains of gaiety. (Stevenson, 1886, p. 43)

> The hall, when they entered it, was brightly lighted up; the fire was built high; and about the hearth the whole of the servants, men and women, stood huddled together like a flock of sheep. At the sight of Mr Utterson, the housemaid broke into hysterical whimpering: and the cook crying out, "Bless God! It's Mr Utterson", ran forward as if to take him in her arms.
> "What, what? Are you all here?" said the lawyer, peevishly.
> "Very irregular, very unseemly: your master would be far from pleased." (Stevenson, 1886, pp. 63–64)

In a story replete with unspeakable vices, nameless desires, and inexplicable character shifts, where are, or *are* there, any secure foundations on which social order can be anchored? One possible foundation is represented by the domestic setting, replete with ritual, convention, and servants, and another, related to it, lies in geography. In both passages, peace and order are both present and disturbed: in the first due to Utterson's doubts about his friend's state of being (and the reason why he lingers on); and in the second, more seriously, in the aftermath of a succession of serious incidents and which culminates in Utterson's instruction to Poole to break down the door. The world of male, bourgeois domesticity needs defending, against anonymous blackmailers or predatory criminals and against any sign of weakening (hysterical servants cannot support the structure) or violent intrusion (as in the second scene, when decisive action is called for).

Here, as in other areas we have considered, the novel's strength consists of its ability to play with the contradictory, to exploit the very "within-ness" that creates the suspense; for example, "It is precisely Jeykll's "high views" which produce morbidity in his relations with his own desires" (Punter, 1996b, p. 3). In other words, order can be dismantled from within and, not only this, but turned upside down. Inversion of order is a real possibility, with the normative becoming the problematic and the civilised world invaded by the lower forms that it had supposedly superseded (Greensdale, 1994). As we have argued, there is considerable scope as to what might constitute the master trope of disorder in the novel (e.g., criminality, madness, addiction, homosexuality, etc.), if one such there be, but let us examine further the social dimension of spaces in the novel.

Slums exist adjacent to fine squares, even citadels; "sinister blocks" disturb the eye and vibrant trading streets stand in contrast to their "dingy neighbourhoods", "like a fire in a forest" (Stevenson, 1886, p. 30). The city that contains the spaces that contain the professional men, regular traders, and obedient servants is also inhabited by the women of "different nationalities", "wild harpies", "ragged children", and other "lower elements" (p. 48). The grand whole, the Imperial City, contains the parts enveloped by fog, vapours, and "chocolate coloured pall". Take, for example, the significance of Hyde's Soho residence, which Utterson describes as "like a district of some city in a nightmare" (p. 48). A poor district at the time, Soho's "muddy ways" abuts the grandeur of the West End, signifying clear social/geographical division. Davidson (1995) analyses the echoing in which the slum and body are described, suggesting he argues, "the novella's mobilization of the body/society chiasmus, widely deployed in nineteen-century discourses, in which body and society are legible in terms of the attributes of the other" (p. 39). Undesirable spaces are inhabited by groups who threaten *disorder* of the respectable spaces nearby, constituting a major problem for the established hierarchies. One could argue that a tension is established between an "upstairs/downstairs" world and an "alongside" world, in which reversal or undesirable mixing can occur. Social actors can get out of place. Is, then, social class the master trope of disorder or is class merely part of the background scenery?

Generally, Gothic fiction amplifies fear in connection to social class, whether it be that of a decaying aristocracy, a striving, conformist middle class, or a potentially resentful, if not violent, working class. "Low life", associated with lowly social position, is gothicised (Mighall, 1999; Punter, 1996a, 1996b). Arata (1996) draws attention to those powerful resonances between descriptions of criminal deviance and a variety of discourses of social class, particularly associated to the urban poor. One complication, as far as Hyde is concerned, is that he is both potentially working-class thug, working his way into quarters that are not intended for his like, *and* moneyed gentleman, protégé, and class riser. As for middle-class self-anxiety, Arata (1996) notes the ambivalence surrounding the image of the hearth in the novella, as representing domestic bliss as well as the isolation of the solitary gentleman/bachelor.[3] The "pleasant dinner" party quoted at the start of this section is another instance of comfort being undermined by disquiet.

The presence of "dark", foreign elements is a final contender in the location of disturbance, whether or not it is merged to a discourse around social class. Davidson (1995) talks about the possibility of Stevenson referring indirectly to Irish agitators as source of social threat (Hyde is an Irish surname). We know that Stevenson was concerned about the growing Fenian attacks sweeping England during the 1880s (Callow, 2001; Rankin, 1987) and in this regard, Hyde's frenzied murder of MP, Sir Danvers Carew, may have additional salience.[4] The witness to the murder describes Carew as "an aged and beautiful gentleman with white hair drawing near along the lane" (Stevenson, 1886, p. 46), whom the "madman" Hyde clubs to death. Read in terms of representing the Irish, what better way could there be to counterpoise English civility versus Irish barbarism?

Conclusion

It could be argued that whatever was "in" Stevenson's mind is of less interest than the notions within cultural circulation upon which he drew, contemporary notions of criminal depravity, evolution, perverse processes, discourses of social class, or speculations on the nature of human mind; of course, Stevenson, had the genius to smelt the elements and, in so doing, captured the public imagination. Gothic, like other novelistic forms, is not merely reflective of reality, but is generative and productive. Macherey (1978), in his theory of literary production, argues that "the work never arrives unaccompanied; it is always determined by the existence of other works ... novelty and originality, in literature as in other fields, are always defined by relationships" (1978).

Is it a pessimistic work? Certainly in bringing Jekyll's tortured life to an end, Stevenson dispensed with the pretence of a good ending. Worse still, with the expiry of the host subject, the parasite triumphs, "usurping the offices of life" (Stevenson, 1886, p. 95): "Half an hour from now, when I shall again and forever reindue that hated personality …" (p. 97). Gone is the idea of struggle, of polar twins, as the denigrated part of the bifurcated body is released.

Is the outcome inevitable or cautionary? If order does fragment, then the social world certainty can enter the domains of revolution, usurpation, anarchy.

That there are no guarantors to order is clear, neither from law nor medicine. The persecutory logic is powerful and challenges the reader, or the witness, not to take what is "normal" for granted. Further, in the Victorian sciences of divided minds, abject bodies, and anti-evolutionary prospects, even the idea of man's double nature may be limited. Stevenson believes that even worse may come: "Others will follow, others will outstrip me on the same lines: and I hazard the guess that man will ultimately known for a mere polity of multifarious, incongruous and independent denizens" (p. 82).

CHAPTER EIGHT

"And thereby hangs a tale": narrative dimensions of human life

Whether or not there has been the often-claimed, grand scale "narrative turn" in social sciences, is open to question (Atkinson, 1997); that a whole range of disciplines have looked to narrative theory and narrative-based research is undeniable. In his manifesto of narrative psychology, Sarbin (1986, p. 8) proposed that we all, "think, perceive, imagine and make moral choices according to narrative structures". Narratives create meanings by organising episodes, aspects, and, subsequently, accounts of our actions; in the words of the philosopher, we are "story-telling animals" (MacIntyre, 1984). And just as Tomasello (1999) argued that the human species is distinguishable from other primates by our elaborate intersubjectivity and ability to "mind read" each other, so Bruner (2002) argued that our very collective life depends on our ability to organise and express our experience in narrative forms. Time only becomes human time to the extent to which it incorporates this narrative, lived dimension; simply put, there are no people who exist without narrative.

So far in this book, I have used narrative examples several times, as in Nietzsche's notion of human beings as metaphorical creatures (Chapter Three), in the discussion of the sixteenth-century spiritual dialogue between a son and his mother (Chapter Five), and the analysis of Stevenson's novella (Chapter Seven), to name a few. Central to my formulation of social unconsciousness as discursive work of articulation and field of identity, is the assumption that we are continually bathed in the waters of narrative; the bath never empties and the water keeps flowing. Stories are building blocks for identity, providing a stock of ways of portraying ourselves, expressing our dominant possibilities, intimately connected to the culture in which we live.

Although "communication" is central to Foulksean group analysis, like many of his concepts, he did not develop its theory. This chapter addresses aspects of narrative theory, suggesting its value as a means of developing the concept of communication; given the ubiquity of stories, it is puzzling that group analysis, with few exceptions, has had so little to say about it.[1]

Group analysis is usefully regarded as the emergence and encouragement of narratives of group members; those narratives are braided products, performative creations shaped by, whilst populating, the group matrix. There is always a surplus of narrative, a view consonant with my philosophical position, of group analysis as a perspectival world built around successive layers and multilateral dialogue. If the "narrative turn" in social sciences is ignored, group analysis fails to benefit from this hugely productive, interdisciplinary paradigm, but, if embraced, we have a better basis for understanding that drive in group towards "an ever more articulate form of communication" (Foulkes & Anthony, 1957, p. 11).

Let us illustrate, through a simple example, how narratives connect and animate, create interest, and consolidate memory.

A tale of minor heroism

Imagine a child who seizes the attention of those gathered at mealtime with the declaration, "Remember that time when ...!" Memories—in this case reminiscing—have a relational, conversational context for their (re)telling with, let us say, in this case, the whole family, who respond with warm interest; they join in, adding their own memories and extensions: "Yes, and ...", or, "Gosh, what a legend, what a swim!" Part of contextualisation of "remembered occasions" involves the mode in which they are shared, in a sense their social rhetoric and illocutionary force—for example, as entertainment, amusing anecdote, showing-off, assertion, moral anecdote, and many other possibilities. In other words, memories are inserted within socio-narrative structure, signaled as an event "worth recalling", as aspect of family heritage, reference point, moral theme, and so on. In group terms, it creates coherence and familiarity. Fivush (2003) puts it well, when he contends that, "At least part of children's developing self-concept is formed in social interaction with others who help provide an evaluative and interpretive framework for understanding past experiences" (p. 10). It is a good illustration of the subtlety of social intelligence, how memories and moments are aligned, so as to maximise their import in the telling.

Perhaps this story has been voiced many times before and constitutes a quick link, as it were, to family reassurance, for example, "We are an adventurous family", or, "We are always so lucky". There may be photographs related to the occasion and pleasant feelings of solidarity may have been kindled through multiple, previous acts of remembering (of course, given modern technology, more and more of our lives have this photographic supplement). This secondary memory and shared narrative is important to many recollections, as the way a person recalls emotions and meanings associates to previous acts of remembering and sharing, in addition to the original event. Let us take up the story once more.

One (jealous? more objective? both?) sibling discounts the whole affair, saying it was "nothing special". Whose memory is accurate, or whose version is dominant? Now, to give the event more content, let us assume that the story concerns the saving of the family dog, "Lucky", from drowning, whilst on holiday. Perhaps the teller weaves an implicit story of his own heroism into the recollection, and, reinforced by family, it is told with pride. Perhaps the teller was six at the time and he loves to retell the occasion. Several years later, however, he cringes with annoyance that his parents still harp on about the time when he supposedly saved the dog from drowning, knowing full well that his dad got there first. In this case, perhaps the memory of saving Lucky was harmlessly sustained as childhood semi-fiction, now outgrown. A few years elapse. Ignored, because it no longer has salience, the memory stays dormant until late teens, when Lucky dies; the memory is briefly rekindled as an emblem of the family's attachment to its dog, who might even have been renamed on account of the incident; "lucky" by name, lucky by nature.

I trust it is clear that the "autobiographical" memory in question is saturated with meanings and organised through narrative structures, some reinforced by family group, others influenced by more internal sources (e.g., the child's maturational changes). These internal sources may, however, be also supported by cultural motifs, such as stories of heroism, nascent maleness, and the like—"Wow, you were a strong lad, just like father!" In another culture, the incident might be viewed less personally and more as a signal of some sort, for example, "There are no such things as accidents". But it also remains unique, relative to age and personal fantasies; as Ricouer (2004b) suggests, there is a real, irreducible "mineness" about memory.

Gergen (1994) offers a modern, constructivist view of memory that lifts it from simply being a private act of storage and retrieval within the self-enclosed mind (or brain). Invariably such memories are, or were, part of a conversational (i.e., narrative) exchange, which endow it with an intersubjective reality; in all-too-brief remarks, Foulkes and Anthony (1957) comment on the nature of group memory and the "social togetherness" of our experiences. Similarly, in expounding a narrative-based view of personal identity and remembering, Bruner (1994) underlines the selectivity and discursivity of memory, such as in the idea that one might exaggerate agency in many situations, especially if they concern positive outcomes and which might have a cultural as well as personal function. If human beings have a tendency towards maintaining consistency ("narrative smoothing"), this is sure to apply to memory of our pasts.

What is good narrative?

Definitions as to what constitutes a "good story" take us back to Aristotle's *Poetics* (1997), the starting point of dramatic and literary theory. According to him, the unifying element of all drama is the plot (*mythos*), with its plausible beginning, middle, and end. Actors, scenes, agency, and purpose are brought into meaningful connection through structured unities of time, and the point about a "good story" is not the absence of problems, but that it is the trouble, the unexpected (*peripeteia*) which makes the story interesting. Narratives require tellers, with Bruner (2002) making the important point that in etymology, "'to narrate' derives from both 'telling' (*narrare*) and 'knowing in some particular way' (*gnarus*)—the two tangled beyond sorting" (p. 27). Narratives assume significant others, audiences of some kind, who are recipients, although this group dimension has attracted relatively little theoretical elaboration compared to its other aspects (except the idea of "audience" or "reader"). Bahktin (1981), in his approach to dialogue, argues that all words ("utterances") are marked by both "addressivity" and "answerability", but does not bring in the group as such.

If these principles are broadly true of the literary, how do they apply to the personal? The following list summarises some of the assumed features of "good" personal stories (in part, based on Dimaggio & Semarari, 2001).

- A firm sense of authorship. In other words, the teller is centred and relatively confident in his narrating
- Good space-time consistency. Good stories have this expansive and elaborated quality, with past/present differentiation
- Reference to inner states. Good stories do not just refer to external happenings, but to motives, intentions, and a range of feelings
- Relevant to the relationship context. Adaptive narrative is appropriate to context and adaptive to the others who receive it
- Thematically coherent, relevant. Coherence is a hallmark of a "good account"
- Integrated. Good stories connect different elements and strands of experience, so as to link them well
- Good self-other differentiation. A good author is able to distinguish who is doing what and to whom.

In group terms, improved narrative capacity includes greater freedom of voice, a quality which I describe in Chapter Nine as one of "discursive democracy". This involves flexibility with respect to receptivity and expressivity, and the ability to "feel 'both' or 'many' sides to their story, without falling back into closing one side down" (Angus & McLeod, 2004, p. 82). If Foulkes and Anthony (1957), referring to psychoanalysis, regard treatment as "panorama", allowing the emergence of new "interpersonal subtleties" (p. 143), then group is equally panorama in which subtle narrative capacities are enhanced. This includes openess to matters being told differently and to letting others "in" on the revision of stories; in the language of Gadamer, expanded, more flexible horizons.

These are ideal qualities and it is important to acknowledge an ambiguity at the heart of the notion of story. On the one hand, story is elevated as a noble aspect of human life and in this light there has been a veritable cultural celebration around "telling one's story", "finding one's voice", "unique life stories", and the like. Everyone is said to have "a story", whether realised or not, whose expression, whether as individual or community, is a central part of identity and expression. The recovery movement in modern psychiatry is an example, replete as it is with reference to stories and "owning". Even politicians talk the language and accuse each other of that most embarrassing of modern sins, having "no narrative", for example, on the economy. And yet, at the same time that the nobility of story and desirability of coherence are emphasised, there is a whole other side to story that contains suspicion, a suspicion centred on seduction or deception. Nietzsche knew this, expressing it with characteristic sting in his observation of man as "clever animal" (as in "too clever for his own good"). It is expressed in countless everyday expressions—"cover story", "old wives' tale", "same old story", "or so the story goes …", etc., as well as in the denigrated language of "tale", "fiction", "anecdote", "spiel", and so forth. A story can be said to be "too good (coherent? smooth?) to be true" and "too subjective" to rely upon as evidence. Identical polarities arose within that ancient tradition of rhetoric, both a noble art of discourse and persuasion and a dangerous act of sophistry, which in modern versions is seen as an empty claim or exaggeration—"mere rhetoric"; even so, the older tradition of rhetoric has been revived. In a nutshell, story suffers from the very subjectivity which defines it.

What constitutes "good story", then, is seemingly characterised by this central ambiguity. In terms of therapy, part of the skill lies not only in helping clients to tell their stories, maybe for the first time, but in seeing the uses, misuses, and flexibility or otherwise of their stories. Some psychoanalysts have described psychoanalysis as tantamount to narrative therapy, such as Spence (1982), who viewed psychoanalytic discourse more as construction than as reconstruction, unlike Freud's archaeological metaphor (see Chapter One). Schaffer (1992), too, saw analysis as akin to a developing story—giving an account, articulating successive versions of oneself—the culmination of which is the retelling of the analysand's life history. Those narrative accounts containing the widest, most integrated coverage of the person's predicament are seen as being the most adaptive and helpful.

As regards group analysis, does narrative theory offer added value or something radically new? Is Foulkes' (1975, p. 11) ideal of groups "working towards an ever more articulate form of communication", one which lends itself to narrative theory? My answer is in the affirmative. Just as the individual mind can be seen as populated by a cast of "characters" or "voices" (e.g., Dimaggio, Salvatore & Azzara, 2003; Hermans, 2003; etc.), group life not only contains this dimension, but also that of a multiplicity of stories, exchanges, positions, harmonies, and dissonances between persons; in group we cannot but help be "in the thick of it".

Disordered narrative

At a simple level, disordered narratives are the converse of good narratives, in so far as they might lack basic coherence (we talk tellingly of someone "losing the plot", as in thought-disorder), express poor authorship and differentiation (an "all-over-the-place" quality), and have a restrictive, thin, or repetitive quality. According to attachment theory, healthy, secure attachment correlates with coherent narratives (*not* necessarily to "happy lives"), with the reverse true of disordered narratives. Those manifesting insecurities of attachment have inadequate self-representations, with poor self-reflection, and hence inhibited regulatory capacities. Some refer to specific disorders of narrative, whether of the emotion kind (e.g., *alexythymia*; absence of words for emotions), or as related to organic conditions (e.g., *dysnarrativia*, a severe impairment in the ability to tell or understand stories, associated e.g., with dementia). The latter is a particularly stark example of the dependence of identity on/in narrative, reducing those with the disorder to "no longer the people who they were ..."

Never on your own: parable of the "first word"

In a child and family service setting, I was privileged to see two sets of parents announcing their respective infants' "first word". Each was delighted and imitated the sound made by their babies, something like "Ada, ada". The first parents were overjoyed that their baby's first word was "Allah"; the other parents exclaimed in all conviction, "He was calling for dada!"

Infant derives from the Latin *infans*, "unable to speak", and parental delight in response to "first words" is probably universal; "first words" are marked because they imply a new kind of joining-in with the world (hence "talk") and are symbolic of the beginning of the long end of infancy. Part of the delight consists in the fact that something new has occurred, an expression of baby initiative; baby has "gone public" in a new way. Can, however, these truly be called words or early speech, as distinct from mere utterances, phonemes with no semantic content and limited in sound, as a result of an immature voice box? Surely there is something mythical about the quest for "first words". What is certain is that the baby is born into a world already saturated by speech, reference, and commentary, and is bestowed with all manner of attributions and desires from day one, and before. The phenomenon of "baby talk" by parents is a good illustration of this; we put words in babies' mouths. The scenario usefully demonstrates the work of culture and symbolic encouragement, the two babies "willed" into the speech and position desired by their parents within their respective cultures. Neither infant is disadvantaged by this, for it is not as if one set of parents is right and the other wrong, simply that each lends different semantic interpretations to the same, vaguely distinguishable baby sounds. The example brings home how from the "beginning", the infant is imbricated in the sheer delight and buoyancy of a shared world full of illocutionary potential. Early communications are prototypical in this sense of later language-use and speech-acts (Unwin, 1984), as well as being emblematic of the early intersubjecivity of life. As for the vitality and wider developmental significance of such communications, Stern (1992) uses the evocative imagery of narrative and pre-narrative "envelopes".

The concept of *interpellation* is useful here, using Althusser's (1971) classic essay as a point of departure. Drawing upon existential and Lacanian ideas, Althusser defines interpellation as a process of recognition, of how individuals are addressed and "hailed" as subjects in relation to a master Subject. Consider expressions as divergent as, "What a strong boy!", "We, the fellow members of this Communist Party, oppose ...", or "God expects ... ." In these cases, an agent or agents are positioned, "called upon", for example, as masculine subject, loyal political comrades, devout believer, and so on. Each depends, to put it crudely, on a recognising agent: a parent, the Party, Church. Thus, individuals are not so much pre-given as pre-constructed, invited to see themselves in the images presented, constituting the *imaginary* (but not false) dimension of identity—for example, "I am a growing boy", "We are proud members of this glorious Party", "I obey the Will of God", and so on. Hirst (1979) summarises Althusser's argument clearly: "It is the recognition in the 'imaginary', in the mirror form of the Other which (to use Althusser's phrase) 'interpellates individuals as subjects'" (p. 57). There are limitations to Althusser's view, not dealt with here (Hirst, 1979), and it should not be assumed that interpellation is passive in operation or is uniform in effect; far from it. Individuals are not empty subjects.

As for so-called first words, an active process of interpellation is in evidence, the baby offered, as it were, a relational incentive, a place beyond the crib, even rudimentary cultural "identity projects" in which to grow (Harré, 1983).[2] The small biological creature known as the human infant is "brought in" to life—the difference between Aristotle's biological life or *zoe* and a human one or *bios*—through endless insertions into the narrative world, of which the emergence of early sounds, bordering verbal/pre-verbal, is but one example. It is not as if there is one, linear moment, or series of moments, within which the process procedes. Stern (1989), in one of his lesser known works, skillfully analyses "crib talk" and observes that, initially, "the production of monologues, however, is quite continuous" (p. 311). His more general argument is that a new sense of self, the "narrative sense of self", emerges slowly, sometimes after the infant's second year. In terms inspired by social theory as much as by developmental psychology, it can be said that "the self" is always dependent on the narratives of surrounding social unconscious life, forever baptising the subject into new possibilities of meaning and articulation, throughout life. The "storied self" is born in the waters of the interpretive world of stories already being told.

From this point of view, what can be called a "narrative concept of self" offers a particularly dynamic notion of identity, capable of expressing both stability and change within the framework of one's lifetime.

Conclusion: bringing the narrative to the group analytic

- First-hand recordings of lived, group narratives would offer a rich source of material for research. Group analysts might be trained to write "process accounts", but something is lost if we do not have accurate transcripts, at least some of the time, which could be subject to principled, reflective inquiry. Having such material to study might help free group analysis from a tendency, all too easy to adopt, in my view, to espouse (premature), analytic formulations.
- Ideas of "positioning" and "illocutionary force", from discourse and speech-act theory respectively, could provide added depth and

dynamism to traditional group analytic concepts such as resonance and mirroring. A great deal could be learned from closer consideration of the uses in group discourse of emphasis, tense, metaphor, tropes, and differing "speech positions".

• Groups carry incredibly complex, densely interwoven threads of narrative interaction. It would, in my view, be helpful to learn more about how individuals find voice, emerging from newcomers to more confident, experienced, contributing agents of group life, learning the art of "discursive democracy" (a theme developed in the final chapter). How do group members and therapists express and develop interest, deepen dialogue, describe, redescribe, and so thicken their accounts of self?

• In his analysis of "narrative space", Cox (Cox & Theilgaard, 1994) uses the dramatological notion of "prompting" as a means of narrative enhancement; as he pithily puts it, "prompting becomes necessary when narrative fails" (p. 89). As crowded arenas, groups contain narrative surplus and become congested; they can become overpopulated, as it were. Cox talks about the importance of "moderation" and helping members in crowded space avoid becoming involved in "near accidents".

CHAPTER NINE

Group analysis in contemporary society

"The community is represented", so argued Foulkes (1966 p. 155), "in the treatment room", including the "valuations" and "norms" of that community. "Community" has changed immeasurably since this was penned and this chapter considers four domains in which group analysis, as therapy and theory, can play a modest role in containing or illuminating some complex issues of the contemporary world. It is not only a question of "modernity" in the singular, for, as Taylor (2004) argues, we live in an era of "multiple modernities", consisting of divergent amalgams of practices, institutions, and ways of life. And, as Giddens (1991) argues, "... because of the 'openness' of social life today, the pluralisation of contexts of action and the diversity of 'authorities', lifestyle choice is increasingly important in the constitution of self-identity and daily activity" (p. 5).

Based on the United Kingdom context, but applicable beyond it, the four domains to be addressed are: (a) democracy, where it is argued that group analysis not only promotes novel democratic processes but that such processes have important effects on subjectivity and experiences of agency; (b) an increasing, older adult population, where the contribution of group analysis in assisting older adults to deal with the pressures they face is explored; (c) identity politics, where it is suggested that group-analytic practice can enable new voices to be heard, in this instance that of "carers"; and (d) values, in which it is argued that group analysis exemplifies values of diversity and difference and can actively contribute to the understanding and enhancement of the plural world(s) we now inhabit. At the same time, what group analysis offers needs to be subject to critical scrutiny, so that its own regulative ideals and historical location can be discerned.

Group analysis—democracy in practice?

As a therapy, does group analysis represent an instance of what a contrived, associative democracy between strangers might look like? The historical rise of group analysis (indeed, social psychology) can certainly be linked to post-war values of social democracy (Rose, 1990, 1998). "Group", like "community", was born around this era, as a social means and end, from school to factory, neighbourhood to clinic. Using a similar social comparison, Nitzgen (2001) regards the group-analytic process as "training in citizenship".[1] One question is whether the "communicative optimism" of group analysis is based on an idealisation of its democratic potential, and an occlusion of power, or is it just one part of constant dialectic, involving progressive *and* defensive movements? The person, below, on whom I mainly concentrate illustrates something of this complicated dialectic and how his progress was interwoven with issues of intergeneration self-concept and emergent voice, as facilitated through expanding group dialogue.

Prakesh and Andrea: group life

Prakesh accepted prospect of group analysis only on the basis that it was "the sound recommendation" of his clinician (who also conducted the group). Otherwise, he had no ready concept of what "talking in a group" would mean. Thus, within the pre-group assessment, there was deferential attitude to authority, based on reliance on supposed, expert "superior knowledge"; he presented as the gentleman and compliant patient. In my attempts to understand his experiential world, it was clear that Prakesh was adept at fitting in and satisfying his family, bosses, and colleagues (and now therapist). He had always valued advancement and took obvious pride in his children, the next generation. He came to the UK as a teenager, effectively as the family envoy, hoping to forge a better life from his native Africa. The rest of his family joined him. The central irritant in an idealised family portrait was his father, for whom Prakesh's efforts were said to be never good enough. Prakesh nursed a grievance against him, made worse by his father's failing health. It was within this context, looking after (nursing) a deeply resented father, that I understood his presenting anxiety symptoms. Psychoanalytic concepts offered useful pointers: had Prakesh internalised a frustrated-frustrating father? Was Prakesh's characterological deference the result of having split off and denied aggressive resources? Were his anxiety symptoms expressive of an oedipal constellation involving rivalry and between siblings over psychic inheritance—that is, who carries the family future? Were these, however, sufficient explanations?

In many ways, Prakesh identified with a non-democratising traditional culture, within which deference to a patriarchal family structure was central. There was a problem, however, in so far as, while such identification provided security—knowing where he stood—it inhibited change. Fitting in to family-of-origin expectations and with work colleagues/managers ("elders and betters") provided him with (limited) approval, but was detrimental to his growth and initiative.

His father's personality proved a problematic model and Prakesh consciously sought to be different. Prakesh created an avowedly non-patriarchal structure with his own family (wife and children), based on egalitarian values and a non-dominant partnership between himself and his wife. He faced troubling psychic choices, however, in that in order to be the more equal person he aspired to be, he needed to construct a different sort of inner authority and to displace the critical father and certain elements of his conservative culture.

Prakesh had things in common with group member Andrea, an English woman who had internalised highly restricting, avoidant attitudes that severely limited her horizons. Prakesh was limited by contradictory aspirations of self whilst Andrea was crushed by a pervasive, negative self-image. Consistent with this, Andrea found it hard to initiate or to elaborate on her difficulties (i.e., did not believe she had "speech rights") and regarded others as "clever" or "interesting" (unlike herself). She was described by group members as "downtrodden", whilst Prakesh was described as "inhibited" or "frustrated"; both complained about relative disadvantage in terms of material resources and an implied absence of power in their social situations. In the unfolding group dialogue, Prakesh and Andrea encouraged each other, as if seeing split-off needs and ambitions in the other (benign mirroring), but both needed considerable group support and permission in order to be able to take more group time and consolidate confidence in their contributions. In the transference, to both Andrea and Prakesh, I represented both an unchallengeable authority—the group boss/professional/ father—and a potentially transformative figure, able to facilitate novel selfobject experiences through the very refusal to occupy the omniscience attributed to me.

Reflections

Warren (1995) and Giddens (1991) compellingly describe the decline of traditional "lifeworld" horizons, including traditional family structures in many parts of the world. Individuals, however, are burdened in different ways by multiplying choices and the prospect of inhabiting multiple and pluralistic roles. Prakesh had moved between different cultures and tried to negotiate a different sort of identity from past models, which created anxiety; of course, it was not a simple matter of disavowing his culture of origin, as this culture contained many elements that he continued to value highly (e.g., community-oriented values). Warren's approach links democratic values with the development of autonomy and "communicative competencies", including the reciprocal recognition of speaking subjects. Although group analysis may chiefly be a form of treatment, its spirit is consistent with democratic processes and the building up of "citizenship", with reflexive attitudes towards one's issues, traditions, and preferences.

Political theorists argue that the vigorous democratic expansion of civil society is important in containing an evermore complex world and in creating conditions for improved governance (e.g., transformed interconnection, pluralism, cosmopolitanism, a "democratising of democracy"; Giddens, 1998; Habermas, 2004; Held, 1993). Conceptualising the realm of democracy beyond the state, Giddens (1992, 1998) explores the equalising, negotiation-based tendencies within modern personal relationships and the rise, for example, of "democratically-oriented" families and the decline in reliance on "old authority" and notions of the "way it was always done". Warren (1992, 1995), drawing on Habermasian theory, proposes a self-transformation theory of democracy, whereby democracy is seen as integral to values and conditions of self-development, autonomy, and self-governance. In other words, democratic experiences foster individuals who are likely to be more "public spirited, tolerant, knowledgeable and self-reflective than they would otherwise be" (Warren, 1992, p. 8). Warren (1995) defines autonomy as a capacity of judgment, an ability to reflect upon one's wants, needs, and values. More than this, democracy presupposes and encourages multiple discourses, an expanding range of communicative possibilities and "the reciprocal recognition of speaking subjects" (p. 140). Consistent with this model, neurosis is regarded as a form of "blocked autonomy". Is this, then, how Prakesh came to be immobilised? And is this where, through democratic and challenging group immersion, he was enabled to better articulate his position and develop more confident speaking and being rights, so to speak?

Power is never absent from the picture and at different times I also represented a distrusted (ex-)colonial country for Prakesh ("white authority") and an advantaged, middle-class professional world in the case of Andrea. Prakesh and Andrea were threatened by and assisted through the democratising forces of group dialogue; after all, no one was telling them what to do, which undermined their respective, deferential postures. The group analyst bears a complex responsibility in a contrived democracy, such as the therapy group, both as a figure of authority and as someone who disappoints omniscient expectations and attributions. It was for similar concerns, that Foulkes (1975c) preferred the term "conductor" as distinct from "leader", in his conceptualisation of the group analyst's task.

The idea of "therapeutic authority" has expanded considerably in the last few decades, subjecting most, if not all, areas of "subjective" and relational life to the potential constructions and interventions of "psy" experts (Miller & Rose, 1994). Correspondingly, there has been an ever-expanding diversification of what it means to live well, with no overarching guidelines or consensus on "how to live" (McAdams, 2008). This development in governance, indeed a regulative ideal of self-governance, is associated with advanced liberalism. That power derives from such authority is undeniable, but it is a power simultaneously open to challenge, dispute, research, support, and complaint in a way that was not the case in earlier decades.

Returning to a more general observation, philosopher John Dewey, like many social and political theorists nowadays, saw democracy as not simply residing in places such as the voting booth or parliamentary assembly, but as integral to "the attitudes which human beings display towards each other in all the incidents and relations of daily life" (Dewey, 1988, p. 226). For him, democracy was a guiding and pervasive moral ideal. Is this also the ideal that permeates the group analytic enterprise? Therapeutic inquiry is continual and, in theory, promotes communicative tolerance and "inner distance" (Woods, 2003), and, to put it even more grandly, a valuing of the "needs and interests and views of more and more diverse human beings" (Rorty, 1999, p. 82).

Therapy for the life-cycle: an older adult

Group analysis must continually adjust to changing social realities, policies, and priorities, as they affect different population groups. In this way, group analysis has a useful role to play across the lifespan. Consider the case of older adults. Smaller families and considerably longer lives mean that there have been dramatic shifts in the generational balance; commentators refer to a "revolution in longevity, radically challenging both the fatalism traditionally associated with aging as well as the social myths that consign the 'elderly' to certain positions and characteristics (Kirkwood, 1999). Giddens (1998) quips that with improved healthcare and conditions, the elderly are becoming younger. In *Everybody's Business* (CSIP, 2005), a document designed to guide health policy and service provision for older adults, the rhetoric is clear, that older adults are a valued resource in society, who should be assisted to remain as independent as is feasible, with or without the panoply of assistive technologies and support. Successive government reports and guidelines emphasise ideas of "social inclusion" and "recovery", enabling older adults, in this context, to continue to lead full and purposeful lives in their communities (Social Exclusion Unit, 2004). In his conclusion to a report, the then mental health "Tsar", Louis Appleby (2007) states, "Public expectation, technological advances and an ageing population are driving change in mental health care, just as they are in every other medical speciality" (p. 10). Whilst "active citizenship", "independence", and "life-long learning" are laudable aims, a host of anxieties, real and imagined deprivations, chance circumstances, and bodily limitations frequently intercede to make their realisation problematic. Adaptation to growing old is not simply a matter of the "internal world" per se, the world most emphasised in psychoanalytic accounts (e.g., Quinodoz, 2009), but of changing norms and practices associated with the modern cultivation of self.

Grace's life

Grace (mid-sixties on joining) joined a group which included a wide age range and felt conspicuous as the significantly oldest member. A core fear on joining was that she would not find a place because others would see her as "past it". Hudson (2005) comments on a common perception and prejudice that "change is no longer worth it or possible for older people" (p. 1). There was a risk that Grace might "carry" negative group representations concerning age, reconfirming a fear that she would once more become a burden to others. This mirrored a preoccupation about her place in society, as unproductive, unwanted, and psychologically redundant. Grace worried about "complaining" and becoming a "bitter old lady". In this way, there was a kind of homology of society/group, group/society.

Grace suffered considerable childhood adversity and disruption. Her mother had mental illness, with hospitalisations, and her father was said to be "kind, but undemonstrative". Nursing a disturbed mother and caring for siblings were themes that rapidly entered the life of the group, with others both enjoying her care-giving, "maternal" sensitivity whilst challenging her gravitation towards the caring role. Grace could be thought of as a "cork-child" (McDougall, 1986), whose psychic duty was to hold a would-be, should-be container (the mother/ the group) together. The fear, were she not to perform, was that the container would explode. Care-giving provided reassurance and was a source of life-long self-esteem. However, this psychological view was not an altogether satisfactory explanation, and possibly reductive, since Grace was also culturally presenting aspects of "her times", when patterns of intra-family caring were more normative, particularly for females. She had lived through the war and austerity years and her parents had lived though two world wars and experienced real poverty. The idea of "talking out" problems was far from easy, as she had been brought up to identify with "keeping things in" and, when group members challenged her reliance on "caring for", they implicitly challenged an organising principle of an internalised culture. Their pleas that Grace "be more selfish" and "put herself first" were understandable acts of encouragement by significantly younger people, raised during times influenced by markedly different values and regulative ideals;[2] indeed, in an unhelpful group polarity, Grace accused the younger people of being part of the "self-regarding, me-generation", whilst she was accused of being "old-fashioned". Nevertheless, Grace found some of the challenges helpful, as well as limited; caring could be a burden, but it was also a long-established, crafted ability. This kind of interactional tension and exchange is precisely how group analysis can be effective, with Grace "taking on" some of the goup members' challenges whilst also challenging pre-reflective views held by others.

Experiences of job redundancy were another focus, for Grace and others. In her work career, she was displaced by a younger, more energetic "entrepreneur", leaving her on the sidelines. Increasing losses reduced the prospects of support outside. It was hard for Grace not to sink into an "internal society" which conspired to deny her the right to a purposeful life—and not to sink into a negative group role in which she would embody such a position. Grace faced the formidable task of rebuilding and countering feelings of inner destruction; the fact that acquired patterns meant that it was hard to be seen to complain or to burden others, made the task considerably more difficult. Group analysis, based on an ethic of communication, did not sit easily with this and, not surprisingly, there were periods during which Grace wanted to "give up", on the group and sometimes on life.

Reflections

At times—perhaps always (Schermer, 2006)—group analysis acts as a spiritual resource, within which existential crisis and depletion is addressed; "defences" often fail through lifelong wear and tear. The clinical material illustrates the role that group analysis might play in sensitising ourselves to the changing life positions, transitions, and thresholds associated with the fact of living longer lives. There is a particular story here, that of Grace, but also a universal theme; after all, the younger members had future lives, prospects, and fantasies of being old(er). How does anyone manage adjustment to changing culture and mores over time, or construct a non-work identity after one's working life, and so on? Significantly, Grace's struggle to keep going inspired the younger members, some of whom were tempted to seek destructive shortcuts or anti-growth solutions to their dilemmas; perhaps she lent them spiritual resources.

An ethics of communication, of dialogical optimism, grounds group analytic operations; talking and taking, giving and receiving, seeing self-in-other and other-in-self, are core to its practice. This, like other social-moral expectations of living actively and fully, can be a source of real pressure, whilst constituting the very norm through which it is supposed to work. In a psychologised society, a "psy complex" as it was, there seems no alternative to "working on ourselves" (Rose, 1992). We have seen that Grace did not readily "take" to such confessional group values, even though she felt she had "nowhere else" to turn. In this way, group analysis offered no easy resolutions or consolations, but through a sometimes co-operative and sometimes agonistic exploration, some growth and reconciliation, albeit it with much sadness, was possible. A painful aspect of any therapy, and one certainly true of group analysis, is how clients figure out their realistic limitations, at whatever stage in life, and appreciate and actualise their assets.

The articulation of identity politics: "carers"

The concept of identity has come to encompass a wide range of social and psychic issues that address the constitution of self as a constructed, continuing, never-completed process. So open are modern possibilities of "active citizenship" and "lifestyle maximisation" that we are encouraged to think that we can make and remake ourselves at will, seize the opportunities "out there", and realise our core ambitions (Giddens, 1991; Rose, 1998). The world is our oyster, or so it seems. Social groups likewise are encouraged to think in terms of collective identities, based on shared "natural interests" and/or to "own" identities that were previously maginalised. This is often described in terms of "identity politics", and sociologists have explored interesting links between identity-formation and proliferating small-group affiliation (Wuthnow, 1994).[3] In the UK, with governmental emphasis on "social inclusion", everyone, it is said, deserves to "have a voice"; no person, group, in short, no constituent of identity, should be left out.

It is commonplace to think of self as a composite, a polity of formations—for example, husband, carer, parent, citizen, doctor, higher-tax earner, middle-aged person, church goer, etc. Group analysis is quite at home with plural views of selfhood, engaged and constructed as we are in the crowded "traffic" of human connection. It is not that people have not always been conceivable as a "collection" in these terms, but that the distinction between various properties seems to have become more explicit and differentiated in contemporary society. Identities are everywhere. A person's ability to "own" and assert a particular identity is celebrated and many modern social movements (e.g., the women's movement, gay/lesbian liberation, survivors, etc.) were forged on the basis of identity struggles, opposing other, dominant identities. To "have a voice" and to express "an identity", increasingly coincide. To explore this paradox, consider the rapid rise to prominence of the "carer".

Carers have always existed, in the sense of individuals or groups of persons who spend a significant proportion of their time helping others, aiding the sick, whether in an occupational or a personal ("private") capacity. Until recently, however, such agents seldom defined themselves *as* carers. Carers have come to be identified as bearers of rights, as legal, social, psychological, if often burdened, agents. A person who introduces themselves in a group or conversation with "and I am a carer", is readily understood as making a socially legitimised claim to a core identity and we "know" what they mean.

The relatives group

In the 1990s, I established a relatives group for carers who live with or "support" someone with substance misuse issues. Hosted within a substance misuse service, I drew upon group-analytic thinking as an aid to negotiation and practice. The substance misuse service was aware of a large, neglected relative population; that for every one individual drug/drink user, many others, particularly nearest and dearest, are deeply affected. In group-analytic or systems terms, the addict creates major dissonance within their relational network, generating helplessness in others and anxiety that everyone will be sucked into the chaos; in response, carers might blame themselves, try to control the addict, or believe that if only the user was taken from them and "put somewhere" (e.g., detox, rehab), the problem would be solved.

What seemed a rational proposal—to set up a service for these carers—met with resistance: "Will we be swamped?", "Won't they interfere with the treatment of the user?", and so on. The service was anxious about the prospect of moving away from an individual model of treatment. I presented audit evidence, confirming the fact that relatives did indeed feel treated "second best" twice—at home, with the user, but also by lack of provision by our service. Careful listening to service resistances or concerns, as expressed by different organisational subgroups—drug team, alcohol team, managers, nurses—paid dividends and I was charged with the task of delivering the service for carers.

The relatives group service was a slow-open, weekly group, strongly influenced by group analysis and which could accommodate newcomers at short notice. The group was a "unilateral intervention" for carers, regardless of whether their loved one was in treatment. Thus, the ticket for entry was simple, in so far as any "affected" partner, spouse, son, daughter, sibling, or friend could join. The aim was to help relatives examine their own, submerged and neglected needs and to gain more "say" and protection in their lives. The group worked actively to improve self/other differentiation; one member spoke of the importance of the group in supporting "healthy detachment" from her alcoholic spouse, enabling her to establish boundaries, limits, and to safeguard her health. The group was a maelstrom of acute emotions, such as anger, shock, fear, and chronic feelings of depletion, demoralisation, bereavement—an impotent sense of "What can I do?" But it also fermented hope and clarity. Carers could, in time, gain more choice in their lives and freedom to decide how best to cope, with or without the direct presence in their lives of the problem drug user.

Reflections

The contemporary carer identity emerges in at least three domains; (a) carers constitute a social and legally protected constituency, in the UK, whose contribution and burdens are recognised in, say, the Carers Recognition Act, 1995; (b) in its idea of a "patient-led" National Health Service, the Department of Health promotes the involvement of carers as well as service users (Simpson & Ramsay, 2004); (c) carers occupy a role that whilst at some levels is applauded—for example, is selfless, devoted, dependable, heroic even—has a shadow side, for example, is a burden, source of guilt, overlooked misery, suppressed need, and so on. If group analysts, like sociologists, are centrally interested in the formation of group identities, then the rise of the carer is a remarkable phenomenon, involving the creation and mobilisation of an entire new constituency as well as a field of psychological subspeciality.

The relatives service not only met an important clinical need but helped to ferment an influential constituency, expressive of the "carer voice". The relatives group paved the way for diversifications, such as family and couple therapy, that had not existed before. As a consequence, carers had an extended menu of choices within the substance misuse service. Not only this, but the "carer awareness" that grew through participation and practice lead to the formation of a lobby group. At one point, for example, when the group was felt to be under threat (the reality was hard to discern), members took up an active campaigning role and made sure managers knew their concerns.

It is one of the paradoxes of identity that people can become constrained by the identity envelope in which they have come to define their position. "Identity" both helps groups to fight for positions, rights, etc., and to cohere, but can also entrap, confining groups to an enclave and creating stereotypes. Butler (1999) suggests that over-emphasis on identity creates a "metaphysics of substance", in which subjects are unable to move out of the "property" that is said to constitute them. Consistent with this, some members of the group increasingly objected to the term "carer", on the grounds that it implied a particular role, suggestive of certain relational obligations. "Being a carer" could trap individuals in the very thing of which they complained, especially as the group encouraged autonomy. Consequently there was much (unresolved) discussion about alternative names to that of "carer", and obvious evidence of a greater sense of authority in their negotiation and requests. There was certainly far less passivity and resignation in their lives and outlooks. In the institutional transference, perhaps I was seen as "caring for the carers", ensuring their provision within the service as a whole. In this way I held a certain "power" in the very act of trying to give it away—one of the many paradoxes of group analysis conceived as a form of therapeutic, democratic association.

Group analysis: values with which to explore values?

"Values-based practice" (VBP) is an interesting development in mental health practice, emerging as a corrective to the inordinate influence of "evidence-based practice" (NIMHE, 2004; Woodbridge & Fulford, 2004). VBP supports the key principles of: (a) recognition—that values are vitally important factors that are implicated in all areas of mental health practice; (b) awareness-raising—that unspoken, underlying values continually influence our practice and judgments, as clinicians and clients; and (c) the cultivation of respect—it is on the basis of this recognition and practice-reflection that true "anti-discriminatory" practice can be founded on respect for the diversity of values that exist in contemporary society. The importance of valuing diversity succeeds, or so it would seem, the decline of more monolithic traditions or singular sources of authority, being part of a process that Berger (1969) refers to as the "pluralisation of life-worlds". To the authors of VBP, such sensitivity and development is an essential component in the ongoing training and cultivation of a capable work-force, indeed citizenry. Woodbridge and Fulford (2004) offer a political analogy: "VBP as being rather like a political democracy" (p. 17), as opposed to authoritarian or totalitarian regimes. But far from being "anything goes", VBP argues that it is more important to promote a "right approach", to facilitate a culture in order to access and understand the values of other people—and potential conflicts between values—than to impose "right values". VBP is a useful way of helping practitioners and policy-makers improve awareness of the implied value assumptions that govern their practice and language.

In his famous psychoanalytic paper, Rey (1988) posed the question, "What is it that the patient brings to analysis?" Rey's answer is that they bring damaged internal objects with the expectation of repair; given the lateral perspective of group analysis, it is important to insist that clients also "bring" the wider worlds which they inhabit, and not only damaged features, including values, sustaining beliefs, backgrounds ideals, and horizons. Values surround us like the air we breathe and, hence, from a certain point of view, group analysis could be thought of as a particular form of values-based practice, or at least, as a medium in which this can occur.

Clinical reflections: a synthesis

Prakesh and Andrea were torn between a deferential or submissive attitude ("Tell me what to do", "You are the expert", "You others are more interesting/clever than me", etc.) and the desire for greater power and equality in relationships. Their conservative positions predominated for a long time, which the group accepted in some ways but did not reinforce. I have suggested that democratic processes and values were an integral part of what helped Prakesh and Andrea to develop autonomy and thus to see themselves differently. In Grace's group, I proposed that her struggles as an older adult, could partly be thought of in terms of a struggle between competing internal values (e.g., "I like to care for others" versus "I want more independence") and that there were conflictual values between group members, some of which had a generational dimension. Thus, Grace was influenced by regulative ideals concerning caring, loyalty, and serving family (in the past, actual, in the present, internal), whilst her group contemporaries were influenced by other regulative ideals, such as the priority of self-expression and independence from family. In many senses we are all multicultural[4] and "more free to decide" (Laclau & Mouffe, 1985) as we move through life and manage differing contexts (including the context of the therapy group). In these examples, and is particularly interesting in terms of value-change, Prakesh had moved from one culture to another, Andrea felt like a fish out of water in a supposedly "educated" group of people (this was partly her perception and based on inferiority feelings), and Grace had lived through many sea-changes in the social world over more than sixty years; each was attempting to forge a satisfactory resolution or reconciliation in the contemporary world and in each instance, the spirit of group analysis was intended to promote useful group and democratising processes rather than to impose "answers". Finally, in the case of the relatives group, the host service grew to recognise, and so to better value, the "carer identity" alongside that of immediate service users. This could only happen as part of a wider shift in society, enabling new constituencies—such as carers—to find an assertive voice.

Reflections

We are said to live in more open, but increasingly complex and risk-dominated societies (Beck, 1992). In a world of multiple expertise and divergent sources of authority, Rose (1990) acknowledges the proliferation of psychotherapies in modern society and the "therapeutic culture of the self". He argues that this is manifested by the invention of a whole new apparatus of living, self-enhancement, and lifestyle, each with differing notions of what is "right" and what helps, a proliferation of ways of crafting the self. Of course, clients primarily wish to overcome their problems and suffering, but are often, implicitly, also seeking a way to live a good life, what the Greek philosophers termed *eudaimonia*. What nowadays counts as *eudaimonia* is thoroughly saturated with psychological discourses of personhood and subjectivity; "the problems of defining and living a good life have been transposed from an ethical to a psychological register" (Rose, 1990, p. xiii). Whilst group analysis is a rich theatre within which value concerns can be located and opened out, like any other psychotherapy, it is not a neutral stage but is premised on values or background notions of what good, fulfilled, and duly co-operative lives might look like. Extending Gadamer's notion of horizons, as discussed in Chapter Two, the ethical can be seen as the horizon which pulls us forward and which tells us how we are doing, "being transformed into a communion in which we do not remain what we were" (Gadmader, 1975, p. 379). Hence, group analysts talk a particular vocabulary, comport themselves in particular ways, arrange furniture, and work, implicitly or explicitly, with particular conceptions of what is healthy, problematic, and desirable. They are installed, as any expert, within what can be called specific therapeutic "enclosures": "relatively bounded locales or types of judgment within which their power and authority is concentrated, intensified and defended" (Rose & Miller, 1992, p. 188). Of course, true to liberal rationale, no one would seek to "impose" these, but all the same there can be no group without the operation of therapeutic desire; this appears the reverse of Bion's (1967) alternative regulative ideal of the analyst working "without memory or desire" (even though this, paradoxically, rests on a different kind of desire). In many ways, and much like the rhetoric of VBP, group-analytic values appear as benign—who could possibly disagree with them? An example is the congruence between group-analytic values and those wider, often celebrated, values of diversity and pluralism. Surely, few would object to Foulkes' (1973) observation that, "it is not the case that one viewpoint is right and the other wrong. It is rather as if we took photographs from various positions ... all of them show what is true from the position from which they are taken" (p. 230). Earlier, I suggested that the democratic ethos of group analysis can foster the development of autonomy, a kind of internal democracy. At one level, there seems to be a perfect fit between group-analytic values and those of the wider, liberal social imaginary in which we live, and surely, using the political analogy of VBP, most of us would prefer to live in freedom than the equivalent of an authoritarian regime.

At the point at which such assumptions rest, it would seem important to subject the group-analytic ethic to critical scrutiny, not in order to undermine it but to make fuller and honest use of its potential and limitations. As has been argued with respect to the tendency to idealise positive "therapeutic group factors", there are also non-therapeutic, "anti-group" processes whose operation can be just as powerful (Nitsun, 1996). Yet even the term "anti-" implies something to be overcome, a standard around which judgments can be made about what is considered "therapeutic" and what "non-therapeutic". The following list, therefore, is not so much labeled in terms of anti-group process, but in terms of the inevitable points of contradiction within group analysis, as it sits within the range of modern psychotherapies.

Aporias of group analysis

- Just as "therapy" and "counselling" is ascribed a pre-given importance within the modern, "therapeutic culture of the self" (Rose, 1990), so too, group analysis as confessional-supportive arena, assumes that talking openly about oneself is inherently good. It partakes of, whilst adding a particular dialect to, relatively recent, historically speaking, psychological language. Clearly there is a self-familiarising effect of such language and, as with all therapies, a potentially "seductive territory of truth" (Rose & Miller, 1992, p. 188). What then about those who do not find this so, those for whom words do not come easily, or those for whom words between people does *not* increase trust?
- In its communicative optimism, group analysis assumes that mirroring and free exchange ultimately help, even though there are many who find it hard to learn in this way and for whom the mirror of group, so to speak, fails; they cannot recognise themselves in its operation or discover points of alleged commonality.
- Group analysis lays claims to the value of "acceptance", but there are many for whom groups alienate or even reject.
- Based as it is on free, group association, what about those unconvinced by the seemingly uncontrolled, lateral unfolding of communication, those for whom what we might see as a "surplus of narrative" sounds like a babble or baffling noise?
- The principle of pluralism appears consonant with the ethic of group analysis, in so far as both are based on the need for, and practice of, active dialogue, authentic exchange, and co-existence. What then when there is a serious conflict of competing values or the appearance of values that threaten our own, cherished ones? Group analysis and VBP are confident of their standing when it comes to "positive differences", but might struggle in relation to values that are contrary to what we identify with. What are the limits to our tolerance and supposed liberality in such circumstances?
- Better self-governance and autonomy seem inherently good values, in a liberal-value world, but there will always be some who lean towards conservative positions and who desire the role of structured authority in their lives. The liberal social imaginary might "oblige

us to be free", but not all are ready, willing, or able to assume the complex responsibility and associated anxiety that accompanies this, or, certainly, not in all contexts of life. Equally, ideals related to living committed, fulfilled, and generative lives have a liberal appeal, but are often at considerable odds with the preferences and possibilities of many.

Conclusion

The modern world seems to demand and cultivate more variegated reflexivity than was the case for previous generations; we experience "greater indeterminacy" with its corresponding freedom "to decide our movements and identity" (Laclau, 1990, p. 68). Group analysis is quite different from many popular, lifestyle psychological approaches but is but one amongst a whole field of competing professional therapies and reflexive approaches, and one based on its own ethic of communication and corresponding assumptions about "what helps". It, too, cultivates, either as aim, or side-product, particular values of living.

Group analysis has been explored in terms of how it enables, in small steps, the extension of "democracy" into subjectivity and the heartlands of self-governance. In the final section, however, some of these claims were turned in on themselves. It was argued that group analysis has also to be seen as part of the very "techniques", as it were, of modern self- and grouphood. In this regard, it is not neutral, but immersed in all those forms of modern "power-knowledge" that are integral to how we regard the "good life".

Group analysis cannot be considered separately from "community" and social matrix; it has been argued, through four examples, that group analysis offers space within which modern dilemmas can be worked upon, by helping people with the different pressures they face. This is by no means easy, as new forms of anxiety replace older forms. Whilst group analysis has no therapeutic monopoly in a post-monopoly world, it can assist people with some of the navigation of complexity that is required. If Erikson (1950) was right that "the patient of today suffers most under the problem of what he should believe in and who he should—or, indeed, might—be or become" (p. 242), then group analysis offers a resource within which individuals can acquire a more substantial view of themselves. With longer lives, proliferating "identities", and more role possibilities, it seems clear that there are more borders, thresholds, and crossroads to negotiate than ever before.

POSTSCRIPT

I believe it was the analyst John Klauber who once remarked that it takes ten years of post-training practice to truly "become" a psychoanalyst. Presumably what he meant by this was that it takes years of reflection, accumulated professional experience, and plain personal growth to come to one's own mind, as it were, on what one is about. I think the same applies to becoming a group analyst, even if there is no magic in the number ten. Part of becoming a group analyst, at least for those with an active interest in theory, is deepening one's understanding of the basis and potential of group analytic concepts. My contribution in this book has taken approximately eight years; that is how long it took to come to my own mind (critical distance?), albeit in fits and starts and with prolonged bursts and a few respites.

The World within the Group is my endeavour to connect group analysis to several developments in philosophy, historical inquiry, and modern social theory, which group analysis can both contribute to and be nourished by. I did not set out with the idea of a book, but as a result of several disparate adventures in writing, the idea of bringing something together, in one place, fermented. There is no single theme or central hypothesis, but rather a number of inquiries and themes that are in effect multiple promptings, whose purpose is to expand the horizons

163

of group analysis. Each chapter should be read as an essay, using that word in the old sense of "attempt" or "trial", as in an attempt to develop a theory or to trial an idea. They can be read separately or together, as there are several threads connecting them. In fact, I have come to prefer the essay form as a way of saying things, of venturing ideas.

Writing style is hardly a secondary matter. The aesthetic dimension of writing matters to me. How we put things and find our way in and through words matters to me. My training supervisor (Dr Harold Behr) underlined for me the importance of crafting our language with our clients. After all, as Wittgenstein reminded us, words, and also deeds, are acts of intervention. As for this act of intervention, this traveling of theory, I have now "let it go", with the trust that it will prompt new and interesting dialogues …

Martin Weegmann
London

GLOSSARY

The glossary is not comprehensive, but selects the main terms which appear more than once, or which contain a concept/theme that travels between more than one chapter.

Abjection

The abject, and abjection, derives from the Latin *abicere* (to cast out, to degrade, and so on); Julia Kristeva uses it as an emblem of pollution, referring to those elements that disturb and threaten the social body or self.

Articulation

In the political theory of Ernesto Laclau, articulation concerns struggles to fix meaning and so to define reality, at least temporarily. It performs an ordering function with respect to discursive elements.

Contingency

In a formal sense, contingency refers to events or circumstances that are possible but which cannot be predicted. Ernesto Laclau develops a theory of the social that is characterised by contingency and articulations which can never be closed or totalised; something always escapes and thus the social is subject to continual rearticulation.

Degeneration

An influential nineteenth-century "theory" of regression and deviation, bodies could be said to be degenerate, whole societies could degenerate and be threatened by the existence of "dangerous groups".

Dialogue

Plato suggested that thinking is a form of "dialogue with oneself". Actual dialogue requires interplay between persons, involving an unfolding, never completed process, to which each and every partner contributes; no one stays where they started, as it were. In the theory of the dialogical self, as developed by psychologists Hubert Hermans and Giancarlo Dimaggio, self is seen as multivoiced, as "society of mind".

Discursive

In general, the discursive pertains to any aspect of meaning, whether linguistic or otherwise.

Effective history

Understanding occurs against a background of our prior involvement, on the basis of our *history*; understanding and interpretation for Hans Georg Gadamer always occurs from within a particular "horizon" that is determined by our historically determined positions.

Emotional communities

Emotional communities are networks of mental and emotional association, occurring in social communities. Historian Barbara Rosenwein is interested in the "systems of feeling" that occur in such communities and what this tells us about their outlook, bonds, and the kinds of emotional expression they expect, encourage, and prohibit.

Exclusionary matrix

Medieval historian Robert Mills uses the phrase to describe dangerous, abject regions and figures within society, representing a counter-side to order and reason. I have used in in a nineteenth-century context.

Figurations

The concept used by Norbert Elias to describe human interdependencies and their evolution. It is said that his earlier medical studies, when he saw the interconnections and interweaving of bones, muscles, and nerves, made a lasting impression and one that he transported to the social/historical realm.

Foundational (matrix)

S. H. Foulkes defined the "foundation matrix" as a store of shared communication and archaic meanings that pre-exist and inform the emergence of current and new groups, including the therapy group.

Hegemony

The Marxist theorist Antonio Gramsci outlined a theory of hegemony concerning the manufacture of consent and legitimisation in society ("common sense"). Counter-hegemonic struggle, by contrast, pursues alternatives to the dominant culture. Ernesto Laclau extends Gramsi's views, arguing that hegemonic struggle centres around "floating signifiers" that are open to rearticulation and contestation.

Historical psychology

Norbert Elias proposed a new discipline of historical psychology (and historical sociology). In his view, "minds" and mentalities could only be understood when placed within the processes that shaped and defined them; human beings are forever interdependent creatures.

Horizon

For Hans Goerg Gadamer, horizon is the larger context of meaning in which particular understandings take place. Understanding involves a "fusion of horizons" and the formation of new contexts of meaning. Personal horizons carve out experiential planes, creating possibilities and limitations to articulation.

Imagined communities

Benedict Anderson develops the notion of imagined communities with respect to the case of nationalism, where he notes that it cannot possibly arise from face-to-face familiarity. Instead, members hold an image and symbols of their affinity and mutual identification. The concept can be productively applied to many groups other than national ones.

Interpellation

Interpellation is a process of recognition, of how individuals are addressed and "hailed" as subjects, in relation to a master Subject/ Term, who "calls" them. Political philosopher Louis Althusser used the idea as a component of his theory of ideology.

Intersubjectivity

In the psychoanalytic theory of Robert Stolorow and colleagues, inter-subjectivity is a paradigm inspired by several traditions, philosophic and analytic. Intersubjectivity rejects what it sees as the "myth of the isolated mind" and of fixed intrapsychic structures, emphasising intsead the constitutive interplay of subjective worlds and dynamic and interderminate processes of development.

Matrix

S. H. Foulkes characterised the matrix as a "hypothetical web of com-munication and relationship". He distinguished the "dynamic matrix" observed in the active life of the therapy group and the "foundation matrix" of shared meanings, cultural images, and other aspects of human life and emotionality.

Narrative

Narrative refers to an account or description and, according to Paul Ricoeur, involves an ordering of the world by the imagination. "Narrate" derives from both "telling" (*narrare*) and "knowing in some particular way" (*gnarus*). Many theorists have developed theories of narrative and how humans tell the stories of their lives, as it were.

Perspectivism

Friedrich Nietzsche's perspectivism rejected the idea of absolute knowledge, independent of particular perspectives about the world. Perspectives depend on language, rhetoric, culture, and history.

Population

Borrowing this metaphor from eighteenth-century faculty psychology, I use the term to describe the "filling out" and expansion of the group matrix and group horizons. It is also linked to nineteenth-century accounts of group/mass and social body.

Pragmatism

Pragmatism is associated with a number of American philosophers, particularly James, Dewey, and Pierce. According to pragmatists, thought does not so much represent or mirror reality, but is an instrument of inquiry, action, and problem-solving. Pragmatists sought to overcome many of the traditional polarities and concerns of philosophy. Rejecting the idea of the detached observer, they acknowleged the social, adaptive nature of all inquiry.

Protestantisation

I use the term to describe the "long history" of the English Reformation and its manifold implications on the reformation of social and personal life, including the emphasis on a more personal God and new narratives of conduct, conscience, and self-inspection.

Reflexivity

In the sociology of Anthony Giddens, reflexivity refers to acts of self-reference, with examination or action "looping back" on itself and hence instituting a cycle of change. In his theory of "reflexive modernity" he argues that modern society is "post-traditional" and increasingly self-aware and reflective. Amongst those changes are new versions of intimacy and "equal" relationships.

Social body

In the nineteenth century, the notion of social body concerned representation of the population as an aggregate. Linked to governance, the notion enabled new definitions of the public and private realms, and influenced targets of reform and improvement. Foucault's work is especially concerned with the relations between political power and the body, and the varied historical ways that bodies were trained and discursively configured.

Social imaginary

Social theorist Charles Taylor sees the social imaginary as a creative and symbolic aspect of the social world, reflective of how individuals imagine their existence and collective life.

Social unconsciousness

I propose a theory of social unconsciousness based on a work of articulation and composition—social unconsciousness as movement, generation, fluidity. It is impossible to finally fix social horizons or to know social unconsciousness once and for all, since it is always behind, before, and around us.

Tradition

Sociologist Edward Shils notes that the traditional is based on *traditum*, something handed down from past to present, also *tradere* or *traderer*, meaning to transmit. Not all inherited meaning has the same value, as a selective and hegemonic process operates. For Hans-Georg Gadamer, tradition refers to this dimension of legacy or historicity.

Traffic

S. H. Foulkes uses the metaphor of traffic to describe the flow that happens between groups, or to characterise transpersonal processes.

Unthought known

Christopher Bollas used the term to describe experiences or inarticulate psychic elements that are "known", but not yet thought. The unthought known becomes the thought known by articulation and reliving in language. There are similarities to Donnel Stern's notion of "unformulated experience".

World-making/World-building

The image of world-making suggests a process ofdefinition, making distinctions, of taking apart and putting together. Philosopher Nelson Goodman uses the notion in relation to his aesthetic theory whilst sociologist Peter Berger argues that evey society is an enterprise of world-building.

NOTES

Chapter One

1. A contentious issue concerning earlier formulations of intersubjectivity was that although it challenged the "myth of the isolated mind" and "myth of neutrality", it concentrated on the analytic partnership or dyad in isolation (Zeddies, 2000; Zeddies & Richardson, 1999). To be fair, this over-emphasis has been subsequently corrected by Stolorow, Atwood & Orange (2002). Greenberg (1999a, 1999b) helpfully explores the embedded dimension of analytic treatment and how definitions of therapeutic authority invoke the cultural milieu in which they operate.
2. Bachelard's (1964) "topoanalysis" uses house as metaphor for the self, replete with its "nooks and corners of solitude". He notes the balance of security and precariousness that homes represent, with home conceived as cradle, the place where we start from, rather than fixed container.

Chapter Two

1. In English translation, "fusion" seems a somewhat inadequate term, implying that two horizons simply bond together (Kidder, 2013).
2. Several group analysts (Pines, 1996a; Zinkin, 1996) have developed the concept of dialogue and it is to Bakhtin that they have referred, rather

than Gadamer. Bakhtin postulated a "surplus of seeing", in which each person occupies a unique perspective. In Chapter Eight I develop the complementary idea of groups as "surplus of narrative". Brown (1986) makes the point that neither the word "dialogue" nor "conversation" appear in Foulkes' writings.

Thornton's (2004) illuminating paper opens up the potential in Foulkes' poorly elaborated idea of "exchange". She writes: "The individual in the group takes in from the others in the group (including the conductor) different ways of being, seeing and acting which broaden the range available to her/him in the real world. Not that we always see this happening; it is partly or wholly unconscious. In the complex and fluid dynamic of group interactions, it can be hard at times to know what belongs to whom ..." (p. 310). This, and her related imagery of "borrowing my self", bears resemblance to my use of Gadamer's philosophy.

3. Eaton (1998) argues that Gadamer's hermeneutics could be a basis for "non-dogmatic psychotherapy", highlighting aspects in this approach which resonate with the so-called "non-specific factors" underlying therapeutic relationships.

4. Foulkes' collaborator, James Anthony (Anthony, 1983) said: "Perhaps the most valuable lesson I received from Foulkes was on the value of unobtrusiveness on the part of the therapist and on the limitations of explicitness" (p. 30). Foulkes (1990), in his emphasis on configurational analysis in groups argued that "one need not jump from what is going on to what is behind it. This also has a bearing on a partially mistaken idea of interpretation" (p. 280).

Chapter Three

1. Nietzsche"s perspectivism is, of course, open to challenge, not least because of his inconsistencies. Houlgate (1986) explores this and poses the apt question, does Nietzsche regard his own (Dionysian, irrationalist) perspective as the privileged (even if, in societal terms, an "untimely") one? Danto (1980) presents an analysis of the radicalism and inherent tensions of Nietzsche's perspectivism.

2. Nietzsche's (1886) suggestion that "My judgment is my judgment; no one else is easily entitled to it ..." has similarities to Freud's (1923b) "narcissism of small differences".

3. It is of interest to note that Nietzsche and Dewey were both influenced by the essayist and poet Ralph Waldo Emerson (1803–82), who developed an ethics of self-reliance and self-improvement (Rorty, 1989).

4. Nietzsche is not a democratic thinker, indeed, is usually thought of as the reverse; many of his statements appall modern sensibilities.

Then again, who, in the nineteenth century, was a democratic theorist, in the way we now understand it? Critchely (2008) notes that most philosophers, prior to the twentieth century, had "aversive reactions" (p. 220) to the notion of democracy. Nietzsche is more correctly thought of as a "philosopher of self-creation", who emphasises the singular, the romantic, the heroic (Rorty, 1999, p. 26). In a rare reference to the philosopher, Foulkes (1975a, p. 165) refers to the need in group to help people "to become what they are, to use Nietzsche's dictum". However, at the same time, perspectivism underpins democratic values and pluralism, supporting a dynamic, agonistic, and contextualist view of democracy (Hatab, 1999). Rorty (1999, p. 267) also points to the importance of the moral perspectivism of Nietzsche, promoting, in theory, the profusion of "new sorts of human lives", in *some* ways as compatible with values of diversity and pluralism.

Chapter Four

1. It is impossible to begin to do justice to the value that other sociological theories can have in bearing upon the notion of social unconsciousness, a fact that Hopper (2003), himself a sociologist, has acknowledged. Another sociologist deserves mention—in his theory of "structuration", Giddens (Giddens & Peirson, 1998) places emphasis on the ongoing nature and flow of social life, to the point that "change and constancy are somehow directly bound up with one another" (p. 89).
2. According to Earl Hopper (personal communication), Eric Fromm was the first to use the phrase "social unconscious", as a cultural surround tantamount to the air people breathed.
3. The role of the "traumatic" in the social unconscious is theorised at length by Hopper (e.g., 2003) and by others. I have no quibble with this emphasis, but it is not the whole story, anymore than is regarding hegemonic meaning as the only type of meaning. To be fair, he does acknowledge this other side. Clealry, the ordinary, non-traumatic, non-dramatic, taken-for-granted features of common sense need equal treatment, that sense that people have that "things have always been this way". Only when someone or some group "steps outside", trouble might start. In this way, societies have integrative, preservative myths as much as those which posit alternatives and ruptures (Ricouer, 2004a).

   A further missing emphasis, but not one addressed in this book, is the realm of social *consciousness*, first addressed by the sociologist, Charles Horton Cooley (1907, p. 98) in his far seeing paper, which, analysing the "social mind", claimed that "most of our reflective consciousness … is social consciousness". In many ways, the phenomena that group analysts cover in the "social" area, including my own speculations, hover around undecidable edges of social conscious *and* social unconscious.

Chapter Five

1. Foulkes (1971) spoke of a "pre-existing and relatively static" area within a given culture, referred to as the "foundation matrix", whose rhythm of change is different to that of the "dynamic matrix", created when particular groups or current associations of individuals come together (Nixon, 1998).

2. Smith (1991) offers an illuminating comparison between the work of Maurice Bloch and that of Elias, pointing out commonalities, such as the importance of networks and ties of dependence, centralising and pacifying processes, *genres de vie*, and change lasting several generations ("longue durée"). In fact several twentieth century continental historians converged in their emphasis on the study of collective mentalities, configurations and the like (Burrow, 2007).

3. Although the Elizabethan Acts of Supremacy and Conformity contained a fervent repudiation of Roman doctrine, they preserved the church hierarchy and enshrined a largely Calvinist theology. Many were dissatisfied with the Elizabethan compromise and sought further reform. By the end of Elizabeth's reign, malcontents and critics of a "but halfy-reformed" church, or "incomplete revolution" were called "precisians" (due to their emphasis on precision) or "puritans" (frequently a word of abuse; Durston & Eales, 1996). Puritans saw themselves as "the godly" and "God"s people", who placed preaching and reading of scripture, rather than the repetition of ritual, above all else. It was their duty on earth to fight God"s battles, enabling Christ's Kingdom, in the words of Milton, Christ as the "shortly expected king".

4. The alternatives to meek, dutiful women are, witches at one end of the extreme and scolds, rough-tongued women, spinsters, and "old hags" at the other. There is a sub-theme surrounding the excluded elements of the then society (I will develop the concept of an "exclusionary matrix" in the next chapter) that associated women with catholic recusancy, an association that in part links back to the "danger" of catholic queens/wives in England. The woman was thus potentially "unruly", spiritually adulterous: "Women and Catholicism were feared as both intrinsically idolatrous, superstition and carnal, if not also physically disgusting" (Marotti, 2005).

5. Botonaki's (1999, 2004) work offers further illumination of the insistence on self-examination and the regulation of conduct, as well as the

possibility of new means of power and effectiveness, as it pertains to women. In her analysis, autobiographical spaces, that were neither entirely private nor public, were "disclosing enclosures" that enabled new forms of assertive femininity to arise; women could be as confident of scripture and equal to men in their capacity to understand God's will. Maternity could represent due spiritual stewardship and not just due care of the young or domestic management per se.

6. There are interesting parallels between the stories of minister John White and diarist Samuel Ward, with respect to the universities that had trained them: Oxford and Cambridge respectively. Both universities were to train the "reaching ministry", although Cambridge was said to be more successful in this regard. Protestant militancy in both universities countered the influence and threat of Catholic Fellows.

Chapter Six

1. Lombroso's ideas are easy to dismiss from a modern viewpoint, perhaps as amusing misconception and conservative pseudoscience; he was certainly not unopposed by other criminologists on the European scene during his time (Nye, 1976). However, it is important to contextualise his ideas of the "born criminal", as Pick (1986) has done, for example, with respect to Italian post-unification politics, where Lombroso was on the side of secular and progressive forces. He was against the interests of a stagnant aristocracy as much as the criminal population, due, in his view, to their respective resistance to modernity. Pick links the concept of the born criminal to racial/regional concerns, whereby, in the "making of Italy", the South became the backward Other to the more advanced North.

2. The idea of degeneracy was applied in the biological sciences, with preoccupations around the definition of "species" and measurement closely tied to racial metaphors; Morel's "species" was easily translated as "races". To this extent degeneracy was a generative signifier, able to travel across disciplinary and social spaces and contributing to racial, class, and nationalistic concerns. With the abolition of slavery and industrialisation, new anxieties emerged, centred on the movement of people, the mixing of races, and the possibility of class migration: "Racial biology, in short, by the mid-nineteenth century was a science of boundaries between groups and the degeneration that threatened when those boundaries were transgressed" (Stepan, 1985). With the eugenic projects later in that century and into the early twentieth century, the biomedical language changed to that of "stock" and "inferior pedigree" (Nye, 1993; Rose, 1985). Mort (1987) clarifies the eugenic

emphasis on racial health and the need to "purify" conditions at their source. He makes the important point however, that eugenics never achieved the hegemony sought by its proponents, with the medical profession deeply divided in its views.

3. Le Bon's seminal contribution to crowd psychology is explored by Nye (1975), who places him within the political context of revolutionary, post-Commune France. Of particular interest is Nye's skilful analysis of the centrality of racial doctrines to the embryonic science of group psychology. Pick (1989) also identifies a misogynistic strand in Le Bon's theory, with woman as symbolic of instability, suggestibility, and emotion, the very qualities he ascribes to crowds. Laclau (2005) offers an interesting analysis of their "denigration of the masses" and the framing of, "their discourses in stock and sterile dichotomies—individual/crowd, rational/irrational, normal/pathological" (p. 40).

4. Terms such as "habitual (or common) drunkenness", "dipsomania", and "inebriety"—the latter used to include all substances, as in "opium inebriety"—were used widely. Inebriety tended to replace common drunkenness as the century moved on, endorsed by the first generation of addiction specialists and the creation of asylums for inebriety. The term "alcoholism" was coined only in the mid-century (White, 1998). "Addict" has a less clear provenance, but was in growing use by the beginning of the twentieth century, associated as it was to narcotics and criminality in particular (Parsinnen, 1983).

5. Nineeteenth-century temperance movements are a remarkable testimony to the power of new social groups, who in a variety of ways redefined the problem of habitual drunkenness and constructed brave progammes of social and personal reform. Temperance movements are easily stereotyped, but in reality were diverse; such movements were sites of resistance to unregulated commercialism and offered alternative spaces within which individuals were supported to change. Augst's (2007) paper offers valuable insights into the iconographic and discursive resources of the Washingtonians, one of the best known American temperance groups, and what he calls their "networks of experience, institutional literacies and the drunkard"s confession" (p. 298). He argues that such groups tried to counter the very exclusions from society their members experienced, by establishing alternative associations.

6. The range of terms included "contrary sexual desire", "inverts" (the term used by the major sexologists and by Freud), "urnings" (used by Ulrichs, the early champion of homosexual emancipation in Germany; Robb, 2003) as well as, in other contexts, acts that could not be named and "crimes against nature". On the legal side, 1885 saw (further) criminalisation in Britain of all acts of "gross indecency" between

men; efforts to extend criminalisation to acts between women failed in England in 1921, with some MP's arguing that silence on the subject was preferable to publicising its existence (Lesbian History Group, 1989; Showalter, 1986)!

Chapter Seven

1. Allegedly Stevenson's wife woke him, in the middle of what she thought was one of his common nightmares. "Why did you wake me", he complained, "I was dreaming a fine bogey tale" (quoted in Callow, 2001, p. 201). Stevenson sets great store by the creativity of dreams, the "inner theatre", because of their congruence with his idea of man's double nature.

2. It is interesting to read Stevenson's novel alongside Freud's (1919b) erudite psychoanalytic/literary study, *The Uncanny (Das Unheimliche)*, where he traces various meanings around the word *unheimliche*: for example, the "uncomfortable", "sinister", "frightening", "un homely", "alien". There he makes reference to the theme of the "double", things of terror, sometimes involving mirrors or shadows. Freud speculates in the essay on unconscious re-enactments, or the "compulsion to repeat". It should be noted that Freud became a corresponding member of the Society for Psychical Research, which was committed to objective investigation into the occult, haunted houses and so on (Pick, 1989). Grotstein (1999) provides an updated psychoanalytic review of such phenomena and notes the dependence of psychoanalysis on eighteenth and nineteenth-century preoccupations with the alter ego. He uses expressions such as "monsters", "demons", phantoms", and "rogue subjects" to depict such states of splitting.

3. Arata (1996, p. 45) explores how biographical contexts shed light on the motivations behind *Jekyll and Hyde*. Stevenson was highly critical of the professionalisation of writing and compares the process to one of prostitution; caught by his own fame, writing the novella "was in part an expression of self-loathing for what Stevenson perceived as the betrayal of his former ideals".

4. Rankin (1987) informs us that the Special Branch of the Metropolitan Police was set up in the 1880s to counter "Fenian outrages".

Chapter Eight

1. While group analysts have addressed dialogue, few, to my knowledge, have commented on narrative. Giancarlo Dimaggio's (e.g., Dimaggio, Salvatore & Azzara, 2003) extensive research in Italy, using cognitive

constructionism and the paradigm of "dialogical self" might be group-analytically influenced, but he does not refer to it in any explicit way (Dimaggio, personal communication). Cox's (Cox & Theilgaard, 1994) book on Shakespeare does, however, contain specific and illuminating reference to narrative concepts.

2. Rom Harré (1983) uses the evocative notion of "identity projects" to signify a trajectory within which the individual carves out a sense of uniqueness.

Chapter Nine

1. In his 1949 New York lecture, Foulkes (1949, p. 64) linked the spirit of group analysis with "concepts of a democratic way of life and for good world citizenship". Hopper (2000) argues that the formation of the "citizen" entails a new model of maturity, beyond that of traditional psychoanalytic theorisation, a view supported by Nitzgen (2001) in his review.

2. The notion of a *regulative ideal* refers to an idea that cannot be realised, but is regulative in so far as it guides or mediates behaviour; regulative ideals inspire, mobilise, and serve as yardsticks to measure progress. Ideals, of whatever nature, have a shadow side, in what they repress or in the alternatives they exclude, those negatives or anti-ideals in a given society.

3. Robert Wuthnow (1994) researches the rapid spread of small-group membership in modern America, which he interprets in terms of a search for bearings and community affiliation, opportunities to make sense of one's life and "journey". He estimates that around forty per cent of Americans (75 million) belong to at least one small group that meets regularly, including church groups, hobby groups, recovery groups, political groups. Such research is a helpful corrective to the simplistic idea that we are more isolated and alienated than ever.

4. Tully's (1995) analysis of the politics of cultural difference extends the meaning of the cultural from ethnicity alone and argues that we all "cross cultures" in different ways; he deconstructs the idea of cultures as homogeneous, colliding entities.

REFERENCES

Almond, R. (2003). The holding function of theory. *Journal of the American Psychoanalytic Association, 51*: 130–153.

Althusser, L. (1971). Ideology and ideological state apparatuses. In: *Lenin and Philosophy and Other Essays*. London: New Left Books.

Amussen, S. (1985). Gender, family and the social order, 1560–1725. In: A. Fletcher & J. Stevenson (Eds.), *Order and Disorder in Early Modern England*. Cambridge: Cambridge University Press.

Anderson, B. (1981). *Imagined Communities*. London: Verso.

Angus, L., & McLeod, J. (2004). Self-multiplicity and narrative expression in psychotherapy. In: H. Hermans & G. Dimaggio (Eds.), *The Dialogical Self in Psychotherapy* (Chapter 5). London, Routledge.

Anthony, J. (1983). The group analytic circle and its ambient network. In: M. Pines (Ed.), *The Evolution of Group Analysis*. London: Routledge and Kegan Paul.

Appleby, L. (2007). *Breaking Down Barriers: Clinical Case for Change*. London: Department of Health.

Arata, S. (1996). *Fictions of Loss in the Victorian Fin de Siècle*. Cambridge: Cambridge University Press.

Aristotle (1997). *Poetics*. New York: Dover.

Arlow, J. (1995). Stilted listening: psychoanalysis as discourse. *Psychoanalytic Quarterly, 64*: 215–233.

Arnold, K., & Atwood. G. (2000). Nietzsche's madness. *Psychoanalytic Review, 87*: 651–698.

Aron, L. (1996). *A Meeting of Minds: Mutuality in Psychoanalysis*. Hillsdale, NJ: Analytic Press.

Atkinson, P. (1997). Narrative turn or blind alley? *Qualitative Health Research, 7*: 325–344.

Augst, T. (2007). Temperance, mass culture and the romance of experience. *American Literary History, 19*: 297–323.

Bacal, H. (1998). Notes on optimal responsiveness in the group process. In: I. Harwood & M. Pines (Eds.), *Self Experiences in Group*. London: Jessica Kingsley.

Bachelard, G. (1964). *The Poetics of Space* (Trans. M. Jolas). Massachusetts, Beacon Press.

Bakhtin, M. (1981). *The Dialogic Imagination. Four Essays*. Texas: University of Texas Press.

Balint, M. (1968). *The Basic Fault: Therapeutic Aspects of Regression*. New York: Bruner/Mazel.

Barrows, S. (1981). *Distorting Mirrors: Visions of the Crowd in Late Nineteenth-century France*. New Haven, CT: Yale University Press.

Barthold, L. (2010). *Gadamer's Dialectical Hermeneutics*. Lexington, KY: Lexington Books.

Basch, M. (1983). Empathic understanding; a review of the concept and some theoretical considerations. *Journal of the American Psychoanalytic Association, 31*: 101–126.

Bauman, Z. (1998). Allosemitism: premodern, modern, postmodern. In: B. Cheyette & L. Marcus (Eds.), *Modernity, Culture and "the Jew"*. California: Stanford University Press.

Beck, U. (1992). *Risk Society: Towards a New Modernity* (Trans. M. Ritter). London: Sage.

Behr, H., & Hearst, L. (2005). *Group Analytic Psychotherapy: A Meeting of Minds*. London: Wiley-Blackwell.

Bejczy, I. (1997). Tolerantia: a medieval concept. *Journal of the History of Ideas, 58*: 365–384.

Berger, P. (1969). *Sacred Canopy: Elements of a Sociological Theory of Religion*. London: Faber & Faber.

Bergmann, M. (1997). The historical roots of psychoanalytic orthodoxy. *International Journal of Psychoanalysis, 78*: 69–89.

Berkovitch, S. (1975). *The Puritan Origins of the American Self*. New Haven, CT: Yale University Press.

Berridge, V., & Edwards, G. (1981). *Opium and the People: Opiate Use in Nineteenth-century England*. London: Allen Lane.

Biggs, R. (1996). "Many reasons why": witchcraft and the problem of multiple explanations. In: J. Barry, M. Hester & and G. Roberts (Eds.), *Witchcraft in Early Modern Europe*. Cambridge: Cambridge University Press.

Bildhauer, B., & Mills, R. (Eds.) (2003). *The Monstrous Middles Ages*. Cardiff: University of Wales Press.

Bion, W. R. (1967). *Second Thoughts*. London: Maresfield.

Bland, L., & Doan, L. (Eds.) (1988). *Sexology in Culture: Labelling Bodies and Desires*. Cambridge: Polity Press.

Bollas, C. (1987). *The Shadow of the Object: the Psychoanalysis of the Unthought Known*. London: Free Association Books.

Bollas, C. (1993). An interview with Christopher Bollas. *Psychoanalytic Dailgoues, 3*: 401–430.

Bostridge, I. (1996). Witchcraft repealed. In: J. Barry, M. Hester & G. Roberts (Eds.), *Witchcraft in Early Modern Europe* (Chapter 12). Cambridge: Cambridge University Press.

Botonaki, E. (1999). Seventeenth-century Englishwomen's spiritual diaries: self examination, covenanting, and account keeping. *Sixteenth Century Journal, 30*: 3–21.

Botonaki, E. (2004). *Seventeenth-century Englishwoman's Autobiographical Writings: Enclosing Disclosures*. New York: Edwin Mellor Press.

Boureau, A. (2006). *Satan and the Heretic: The Birth of Demonology in the Medieval West* (Trans. T. Fagan). Chicago: University of Chicago Press.

Brady, S. (2005). *Masculinity and Male Homosexuality in Britain, 1861–1913*. Basingstoke: Palgrave/McMillan.

Brauner, S. (1995). *Fearless Wives and Frightened Shrews: The Construction of the Witch in Early Modern Germany*. Amherst, MA: University of Massachusetts Press.

Brennan, M. (1997). *The Gothic Psyche: Disintegration and Growth in Nineteenth-Century English Literature*. Columbia: Camden House.

Breuer, J., & Freud, S. (1895). *Studies in Hysteria. S. E., 2*. London: Hogarth Press (1951).

Brickell, C. (2006). Sexology, the homo/hetero binary and the complexities of male sexual history. *Sexualities, 9*: 423–447.

Broedel, H. P. (2003). *The Malleus Maleficarum and the Construction of Witchcraft*. Manchester: Manchester University Press.

Brown, D. (1979). Some reflections on Bion's basic assumptions from a group-analytic viewpoint. *Group Analysis, 12*: 203–210.

Brown, D. (1986). Dialogue for change. *Group Analysis, 19*: 25–38.

Brown, D. (2001). A contribution to the understanding of the social unconscious. *Group Analysis, 34*: 29–38.

Bruner, J. (1994). The "Remembered Self". In: U. Neisser & R. Fivush (Eds.), *The Remembering Self: Construction and Accuracy in the Self-Narrative* (Chapter 2). Boston, MA: Cambridge University Press.

Bruner, J. (2002). *Making Stories: Law, Literature, Life*. Cambridge, MA: Harvard University Press.

Burrow, J. (2007). *A History of Histories*. London: Penguin.

Burrows, S. (1981). *Distorting Mirrors; Visions of the Crowd in Late Nineteenth-century France*. New Haven, CT: Yale University Press.

Butler, J. (1993). *Bodies that Matter: On the Discursive Limits of Sex*. London: Routledge.

Butler, J. (1999). *Gender Trouble: Feminism and the Subversion of Identity*. London: Routledge.

Butler, J. (2000). Restaging the universal; hegemony and the limits of formalism. In: J. Butler, E. Laclau & S. Žižek, *Contingency, Hegemony, Universality: Contemporary Dialogues on the Left* (Chapter 1). London, Verso.

Butler, L. (2006). The discourse of (in) temperance in R. S. Stevenson's *The Strange Case of Jekyll and Hyde*. *Romanticism on the Net: The Gothic Issue, 44*.

Bynum, W. (1984). Alcoholism and degeneration in nineteenth-century European medicine and psychiatry. *British Journal of Addiction, 79*: 59–70.

Callow, P. (2001). *Louis: A Life of Robert Louis Stevenson*. London: Constable.

Capp, B. (1996). Separate Domains? Women and Authority in Early Modern EnglandIn: P. Griffiths, A. Fox & S. Hindle (Eds.), *The Experience of Authority in Early Modern England* (Chapter 4). Basingstoke: Macmillan.

Carlson, E. (1985). Medicine and degeneration; theory and praxis. In: F. Chamberlain & S. Gilman (Eds.), *Degeneration: The Dark Side of Progress*. New York: Columbia University Press.

Carlson, E. (2001). *The Unfit: A History of a Bad Idea*. New York: Cold Spring Harbour Laboratory Press.

Carr, E. H. (1987). *What is History?* London: Penguin.

Chamberlain, F., & Gilman, S. (Eds.) (1985). *Degeneration: The Dark Side of Progress*. New York: Columbia University Press.

Classen, C. (2005). The witch's senses. In: D. Howes (Ed.), *Empire of the Senses: the Sensual Culture Reader* (Chapter 4). Oxford: Berg.

Cohen, J. (Ed.) (1996). *Monster Theory: Reading Culture*. Minneapolis: University of Minnesota Press.

Cohn, H. (1996). The philosophy of S. H. Foulkes: Existential-phenomenological aspects of group analysis. *Group Analysis, 29*: 287–302.

Cohn, H. (1997). *Existential Thought and Therapeutic Practice*. London: Sage.

Collinson, P. (2003). *The Reformation*. London: Phoenix.

Cook, M. (2003). *London and the Culture of Homosexuality, 1885–1914*. Cambridge: Cambridge University Press.

Cooley, C. H. (1907). Social consciousness. *Publications of the American Sociological Society, 1:* 97–109.

Cooper, R. (1996). Philosophy and madness: Sass's Paradoxes of Delusion. *Group Analysis, 29:* 369–384.

Coplestone, F. (1965). *A History of Philosophy Volume 7, Part 2.* New York: Image Books.

Cousins, M. (1978). The logic of deconstruction. *Oxford Literary Review, 3:* 70–77.

Cousins, M., & Hussein, A. (1984). *Michael Foucault.* London: Macmillan.

Cox, M., & Theilgaard, A. (1994). *Shakespeare as Prompter: The Amending Imagination and the Therapeutic Process.* London: Jessica Kingsley.

Critchely, S. (2008). *The Book of Dead Philosophers.* London: Granta.

Crothers, T. D. (1902). *Morphinism and Narcomanias from other Drugs; their Etiology, Treatment and Medico-legal Relations.* Philadelphia & London: W. B. Saunders and Co.

CSIP (Care Services Improvement Partnership) (2005). *Everybody's Business. Securing Mental Health for Older Adults.* London: CSIP.

Dahlin, O. (1991). "Human understanding" in psychoanalysis and group analysis. *Group Analysis, 24:* 21–40.

Dalal, F. (1998). *Taking the Group Seriously.* London: Jessica Kinsley.

Dalal, F. (2001). The social unconscious; a post-Foulksean perspective. *Group Analysis, 34:* 539–555.

Dalal, F. (2002). *Race, Colour and the Process of Racialization.* Hove: Brunner-Routledge.

Danto, A. (1980). *Nietzsche as Philosopher.* New York: Columbia University Press.

Davidson, G. (1995). Sexuality and the degenerate body in Stevenson's *The Strange case of Dr Jekyll and Mr Hyde. Australian Victorian Studies Annual,* 1: 31–40.

De Maré, P. B. (1972). *Perspectives on Group Psychotherapy.* London: Allen and Unwin.

Derrida, J. (1976). *Of Grammatology* (Trans. G. Spivak). Baltimore, MD: John Hopkins University Press.

Derrida, J. (1981). *Positions* (Trans. A. Bass). Chicargo: University of Chicago Press.

Dewey, J. (1958). *Experience and Nature.* New York: Dover.

Dewey, J. (1977a). The influence of Darwinism on philosophy. In: D. Sidorsky (Ed.), *John Dewey: The Essential Writings.* New York: HarperTorchbooks.

Dewey, J. (1977b). The need for recovery in philosophy. In: D. Sidorsky (Ed.), *John Dewey: The Essential Writings.* New York: HarperTorchbooks.

Dewey, J. (1977c). The pattern and structure of inquiry. In: D. Sidorsky (Ed.), *John Dewey: The Essential Writings*. New York: HarperTorchbooks.

Dewey, J. (1988). Creative democracy: the task before us. In: J. A. Boydston (Ed.), *The Later Works of John Dewey, Volume 14*. Carbondale, IL: Southern Illinois University Press.

Diamond, N. (1996). Can we speak of internal and external reality? *Group Analysis, 29*: 303–317.

Dickens, C. (2009). *The Mystery of Edwin Drood*. London: Vintage.

Dimaggio, G., & Semerari, A. (2001). Psychopathological narrative forms. *Journal of Constructivist Psychology, 14*: 1–23.

Dimaggio, G., Salvatore, G., & Azzara, C. (2003). Rewriting self-narratives; the therapeutic process. *Journal of Constructivist Psychology, 16*: 155–181.

Dinshaw, C. (1999). *Getting Medieval: Sexualities and Communities, Pre- and PostModern*. Durham, NC: Duke University Press.

Donnelly, M. (1983). *Managing the Mind: A Study of Medical Psychology in Early Nineteenth-century Britain*. London: Tavistock.

Douglas, M. (1966). *Purity and Danger*. London: Ark.

Douglas, M. (1970). *Natural Symbols: Explorations in Cosmologies*. London: Routledge.

Durston, C., & Eales, J. (1996). The Puritan ethos, 1560–1700. In: C. Durston & J. Eales (Eds.), *The Culture of English Puritanism, 1560–1700*. London: Palgrave Macmillan.

Eales, J. (1998). *Women in Early Modern England, 1500–1700*. London: UCL Press.

Eaton, J. (1998). Gadamer: psychotherapy as conversation. *European Journal of Psychotherapy, Counselling and Health, 1*: 421–433.

Eigen, J. (2003). *Unconscious Crime: Mental Absence and Criminal Responsibility in Victorian London*. Baltimore, MD: John Hopkins University Press.

Eisold, K. (1997). Freud as a leader: the early years of the Viennese society. *International Journal of Psychoanalysis, 78*: 59–103.

Elias, N. (1978). *The Civilising Process: the History of Manners*. Oxford: Basil Blackwell.

Elias, N. (1979). Conversation with Norbert Elias: Interviewed by Dennis Brown. *Group Analysis, 30*: 515–524.

Elias, N. (1982). *The Civilising Process: State Formation and Civilisation*. Oxford: Basil Blackwell.

Elliot, D. (1999). *Fallen Bodies: Pollution, Sexuality and Demonology in the Middle Ages*. Philadelphia: University of Pennsylvania Press.

Elliot, D. (2007). Women in love. In: B. Hanawalt & A. Grotans (Eds.), *Living Dangerouly: On the Margins in Medieval and Early Modern Europe* (Chapter 3). Notre Dame, IN: University of Notre Dame Press.

Erickson, E. (1950). *Childhood and Society*. New York: Norton.

Ezriel, H. (1950). A psychoanalytic approach to group treatment. *British Journal of Medical Psychology, 23*: 59–74.

Ezriel, H. (1952). Notes on psychoanalytic group therapy: interpretation and research. *Psychiatry, 15*: 119–126.

Febvre, L. (1973). Sense and history; how to reconstitute the emotional life of the past. In: P. Burke (Ed.), K. Folca (Trans.), *A New Kind of History: From the Writings of Febvre*. New York: Harper Row.

Fishman, S. (2007). *John Dewey and the Philosophy and Practice of Hope*. Urbana-Champaign, IL: University of Illinois Press.

Fivush, R. (2003). The silenced self; constructing self from memories spoken and unspoken. In: D. Beike, J. Lampinen & D. Behrend (Eds.), *The Self and Memory* (Chapter 1). Kentucky: Psychology Press.

Fosshage, J. (1994). Towards re-conceptualising transference: theoretical and clinical considerations. *International Journal of Psychoanalysis, 75*: 265–280.

Foucault, M. (1965). *Madness and Civilization: A History of Insanity in the Age of Reason*. New York: Vintage.

Foucault, M. (1977). *Discipline and Punish: The Birth of the prison*. London: Allen Lane.

Foucault, M. (1978a). About the concept of the "dangerous individual" in 19th-century legal psychiatry. *International Journal of Law and Psychiatry, 1*: 1–18.

Foucault, M. (1978b). *The History of Sexuality, Volume 1*. London: Allen Lane.

Foulkes, S. H. (1949). Concerning leadership in group-analytic psychotherapy. In: *Therapeutic Group Analysis* (Chapter 4). London: Allen and Unwin.

Foulkes, S. H. (1964). *Therapeutic Group Analysis*. London: Allen and Unwin.

Foulkes, S. H. (1966). Some basic concepts in group psychotherapy. In: *Selected Papers* (Chapter 15). London: Karnac, 1990.

Foulkes, S. H. (1968). Group dynamic processes and group analysis. In: *Selected Papers* (Chapter 18). London: Karnac, 1990.

Foulkes, S. H. (1971). Access to unconscious processes in the group-analytic group. In: *Selected Papers* (Chapter 21). London: Karnac, 1990.

Foulkes, S. H. (1973). The group as a matrix of the individual's mental life. In: *Selected Papers* (Chapter 22). London: Karnac, 1990.

Foulkes, S. H. (1974). My philosophy in psychotherapy. In: *Selected Papers*. London, Karnac, 1990.

Foulkes, S. H. (1975a). *Group Analytic Psychotherapy: Methods and Principles*. London, Maresfield, 1986.

Foulkes, S. H. (1975b). *Problems of the large group*. In: Selected Papers. London: Karnac, 1990.

Foulkes, S. H. (1975c). *The leader in the group*. In: Selected Papers (Chapter 27). London: Karnac, 1990.

Foulkes, S. H. (2003). Mind. *Group Analysis, 36*: 315–321.

Foulkes, S. H., & Anthony, E. J. (1957). *Group Psychotherapy: The Psychoanalytic Approach*. London: Penguin Books.

Foxcroft, L. (2007). *The Making of Addiction: The "Use and Abuse" of Opium in Nineteenth-Century Britain*. Aldershot: Ashgate.

Freud, S. (1905). *Fragment of an Analysis of a Case of Hysteria. S. E., 7*. London: Hogarth.

Freud, S. (1909). *Notes upon a Case of Obsessional Neurosis. S. E., 10*. London: Hogarth.

Freud, S. (1912). *Recommendations to Physicians practicing psychoanalysis. S. E., 12*. London: Hogarth.

Freud, S. (1919a). *Lines of advance in psycho-analytic therapy. S. E., 17*. London: Hogarth.

Freud, S. (1919b). The *"Uncanny"*. *S. E., 17*. London: Hogarth.

Freud, S. (1923a). *Two Encyclopaedia Articles. S. E., 18*. London: Hogarth.

Freud, S. (1923b). *Group Psychology and the Analysis of the Ego. S. E., 18*. London: Hogarth.

Freud, S. (1933). *New Introductory Lectures on Psychoanalysis. S. E., 22*. London: Hogarth.

Frosch, S. (1997). *For and Against Psychoanalysis*. London: Routledge.

Gadamer, H. -G. (1966). The universality of the hermeneutical problem. In: D. Linge (Ed. & Trans.), *Philosophical Hermeneutics*. Berkeley, CA: University of California Press.

Gadamer, H. -G. (1975). *Truth and Method*. (Second edition, Trans. J. Weisheimer & D. Marshall). London: Sheed and Ward.

Gadamer, H. -G, (1985). *Philosophical Apprenticeships*. Cambridge, MA: The MIT Press.

Gadamer, H. -G. (1991). A conflict of interpretations: debate with Hans-Georg Gadamer. In: M. J. Valdés (Ed.), *A Ricoeur Reader: Reflection and Imagination*. Toronto: University of Toronto Press.

Gadamer, H. -G (1995). On the truth of the word. In: L. Schmidt (Ed.), *The Specter of Relativism: Truth, Dialogue and Phronesis in Philosophical Hermeneutics*. Evanston, IL: Northwest University Press.

Gadamer, H. -G. (2006). *A Century of Philosophy: Hans Georg Gadamer in Conversation with Ricardo Dottori* (Trans. S. Koepke). New York: Continuum.

Gergen, K. (1994). Mind, text and society; self-memory in a social context. In: U. Neisser & R. Fivush (Eds.), *The Remembering Self: Construction and Accuracy in the Self-narrative* (Chapter 7). Cambridge: Cambridge University Press.

Giddens, A. (1991). *Modernity and Self-Identity: Self and Society in the Late Modern Age*. Stanford, CA: Stanford University Press.

Giddens, A. (1992). *The Transformation of Intimacy*. Cambridge: Polity.

Giddens, A. (1998). *The Third Way: The Renewal of Social Democracy*. Cambridge: Polity.

Giddens, A., & Pierson, C. (1998). *Conversations with Anthony Giddens*. Palo Alto, CA: Stanford University Press.

Gilbert, P. K. (2007). *The Citizen's Body; Desire, Health, and the Social in Victorian England*. Columbus: Ohio State University Press.

Gilchrist, R. (2000). Unsexing the body; the interior sexuality of medieval religious women. In: R. Schmidt & B. Voss (Eds.), *Archaeologies of Sexuality* (Chapter 4). New York: Routledge.

Gill, M. (1982). Psychoanalysis and psychotherapy: A revision. *International Review of Psychoanalysis, 11*: 161–179.

Gilman, S. (1985). *Difference and Pathology: Stereotypes of Sex, Race and Madness*. New York: Cornell University Press.

Goldberg, A. (2000). Postmodern psychoanalysis. *International Journal of Psychoanalysis, 82*: 123–128.

Goldberg, A. (2002). American pragmatism and American psychoanalysis. *Psychoanalytic Quarterly, LXXXI*: 235–250.

Goldberg, A. (2007). *Moral Stealth: How "Correct Behaviour" insinuates itself into Psychotherapeutic Practice*. Chicago: University of Chicago Press.

Gordon, R. (1991). Intersubjectivity and the efficacy of group analysis. *Group Analysis, 24*: 41–51.

Goodman, N. (1978). *Ways of Worldmaking*. Indiana: Hackett.

Gramsci, A. (1985). *Selections from Cultural Writings*. London: Lawrence & Wishart.

Granier, J. (1985a). Nietzsche's concept of chaos. In: D. Allison (Ed.), *The New Nietzsche*. Cambridge, MA: MIT Press.

Granier, J. (1985b). Perspectivism and interpretation. In: D. Allison (Ed.), *The New Nietzsche*. Cambridge, MA: MIT Press.

Greenberg, J. (1999a). The analysts' participation: a new look. *Journal of the American Psychoanalytic Association, 49*: 383–391.

Greenberg, J. (1999b). Analytic authority and analytic restraint. *Contemporary Psychoanalysis, 35*: 25–41.

Greenblatt, S. (1980). *Renaissance Self-Fashioning: From More to Shakespeare*. Chicago: University of Chicago Press.

Greensdale, W. (1994). *Degeneration, Culture and the Novel, 1880–1994*. Cambridge: Cambridge University Press.

Grotstein, J. (1999). The alter ego and *déjà vu* phenomena. In: J. Rowan & M. Cooper (Eds.), *The Plural Self*. New York: Sage.

Group Analysis Journal (1998). Special issue on philosophy.

Habermas, J. (2004). *The Post-national Constellation* (Trans. M. Pensky). Cambridge: Polity.

Hacking, I. (1991). Double consciousness in Britain, 1815–1875. *Dissociation*, 4: 134–146.

Haggerty, G. (2006). *Queer Gothic*. Urbana: University of Illinois Press.

Haigh, C. (1995). The recent historiography of the English Reformation. In: M. Todd (Ed.), *Reformation to Revolution: Politics and Religion in Early Modern England* (Chapter 1). London: Routledge.

Hales, S., & Welshon, R. (2000). *Nietzsche's Perspectivism*. Urbana: University of Illinois Press.

Hall, S. (1996). Introduction: who needs identity? In: S. Hall & P. Du Gay (Eds.), *Questions of Cultural Identity*. London: Sage.

Harwood, I., & Pines, M. (Eds.) (1998). *Self Experiences in Group*. London: Jessica Kingsley.

Harré, R. (1983). *Personal Being: A Theory for Individual Psychology*. Oxford: Blackwell.

Harrison, R. P. (2003). *The Dominion of the Dead*. Chicago & London: University of Chicago Press.

Hatab, L. (1999). *A Nieztschean Defense of Democracy: Experiments in Postmodern Politics*. New York: Open Court.

Hausman, C. (1999). Evolutionary realism and Charles Pierce's pragmatism. In: S. B. Rosenthal, C. R. Hausman & D. R. Anderson (Eds.) *Classical American Pragmatism: Its Contemporary Vitality* (Chapter 13). Urbana: University of Illinois Press.

Hearst, L. (2000). *Power: Where Does It Reside in Group Analysis?* Unpublished talk.

Heath, S. (1986). Psychopathia sexualis: Stevenson's Strange Case. *Critical Inquiry, 28*: 93–108.

Heidegger, M. (1961). *An Introduction to Metaphysics*. New York: Doubleday Anchor.

Heidegger, M. (1962). *Being and Time* (Trans. J. Macquarrie & E. Robinson). London: SCM Press.

Held, D. (1993). From city states to a cosmopolitan order?I In: D. Held (Ed.), *Prospects for Democracy: North, South, East, West* (Chapter 1). Cambridge: Polity.

Hermans, H. (2003). The construction and reconstruction of a dialogical self. *Journal of Constructivist Psychology, 16*: 89–130.

Hester, M. (1992). *Lewd Women and Wicked Witches*. London: Routledge.

Hilderbrand, D. (2008). *Dewey: A Beginner's Guide*. Oxford: One World.

Hill, C. (1972). *The World Turned Upside Down*. London: Penguin.

Hill, C. (1990). *A Nation of Change and Novelty: RadicalPolitics, Religions and Literature in 17th Century England*. London: Routledge and Kegan Paul.

Hill, C. (1997). *Intellectual Origins of the English Revolution, Revisited*. Oxford: OUP.

Hirst, P. (1979). Althusser and the theory of ideology. In: *On law and Ideology*. London: Macmillan.

Hirst, P., & Woolley, P. (1981). *Social Relations and Human Attributes*. London: Routledge.

Hollingdale, R. (1995). Theories and innovations in Nietzsche; logic, theory of knowledge and metaphysics. In: P. Sedgwick (Ed.), *Nietzsche: A Critical Reader*. Oxford: Blackwell.

Hollingdale, R. (1996). The hero as outsider. In: B. Magnus & K. Higgins (Eds.), *The Cambridge Companion to Nietzsche*. Cambridge: Cambridge University Press.

Hoover, A. (1994). *Fredrick Nietzsche: His Life and Thought*. Westport, CT: Praeger.

Hopper, E. (2000). From objects to subjects to citizens: group analysis and the study of maturity. *Group Analysis, 15*: 29–35.

Hopper, E. (2003). *The Social Unconscious: Selected Papers*. London: Jessica Kingsley.

Hopper, E., & Weinberg, H. (2011). (Eds.). *The Social Unconscious in Persons, Groups and Societies: Volume 1: Mainly Theory*. London: Karnac.

Houlbrooke, R. (2000). The family and pastoral care. In: G. Evans (Ed.), *A History of Pastoral Care* (Chapter 15). Melbourne: Koorong Books.

Houlgate, S. (1986). *Hegel, Nietzsche and the Criticism of Metaphysics*. Cambridge: Cambridge University Press.

Hudson, I. (2005). Group analysis in later life. Unpublished talk given at 13th European Symposium on Group Analysis, Molde, Norway.

Hurley, K. (1996). *The Gothic Body: Sexuality, Materialism and Degeneration at the Fin De Siècle*. Cambridge: Cambridge University Press.

Hurley, K. (2002). British Gothic fiction, 1885–1930. In: J. Hoyle (Ed.), *The Cambridge Companion to Gothic Fiction*. Cambridge: Cambridge University Press.

Jackson, L. (1995). Witches, wives and mothers: witchcraft persecution and women's confessions in seventeenth-century England. *Women's History Review, 4*: 63–84.

James, W. (1902). *A Pluralistic Universe*. New York: Longmans, Green.

Jay, M. (2000). *Emperors of Dreams: Drugs in the Nineteenth Century*. Cambridge: Dedalus.

Johnson, P. (2000). *On Gadamer*. Belmont, CA: Wadsworth.

Jones, N. (2002). *The English Reformation: Religion and Cultural Adaptation.* Oxford: Blackwell.

Kantrowitz, J. (1986). The role of the patient–analyst "match" in the outcome of psychoanalysis. *The Annual of Psychoanalysis, 14:* 273–297.

Kanzer, M. (1983). Freud: the first psychoanalytic group leader. In: H. Kaplan & B. Sadock (Eds.), *Comprehensive Group Psychotherapy.* Baltimore: Williams & Williams.

Karant-Nunn, S. C., & Wiesner-Hanks, M. E. (Eds.) (2003). *Luther on Women: A Sourcebook.* Cambridge: Cambridge University Press.

Karras Mazo, R. (2005). *Sexuality in Medieval Europe: Doing unto Others.* London: Routledge.

Kearney, R. (2003). *Strangers, Gods and Monsters.* London: Routledge.

Keeble, N. H. (Compiler & Ed.) (1994). *The Cultural Identity of Seventeenth-Century Women: A Reader.* London: Routledge.

Kenny, A. (1985). *Wyclif.* Oxford: OUP.

Kerby, A. P. (1991). *Narrative and the Self.* London: Wiley.

Kidder, P. (2013). *Gadamer for Architects.* New York: Routledge.

Kirkwood, T. (1999). *Time of our Lives.* Oxford: OUPress.

Kofman, S. (1993). *Nietzsche and Metaphor.* London: Athlone.

Kohut, H. (1977). *Restoration of the Self.* New York: International University Press.

Kramer, H., & Sprengler, J. (1486). *Malleus Maleficarum* (Trans. Rev. M. Summers). London: Pushkin Press, 1928.

Krieken, R. van (1998). *Norbert Elias.* London: Routledge.

Kristeva, J. (1982). *Powers of Horror: An Essay on Abjection* (Tranl. L. Ruodiez). New York: Columbia University Press.

Kuriloff, E. (2013). *Contemporary Psychoanalysis and the Legacy of the Third Reich.* New York: Routledge.

Lachmann, F. (1986). Interpretation of psychological conflict and adversarial relationships: a self-psychological perspective. *Psychoanalytic Psychology, 3:* 341–355.

Laclau, E. (1990). *New Reflections on the Revolutions of our Times.* London: Verso.

Laclau, E. (2005). *On Populist Reason.* London: Verso.

Laclau, E., & Mouffe, C. (1985). *Hegemony and Socialist Strategy.* London: Verso.

Larner, C. (1981). *Enemies of God: The Witch-Hunt in Scotland.* Oxford: Blackwell.

Larner, C. (1984). *Witchcraft and Religion: The Politics of Popular Belief.* Oxford: Blackwell.

Lawn, C. (2006). *Gadamer: A Guide for the Perplexed.* London: Continuum.

LeBlanc, A. (2001). The origins of the concept of dissociation: Paul Janet, his nephew Pierre, and the problem of post-hypnotic suggestion. *History of Science, xxxix:* 57–69.

Leites, E. (1982). The duty to desire: love, friendship and sexuality in some puritan theories of marriage. *Journal of Social History, 13*: 383–408.

Lesbian History Group (1989). *Not a Passing Phase: Reclaiming Lesbian History, 1840–1985.* London: The Women's Press.

Levack, B. (1987). *Witchcraft in Early Modern Europe.* Harrow: Pearson Education.

Levine, H. (1978). The discovery of addiction: changing conceptions of habitual drunkenness in America. *Journal of Studies on Alcohol, 15*: 493–506.

Lewes, A. (1974). Psychopathic personality: a most elusive category. *Psychological Medicine, 4*: 133–140.

Lichtenberg, J. D. (1983). The influence of values and value judgments on the psychoanalytic encounter. *Psychoanalytic Inquiry, 3*: 647–664.

Linge, D. (1966). Introduction. In: H. -G. Gadamer, *Philosophical Hermeneutics* (Ed. and trans. D. Linge). Berkeley, CA: University of California Press.

MacAdams, D. (2008). Personal narratives and the life story. In: O. John, R. Robins & L. Pervin (Eds.), *Handbook of Personality: Theory and Research* (3rd Edition) (Chapter 8, pp. 242–264). New York: Guildford Press.

Mace, C. (1999). On putting psychoanalysis into Nietzschean perspective. *Philosophy, Psychiatry & Psychology, 6*: 187–189.

MacFarlane, A. (1970). *Witchcraft in Tudor and Stuart England.* London: Routledge and Kegan Paul.

Macherey, P. (1978). *A Theory of Literary Production.* London: Routledge and Kegan Paul.

MacIntyre, A. (1984). *After Virtue: A Study in Moral Theory.* Notre Dame, IN: University of Notre Dame Press.

Maglo, D. (2002). Kierkegaard and Foulkes; the role of group therapy in the treatment of despair. *Group Analysis, 35*: 27–42.

Malan, D. (1976). Group psychotherapy: a long term follow up study. *Archives of General Psychiatry, 33*: 1303–1315.

Mandrou, R. (1979). *From Humanism to Science: 1480–1700.* Hassocks: Harvester.

Marotti, A. (2005). *Religious Ideology and Cultural Fantasy: Catholic and Anticatholic Discourses in Early Modern England.* Indiana: University of Notre Dame Press.

McDougall, J. (1986). *Theatres of the Mind: Illusion of Truth on the Psychoanalytic Stage.* London: Free Association.

McGuiness, B. (1982). Freud and Wittgenstein. In: A. Levy, B. McGuiness, J. C. Nyiri, R. Rhees & G. Von Wright (Eds.), *Wittgenstein and His Times.* Oxford: Basil Blackwell.

McLaughlin, J. (1981). Transference, psychic reality and countertransference. *Psychoanalytic Quarterly, 20*: 639–664.

Mennell, S. (1997). A sociologist at the onset of group analysis: Norbert Elias and his sociology. *Group Analysis, 30*: 489–514.

Middelfort, E. (1972). *Witch-hunting in Southwestern Germany, 1562–1684.* Standford, CA: Stanford University Press.

Mighall, R. (1999). *A Geography of Victorian Gothic Fiction: Mapping History's Nightmares.* Oxford: OUP.

Miller, P., & Rose, N. (1994). On therapeutic authority: psychoanalytic expertise under advanced liberalism. *History of the Human Sciences, 7*: 29–64.

Mills, R. (2005). *Suspended Animation: Pain, Pleasure and Punishment in Medieval Culture.* London: Reaktion.

Mitchell, S. (1988). *Relational Concepts in Psychoanalysis.* Cambridge, MA: Harvard University Press.

Miyoshi, M. (1969). *The Divided Self: A Perspective on the Literature of the Victorians.* New York: New York University Press.

Monter, E. W. (1977). The pedestal and the stake: Courtly love and witchcraft. In: R. Bridenthal & C. Koonz (Eds.), *Becoming Visible: Women in European History* (Chapter 5). Boston: Houghton Mifflin.

Moore, R. (1987). *The Formation of a Persecuting Society.* Oxford: Basil Blackwell.

More, T. (1551). *Utopia.* London, Penguin Books, 1965.

Morris, L. (1994). *Dangerous Class: The Underclass and Social Citizenship.* London: Routledge.

Mort, F. (1987). *Dangerous Sexualities: Medico-moral politics in England since 1830* (2nd Ed). London: Routledge.

Nehamas, A. (1985) *Nietzsche: Life as Literature.* Cambridge, MA: Harvard University Press.

Neve, M. (1997). The influence of degeneration categories in 19th century psychiatry. In: Y. Kawakita, S. Sakai & Y. Isuka (Eds.), *History of Psychiatric Diagnoses.* Tokyo: Ishiyaku EuroAmerican Inc.

Nietzsche, F. (1881). *Daybreak: Thoughts on the Prejudices of Morality* (Trans. R. J. Hollingsdale). Cambridge: Cambridge University Press, 1997.

Nietzsche, F. (1882). *The Gay Science* (Trans. J. Nanchhop). Cambridge: Cambridge University Press, 2001.

Nietzsche, F. (1886). *Beyond Good and Evil* (Trans. R. J. Hollingsdale). London: Penguin Books, 1972.

Nietzsche, F. (1887). *The Genealogy of Morals* (Trans. W. Kaufmann). New York: Vintage.

Nietzsche, F. (1967a). *The Will to Power* (Trans. W. Kaufman & R. J. Hollingsdale). New York: Vintage.

Nietzsche, F. (1967b). Truth and falsehood in an extra-moral sense. In: W. Kaufman (Ed.), *The Portable Nieztsche.* New York: Viking.

NIMHE (2004). *The National Framework for Values in Mental Health*. London: NIMHE, The Salisbury Centre for Mental Health.

Nitsun, M. (1989). Early development; linking the individual and the group. *Group Analysis, 22*: 249–260.

Nitsun, M. (1996). *The Anti-Group: Destructive Forces in the Group and their Creative Potential*. London: Routledge.

Nitzgen, D. (2001). Training in democracy, democracy in training: notes on group analysis and democracy. *Group Analysis, 34*: 331–347.

Nixon, P. (1998). Foulkes, Elias and human figurations. *Group Analysis, 31*: 5–19.

Nye, R. (1975). *The Origins of Crowd Psychology: Gustave LeBon and the Crisis of Mass Democracy in the Third Republic*. London: Sage.

Nye, R. (1976). Heredity or milieu; the foundations of modern European criminological theory. *Isis, 67*: 335–355.

Nye, R. (1989). Sexual difference and male homosexuality in French medical discourse, 1830–1930. *Bulletin of the History of Medicine, 63*: 32–51.

Nye, R. (1993). The rise and fall of the eugenics empire: recent perspectives on the impact of biomedical thought in modern society. *The Historical Journal, 36*: 687–700.

O'Day, M. (1986). *The Debate on the English Reformation*. London: Methuen.

O'Neill, E. (1959). *Long Day's Journey into Night*. London: Jonathan Cape.

Orange, D. (1995). *Emotional Understanding: Studies in Psychoanalytic Epistemology*. New York: The Guilford Press.

Orange, D., Atwood, G., & Stolorow, R. (1997). *Working Intersubjectively*. Hillsdale, NJ: Analytic Press.

Ozment, S. (1980). *The Age of Reform, 1550–1550*. New Haven, CT: Yale University Press.

Ozment, S. (1983). *When Fathers Ruled: Family Life in Reformation Europe*. Cambridge, MA: Harvard University Press.

Ozment, S. (1999). *Flesh and Spirit: Private Life in Early Modern Germany*. London: Penguin.

Parkes, G. (1994). *Composing the Soul: Reading Nietszche's Psychology*. Chicago: University of Chicago Press.

Parssinen, T. (1983). *Secret Passions, Secret Remedies: Narcotic Drugs in British Society, 1820–1930*. Philadelphia: Institute for the Study of Social Issues Inc.

Pasquino, P. (1980). Criminology: the birth of a special savoir. *I and C, 7*: 17–32.

Pecheux, M. (1982). *Language, Semantics and Ideology*. New York: St. Martin's.

Pettegrew, J. (Ed.) (2000). *A Pragmatist's Progress? Richard Rorty and American Intellectual History*. New York: Rowman and Littlefield.

Pick, D. (1986). The faces of anarchy: Lombroso and the politics of criminal science in post-unification Italy. *History Workshop, 21*: 60–86.

Pick, D. (1989). *Faces of Degeneracy: A European Disorder, c. 1848–1918*. Cambridge: Cambridge University Press.

Pines, M. (1996a). Dialogue and selfhood: discovering connections. *Group Analysis, 29*: 327–341.

Pines, M. (1996b). Interpretation, dialogue, response: changing perspectives in psychoanalytic theory and technique. Unpublished talk.

Porter, R. (2003). *Flesh in the Age of Reason*. London: Penguin.

Punter, D. (1996a). *The Literature of Terror: The Gothic Tradition, Volume 1*. London: Longman.

Punter, D. (1996b). *The Literature of Terror: The Modern Gothic, Volume 2*. London: Longman.

Punter, D., & Byron, G. (2006). *The Gothic*. Oxford: Blackwell.

Purkiss, D. (1996). *The Witch in History: Early Modern and Twentieth-century Representations*. London: Routledge.

Puterbaugh, P. (2000). "Your selfe be judge and answer your self": formation of a Protestant identity in *A conference betwixt a mother a devout Recusant and Her sonne a Zealous Protestant*. *Sixteenth Century Journal, 31*: 419–431.

Quinodoz, D. (2009). *Growing Old: A Journey of Self-Discovery*. London: Routledge.

Rankin, N. (1987). *Deadman's Chest: Travels after Robert Louis Stevenson*. London: Phoenix.

Reed, M. (2001). Historicising inversion: or, how to make a homosexual. *History of the Human Sciences, 14*: 1–29.

Rey, H. (1988). That which patients bring to analysis. *International Journal of Psychoanalysis, 69*: 457–470.

Ricoeur, P. (1970). *Freud and Philosophy: An Essay on Interpretation* (Trans. D. Savage). New Haven, CT: Yale University Press.

Ricoeur, P. (2004a). Myth as the bearer of possible worlds. In: R. Kearney, *On Paul Ricoeur: The Owl of Minerva* (Dialogue 1). Aldershot: Ashgate.

Ricoeur, P. (2004b). The creativity of language. In: R. Kearney, *On Paul Ricoeur: The Owl of Minerva* (Dialogue 1). Aldershot: Ashgate.

Roazen, P. (1971). *Freud and his Followers*. London: Penguin Books.

Robb, G. (2003). *Strangers: Homosexual Love in the Nineenth Century*. Oxford: Picador.

Roper, L. (1989). *The Holy Household: Women and Morals in Reformation Augsburg*. Oxford: Clarendon.

Roper, L. (1994). *Oedipus and the Devil: Witchcraft, Sexuality and Religion in Early Modern Europe*. London: Routledge.

Roper, L. (2004). *Witch Craze: Women and Evil in Baroque Germany*. New Haven, CT: Yale University Press.

Rorty, R. (1980). *Philosophy and the Mirror of Nature*. Oxford: Blackwell.

Rorty, R. (1982). *Consequences of Pragmatism*. Minnesota: University of Minnesota Press.

Rorty, R. (1989). *Contingency, Irony, and Solidarity*. Cambridge: Cambridge University Press.

Rorty, R. (1999). *Philosophy and Social Hope*. London: Penguin.

Rorty, R. (2000). Pragmatism. *International Journal of Psychoanalysis, 81*: 819–823.

Rorty, R. (2006). *Take care of freedom and truth will take care of itself. Interviews with Richard Rorty* (Ed. E. Mendieta). Stanford, CA: University of Stanford Press.

Rose, N. (1985). *The Psychological Complex: Psychology, Politics and Society in England, 1869–1939*. London: Routledge & Kegan Paul.

Rose, N. (1990). *Governing the Soul: The Shaping of the Private Self*. London: Routledge.

Rose, N. (1992). Engineering the human soul: analysing psychological expertise. *Science in Context, 5*: 351–369.

Rose, N. (1998). A Science of democracy. In: *Inventing Ourselves: Psychology, Power and Personhood* (Chapter 6). Cambridge: Cambridge University Press.

Rose, N., & Miller, P. (1992). Political power beyond the State: problematics of government. *British Journal of Sociology, 43*: 173–205.

Rosenthal, S., Husman, C., & Anderson, D. (1999). *Classical American Pragmatism*. Urbana, IL: University of Illinois Press.

Rosenwein, B. (2006). *Emotional Communities in the Early Middle Ages*. Ithaca, NY: Cornell University Press.

Rosenwein, B. (2009). Worrying about emotions in history. *American Historical Review, 107*: 821–845.

Roustang, F. (1980). *Dire Mastery: Discipleship from Freud to Lacan* (Trans. N. Lukacher). Baltimore, MD: John Hopkins University Press.

Said, E. (1978). *Orientalism*. London: Penguin.

Salih, S. (2001). *Versions of Virginity in Late Medieval England*. Cambridge: D. S. Brewer.

Saposnik, I. (1974). *Robert Louis Stevenson*. Boston: Twayne.

Sarbin, T. (Ed.) (1986). *Narrative psychology: the storied nature of human conduct*. New York: Praeger.

Scarre, G., & Callow, J. (2001). *Witchcraft and Magic in Sixteenth- and Seventeenth-Century Europe* (2nd Edition). London: Palgrave.

Schaffer, R. (1992). *Retelling a Life: Narration and Dialogue in Psychoanalysis*. London: Basic Books.

Schermer, V. (2006). 30th S. H. Foulkes Annual Lecture: Spirituality and group analysis. *Group Analysis, 39*: 445–466.

Schmitt, C. (2002). Narrating national addictions: de Quincey, opium, tea. In: J. Brodie & M. Redfield (Eds.), *High Anxieties: Cultural studies in Addiction*. Berkeley: University of California Press.

Sedgwick, E. Kosofsky (1985). *Between Men: English Literature and Male Homosocial Desire*. New York: Columbia University Press.

Sedgwick, E. Kosofsky (1994). *Epistemology of the Closet*. London: Penguin.

Sedgwick, P. (1995). Introduction. In: P Sedgwick (Ed.), *Nietzsche: A Critical Reader*. Oxford: Blackwell.

Sharpe, J. (1996). *Instruments of Darkness: Witchcraft in England, 1550–1750*. London: Penguin.

Sharpe, J. (1997). *Early Modern England: A Social History, 1550–1760*. Oxford: Hodder Arnold.

Shawcross, J. (Ed.) (1967). *The Complete Poetry of John Donne*. New York: Doubleday.

Showalter, E. (1986). *The Female Malady: Women, Madness and English Culture* (1830–1980). Llanwarne, Herefordshire: Pandora.

Showalter, E. (1990). *Sexual Anarchy: Gender and Culture at the Fin de Siècle*. London: Bloomsbury.

Simpson, E., & Ramsay, R. (2004). Carers as partners in care. *Advances in Psychiatric Treatment, 10*: 81–84.

Skelly, J. (2010). *The Desire to Fill: Addiction and British Visual Culture, 1751–1919*. Unpublished PhD Thesis, Queen's University, Kingston, Ontario, Canada, July 2010.

Skidelski, R., & Skidelski, E. (2012). *How Much is Enough? Money and the Good Life*. New York: Other Press.

Smith, A. (2004). *Victorian Demons: Medicine, Masculinity and the Gothic at Fin de Siècle*. Manchester: Manchester University Press.

Smith, D. (1991). *The Rise of Historical Sociology*. Oxford: Polity.

Social Exclusion Unit (2004). *Mental Health and Social Exclusion*. London: Social Exclusion Unit, Office of Deputy Prime Minister.

Somerville, S. (1994). Scientific racism and the emergence of the homosexual body. *Journal of the History of Sexuality, 5*: 243–266.

Sournia, J. -C. (1990). *A History of Alcoholism*. Oxford: Basil Blackwell.

Spence, D. (1982). *Narrative Truth and Historical Truth: Meaning and Interpretation in Psychoanalysis*. New York: Norton.

Spence, D. (1987). *The Freudian Metaphor: Toward Paradigm Change in Psychoanalysis*. New York: Norton.

Spurling, L. (1993). Introduction. In: L. Spurling (Ed.), *From the Words of my Mouth: Tradition in Psychotherapy*. London: Tavistock.

Spurr, J. (1998). *English Puritanism 1603–1689*. Basingstoke: Palgrave Macmillan.

Stacey, R. (2001). What can it mean to say that the individual is social through and through? *Group Analysis, 34*: 457–471.

Stacey, R. (2003). *Complexity and Group Process*. Hove: Brunner-Routledge.

Steadman Jones, G. (1971). *Outcast London: A Study in the Relationship between Classes in Victorian Society*. Oxford: Clarendon.

Steele, R. (1979). Psychoanalysis and hermeneutics. *International Review of Psychoanalysis, 6*: 389–411.

Stepan, N. (1985). Biological degeneration: races and proper places. In: F. Chamberlain & S. Gilman (Eds.), *Degeneration: The Dark Side of Progress* (Chapter 5). New York: Columbia University Press.

Sterba, R. (1982). *Reminiscences of a Viennese Psychoanalyst*. Detroit: Wayne University Press.

Stern, D. (1985). *The Interpersonal World of the Infant*. New York: Basic Books.

Stern, D. (1989). Crib monologues from a psychoanalytic perspective. In: K. Nelson (Ed.), *Narratives from the Crib*. Cambridge, MA: Harvard University Press.

Stern, D. (1992). The "pre-narrative envelope": An alternative view of "unconscious phantasy" in infancy. *Bulletin of the Anna Freud Centre, 15*: 291–318.

Stern, D. (1997). *Unformulated Experience: From Dissociation to Imagination in Psychoanalysis*. Hillsdale, NJ: Analytic Press.

Stern, D. N., Sander L. W., Nahum J. P., Harrison, A. M., Lyons-Ruth, K., Morgan, A. C., Bruschweiler-Stern, N., Tronick, E. Z. (1998). Non-interpretive mechanisms in psychoanalytic therapy: the "something more" than interpretation. *International Journal of Psychoanalysis, 79*: 903–921.

Stern, J. P. (1978). *Nietzsche*. Glasgow: Fontana/Collins.

Stevenson, R. L. (1886–1979). *The Strange Case of Dr Jekyll and Mr Hyde and Other Stories* (Ed. J. Calder). London: Penguin, 1979.

Stewart, H. (1990). Interpretation and other agents for psychic change. *International Journal of Psychoanalysis, 17*: 61–69.

Stolorow, R. (1997). Dynamic, dyadic, intersubjective systems: an evolving paradigm of psychoanalysis. *Psychoanalytic Psychology, 14*: 337–346.

Stolorow, R., & Atwood, G. (1979). *Faces in a Cloud: Subjectivity in Personality Theory*. New York: Jason Aronson.

Stolorow, R., & Atwood, G. (1992). *Contexts of Being: The Intersubjective Foundations of Psychological Life*. Hillsdale, NJ: Analytic Press.

Stolorow, R., & Lachmann, F. (1981). Two psychoanalyses or one? *Psychoanalytic Review, 68*: 307–319.

Stolorow, R., Atwood, G., & Orange, D. (2002). *Worlds of Experience.* New York: Basic Books.

Stolorow, R., Brandchaft, B., & Atwood, G. (1987). *Psychoanalytic Treatment: An Intersubjective Approach.* Hillsdale, NJ: Analytic Press.

Stolorow, R., Orange, D., & Atwood, G. (2001). World horizons; A post-Cartesian alternative to the Freudian unconscious. *Contemporary Psychoanalysis, 37:* 43–61.

Stone, L. (1977). *The Family, Sex and Marriage in England, 1500–1800.* London: Penguin.

Strachey, J. (1934). The nature of the therapeutic action of psychoanalysis. *International Journal of Psychoanalysis, 15:* 127–159 (Reproduced in volume 50, 1969).

Strohl, J. (2008). Marriage as discipleship: Luther's praise of married life. *Dialog: A Journal of Theology, 47:* 136–142.

Stuart, K. (1999). *Defiled Trades and Social Outcasts: Honour and Ritual Pollution in Early Modern Germany.* Cambridge: Cambridge University Press.

Szasz, T. (1973). *Ceremonial Chemistry: The Ritual Persecution of Drugs, Addicts and Pushers.* London: Routledge and Kegan Paul.

Taylor, C. (1985). Human agency and language. In: *Philosophical Papers, Volume 1* (Chapter 1). Cambridge: Cambridge University Press.

Taylor, C. (1989). *Sources of the Self: The Making of Modern Identity.* Cambridge University press.

Taylor, C. (1993). Engaged agency and background. In: C. Guigon (Ed.), *The Cambridge Companion to Heidegger* (Chapter 12). Cambridge: Cambridge University Press.

Taylor, C. (2004). *Modern Social Imaginaries.* Durham, NC: Duke University Press.

Terdiman, R. (1984). Ideological voyages: Concerning a Flaubertian dis-orient-ation. In: F. Barker, P. Hulme, M. Iversen and D. Loxley (Eds.), *Europe and Its Others* (Chapter 3). Colchester: University of Essex.

Thiele, L. P. (1990). *Friedrich Nietzsche and the Politics of the Soul.* Princeton, NJ: Princeton University Press.

Thomas, K. (1971). *Religion and the Decline of Magic.* London: Penguin.

Thomas, K. (2009). *The Ends of Life; Roads to Fulfillment in Early Modern England.* Oxford: OUP.

Thornton, C. (2004). Borrowing my self; an exploration of exchange as a group-specific therapeutic factor. *Group Analysis, 37:* 305–320.

Todd, M. (1992). Puritan self-fashioning; the diary of Samuel Ward. *Journal of British Studies, 31:* 236–264.

Tolpin, M. (1971). On the beginnings of a cohesive self. *The Psychoanalytic Study of the Child, 25:* 273–305.

Tomasello, M. (1999). *The Cultural Origins of Human Cognition.* Cambridge MA: Harvard Unversity Press.

Trevor-Roper, H. R. (1978). *The European Witch-Craze of the Sixteenth and Seventeenth Centuries*. London: Penguin.

Tubert-Oklander, J. (2014). *The One and the Many: Relational Psychoanalysis and Group Analysis*. London: Karnac.

Tully, J. (1995). *Strange Multiplicities: Constitutionalism in an Age of Diversity*. Cambridge: Cambridge University Press.

Underdown, D. (1985). The taming of the scold. In: A. Fletcher & J. Stevenson (Eds.), *Order and Disorder in Early Modern England*. Cambridge: Cambridge University Press.

Underdown, D. (1992). *Fire from Heaven: Life in an English Town in the Seventeenth Century*. London: Pimlico.

Unwin, C. (1984). Power relations and the emergence of language. In: J. Henriques, W. Holloway, C. Unwin, C. Venn & V. Walkerdine, *Changing the Subject: Psychology, Social Regulation and Subjectivity*. London: Methuen.

Walkowtiz, J. R. (1992). *City of Dreadful Delight: Narratives of Sexual Danger in Late-Victorian London*. Chicago: University of Chicago Press.

Walter, R. (1956). What became of the degenerate? A brief history of the concept. *Journal of the History of Medicine, 11*: 422–429.

Warnke, G. (1987). *Gadamer: Hermeneutics, Tradition and Reason*. Oxford: Basil Blackwell.

Warren, M. (1992). Democratic theory and self-transformation. *The American Political Science Review, 86*: 8–23.

Warren, M. (1995). The self in discursive democracy. In: S. K. White (Ed.), *The Cambridge Companion to Habermas*. Cambridge: Cambridge University Press.

Webster, T. (1997). *Godly Clergy in Early Stuart England: The Caroline Puritan Movement, c. 1620–1643*. Cambridge: Cambridge University Press.

Weegmann, M. (2001). Working intersubjectively; what does it mean for theory and therapy? *Group Analysis, 34*: 515–530.

Weegmann, M. (2004a). "You're not finished yet": personal horizons and unformulated experience. *Psychodynamic Practice, 10*: 5–26.

Weegmann, M. (2004b). A response to 'Mind' by S. H. Foulkes and Dahlin's challenge—"Group analysis has no theory! Foulkes failed us. Did he?" *Group Analysis, 37*: 361–363.

Weegmann, M. (2005a). Dangerous cocktails; drugs and alcohol in the family. In: M. Bower (Ed.), *Psychoanalytic Perspectives in Social Work*. London: Routledge.

Weegmann, M. (2005b). "If each could be housed in separate personalities …": therapy as conversation between different parts of the self. *Psychoanalytic Psychotherapy, 19*: 279–293.

Weegmann, M. (2006a). Edward Said (1935–2003): his relevance to psychotherapy. *Psychodynamic Practice, 11*: 389–404.

Weegmann, M. (2006b). From tenuous to tenacious: psychodynamic group therapy with substance misusers. *Groups in Addiction and Recovery, 1*: 51–67.

Weegmann, M. (2008). Monsters: the social-unconscious life of "Others" and a note on the origins of group theory. *Group Analysis, 41*: 291–300.

Weegmann, M. (2011). Working intersubjectively: what does it mean for theory and therapy? In: E. Hopper & H. Weinberg (Eds.), *The Social Unconscious in Persons, Groups and Societies: Volume 1* (Chapter 6). London: Karnac.

Weegmann, M. (2015). Social unconsciousness: verb, movement and field of identity. In: E. Hopper & H. Weinberg (Eds.), *The Social Unconscious in Persons, Groups & Societies: Volume 2*. London: Karnac.

Weeks, J. (1977). *Coming Out: Homosexuality and Politics in Britain, from the Nineteenth Century to the Present*. London: Quartet.

Weiner, B., & White, W. (2007). The Journal of Inebriety (1876–1914): history, topical analysis, and photographic images. *Addiction, 102*: 15–23.

Weinsheimer, J. (1985). *Gadamer's Hermeneutics*. New Haven, CT: Yale University Press.

White, W. L. (1998). *Slaying the Dragon: The History of Addiction Treatment and Recovery in America*. Illinois; Chesnut Health Systems.

Williams, D. (1996). *Deformed Discourse: The Function of the Monster in Mediaeval Thought and Literature*. Montreal: McGill-Queen's University Press.

Williams, R. (1977). *Marxism and Literature*. Oxford: OUP.

Wittkower, R. (1942). Marvels of the East: a study in the history of monsters. *Journal of the Warburg and Courtauld Institutes, 5*: 159–197.

Wolberg, L. R. (1967). The technique of short-term psychotherapy. In: L. R. Wolberg (Ed.), *Short-term Psychotherapy*. New York: Grune & Stratton.

Woodbridge, K., & Fulford, B. (2004). *Whose Values? A Workbook for Values-based Practice in Mental Health Care*. Salisbury Centre for Mental Health.

Woods, P. (2003). Building on Weber to understand governance: exploring links between identity, democracy and "inner distance". *Sociology, 37*: 143–163.

Wrightson, K. (1982). *English Society, 1580–1680*. New Brunswick, NJ: Rutgers University Press.

Wuthnow, R. (1994). *Sharing the Journey: Support Groups and America's New Quest for Community*. New York: Free Press.

Wyse, H. (1996). Was Wittgenstein a group analyst? *Group Analysis, 29*: 355–367.

Zeddies, T. (2000). Within, outside and in between: the relational unconscious. *Psychoanalytic Psychology, 17*: 467–487.

Zeddies, T., & Richardson, F. (1999). Analytic authority in historical and critical perspective. *Contemporary Psychoanalysis, 35*: 581–601.

Zieger, S. (2005). "How far am I responsible?": women and morphinism in late nineteenth-century Britain. *Victorian Studies, 48*: 59–81.

Zieger, S. (2008). *Inventing the Addict: Drugs, Race and Sexuality in Nineteenth-Century British and American Literature.* Amherst: University of Massachusetts Press.

Zinkin, L. (1996). A Dialogical model for group analysis: Jung and Bakhin. *Group Analysis, 29*: 343–354.

INDEX

205